# COMPUTERS

# COMPUTERS
## from logic to architecture

**R.D. DOWSING and F.W.D. WOODHAMS**

*School of Information Systems*
*University of East Anglia*
*NORWICH*

**International**

Van Nostrand Reinhold (International)

Published in 1990 by
Van Nostrand Reinhold (International) Co. Ltd
11 New Fetter Lane, London EC4P 4EE

First published in 1985 as Computer Architecture:
A first course

© 1990   R.D. Dowsing and F.W.D. Woodhams

Typeset in 10/12 Times by
Best-Set Typesetter Limited, Hong Kong
Printed in Great Britain by
TJ Press Ltd, Padstow, Cornwall

ISBN 0 278 00093 2

---

**British Library Cataloguing in Publication Data**

---

Dowsing, R. (Roy)
[Computer architecture]. Computers: from
logic to architecture.
1. Computer systems
I. [Computer architecture]   II. Title
III. Woodhams, Frank
004

ISBN 0-278-00093-2

# Contents

# Preface

With the ever increasing use of computers there is an increasing need for students to be trained in the techniques of computing. One specific area which has been targeted by many colleges, polytechnics and universities is that of computer systems engineering; the interface area between computing and electronics. The specific requirements of this area of study are a knowledge of the interaction of the software and hardware of computers, often with reference to microprocessors and their applications.

This book is aimed at providing a first course in computer architecture: the interaction of hardware and software. The reader does not require any specific prior knowledge but the student who has at least a little experience of programming in a high-level language will find the latter half of the book easier reading. The book covers the spectrum of computer architecture topics from technology through to systems software and communications.

As in our previous book, we had the problem of deciding what hardware to use for examples. We decided, eventually, to use two systems, the 8-bit Intel 8085 and the 16/32-bit Motorola 68000 to show the differences between a simple 8-bit system and a sophisticated 16/32-bit machine. Also the use of two different microprocessors enables the student to see the different design choices made by the designers.

The book takes a bottom-up approach to the subject, starting at the lowest level, logic, and building up the hardware and software architecture of the computer from this basis.

Chapter 1 introduces some of the important concepts in understanding computer architecture whilst the next chapter introduces some of the concepts required to understand logic and logic design. It deals with Boolean algebra, truth tables and the different types of electronic logic component. Chapter 3 deals with combinatorial logic design, i.e. the design of circuits whose output depends solely on their inputs. It shows how the combinatorial elements of a computer, such as decoders and multiplexers, can be formed from simple logic networks. Chapter 4 describes sequential logic elements, those whose output is determined by past actions as well as present inputs. Latches, registers and memory elements are discussed in this chapter. The structure of a computer is discussed in the next chapter, showing how the elements of the computer are interconnected. Details of specific computer components are given as well as the general architecture.

Chapter 6 considers the different types of memory available, such as RAM and ROM, and the organization of memory into a hierarchy. Input–output processing techniques such as polling, interrupts and DMA are considered in the next chapter. Microprogramming and how it can be used to implement the control unit of a processor is considered in Chapter 8, and the following chapter presents the design of two small computer systems based on the 8085 and 68000 processors and components described in previous chapters. Chapter 10 describes the different types of data that can be manipulated in a computer and the operations that can be performed on them. Detailed discussion of number systems is dealt with here. Instruction sets and addressing modes found in computers with specific reference to the 8085 and 68000 are considered in the next chapter. Many examples are given and some complete programs are given at the end of the chapter. A chapter introducing system software such as assemblers, linkers and loaders follows. Of necessity, the discussion is brief but most of the software falling into this category is covered. Data communications and the way in which the development of communication networks has led to the introduction of distributed computing is the subject of Chapter 13, whilst the final chapter considers some new approaches to the design of computers, specifically RISC designs and the transputer.

Many people have contributed to the material in this book, including the numerous students to whom we have taught the material. We would like to thank them all, especially our colleagues Ian Marshall and George Turner, for their helpful comments and criticisms of drafts of the manuscript.

**R.D. Dowsing**
**F.W.D. Woodhams**

# Glossary

**Absolute address**   actual memory address used to access data or instructions in memory

**Access time**   delay between time supplying address to memory and receiving data

**Accumulator**   special register in the CPU, often the destination of arithmetic and logical operations and, sometimes, one of the source operands

**Addressing mode**   method of specifying the address of an operand from the address bits in the instruction

**Algorithm**   sequence of steps required to solve a problem

**ALU**   arithmetic and logic unit

**ASCII**   American Standard Code for Information Interchange

**Arithmetic and logic unit**   a hardware unit which performs operations such as addition on its operands according to the function code supplied

**Assembler**   the program which converts input in assembly language to machine code

**Assembly code**   representation of machine instructions where bit patterns are replaced by symbols

**Base**   the radix of the number system in use, for example, 2 for binary

**BCD**   binary coded decimal

**Binary**   representation of numbers in base 2, that is, using the digits 0 and 1 only

**Binary coded decimal**   a method of number representation where each decimal digit is encoded into 4 bits

**Bit**   binary digit, taking one of the values 0 or 1

**Bridge**   a node which connects two networks using similar protocols

**Bus**   a group of wires carrying information between subsystems

**Byte**   a group of 8 bits

**Cache**   small fast memory between processor and main memory

**Central processing unit**   the arithmetic and logic unit together with registers and control logic for decoding and obeying instructions

**Channel**  any medium which carries data

**Circuit switching**  a switching technique in which a route is first set up, then used for data transmission and finally closed down

**Clock**  source of regular pulses to control the system operation

**Combinatorial**  a circuit whose output depends only on its current inputs

**Compiler**  a program which translates a high-level language program into a lower-level one, frequently machine code

**Condition flags**  flags normally used to indicate carry, sign, overflow and zero as the result of the last instruction

**Complement**  1's complement – inverting all the bits of the binary value; 2's complement – 1's complement + 1

**CPU**  central processing unit

**Cycle stealing**  using memory time slots not used by the CPU

**Data selector**  a programmable switch

**Deadlock**  a situation where no processing can proceed because two or more processes are waiting for each other cyclically

**Direct memory access**  method of transferring large quantities of information between memory and an input–output device without intervention from the CPU

**Distributed computing**  computing spread over several processors

**DMA**  direct memory access

**Fetch**  that part of the instruction cycle concerned with bringing the next instruction to be executed from memory into the instruction register

**Flag**  a single-bit hardware marker indicating something about the state of the computer

**Flip-flop**  a single-bit memory device

**Full adder**  a circuit that accepts two single-bit operands and a carry producing their sum and a carry out

**Gateway**  a node which connects together two dissimilar networks

**Half adder**  a circuit that accepts two single-bit operands and produces their sum and carry

**Handshake**  one or more signals controlling (synchronizing) the transfer of data between sender and receiver

**Hardware**  that part of a computer implemented by electronic and mechanical components

**Hexadecimal**  number system using base 16 with symbols digits 0 to 9 and letters A to F

**High-level language**  a language where each statement corresponds to several machine-code instructions; a language which is more expressive than machine code

**Indirect address**  an address which refers to a location containing the address of the required value

**Input–output**  the interface and devices by means of which the computer communicates with the outside world

**Instruction**  a collection of bits containing an operation code and, possibly, one or more operands

**Instruction register** register in the CPU used for holding the current instruction whilst it is being decoded

**Instruction set** the repertoire of instructions available on a particular computer

**Interpreter** a program which directly executes statements in a language without prior translation

**Interrupt** a method of a device informing the CPU that it needs attention

**I/O** input–output

**$K$** 1024, e.g. $2K = 2 \times 1024 = 2048$

**Link editor** program which fills in the cross references between separately compiled subprograms

**Literal** any symbolic value representing a constant

**Loader** program which loads a binary program into memory

**Local area network** a network which extends over a small area such as a building or single site

**LSI** large scale integration – integrated circuits large enough to hold a microprocessor on a single chip

**Macroprocessor** a program which performs text substitution, replacing one input statement by several output statements; can be used for language translation

**Machine code** a representation of the bit pattern of an instruction, often in hexadecimal

**Memory mapped I/O** an addressing scheme where the registers concerned with input–output have addresses in the normal memory address space

**Microprocessor** a CPU implemented in LSI or VLSI

**Microprogram** a set of instructions, normally in read-only memory, which are used to implement the instruction set of the computer

**Mnemonic** in computing, a symbol representing a bit string

**MOS** metal oxide semiconductor

**Multiplexer** a switch which allows several inputs to share the same output, but not at the same time

**Multiprogramming** the running of several processes on a single processor by time-division multiplexing

**Operand** a value to be operated on by the opcode in an instruction

**Operation code** opcode

**Opcode** that part of an instruction which defines the operation to be performed

**OSI model** a standard model for protocol levels in networks

**Packet switching** a technique for sending messages across networks as fixed-sized units

**Page** a contiguous block of memory space

**Paging** a mechanism for swapping information between main memory and backing store

**Peripherals** input–output devices

**PLA** programmable logic array – a regular array of AND and OR gates which may be connected together (programmed) to produce the required logic function

**Polling** interrogation of devices to find their status

**Port** an external entry or exit point from an interface

**Process** a program or subprogram in execution

**Program counter** register in the CPU holding the address of the next instruction to be executed

**PROM** programmable read-only memory – a reusable programmable memory which can be programmed by special equipment and erased by ultraviolet light

**Protocol** a set of rules which sender and receiver have to obey in order to communicate

**RAM** random access memory, often used for read–write memory; access to any location takes the same time irrespective of address

**Refresh** a process whereby a dynamic memory which loses information after a short time has its memory contents rewritten

**Register** a fast memory location, often in the CPU

**Relative address** an address relative to the current contents of the program counter

**Relocation** the process of moving a program from one part of memory to another

**RISC** reduced instruction set computer

**ROM** read-only memory

**Rotate** *see* **Shift**

**Routeing** the process of directing a message through a network

**RS232** a standard for communication

**Sequential** performing in sequence, that is, one after another

**Serial** one after another, often with reference to communication

**Shift** to move sideways in a register

**Software** that part of the computer implemented by a program

**Stack** memory that is used in last-in–first-out fashion

**Stack pointer** register which points to the memory location currently acting as the top of the stack

**Static RAM** memory that needs no refreshing

**Status** condition

**Synchronization** the co-ordination of actions between two or more entities

**Transputer** a RISC machine designed for distributed computing designed by Inmos Ltd

**Tristate** three state, usually logic 0, logic 1 and high impedance

**VDU** visual display unit

**VLSI** very large scale integration

**Wide area network** a network over a large geographical area such as a country or a continent

**Word** a group of bits, usually the size of the data bus

# 1

# Introduction

## 1.1  Approaches to computer architecture

The way in which a human being understands a complex topic is known as 'divide and conquer'. Any complex topic is decomposed into a set of less complex subparts hierarchically until the subparts are simple enough to be understood. Once these simple subparts are understood they are then composed into more complex units whose behaviour can be explained by the action of the subparts and their interaction. This process is continued hierarchically until the complex topic can be explained. This process is illustrated in Fig. 1.1.

Computer architecture is a complex topic and hence the way to understanding is to subdivide it into smaller topics. There are many different ways of subdivision and hence the many different ways of approaching the topic found in textbooks. Here two approaches to computer architecture are considered to show why a mixture of these two approaches is used in this book.

### 1.1.1  Layered approach

One approach to computer architecture is to consider a computer system as consisting of a set of layers of abstraction, a subset of which is used to implement a given computer system. For example, one or more of the lower layers in this model are concerned with the logic elements used to implement an architecture. One level could be solely concerned with the types of element used, for example **AND** and **OR** gates, and the design method for combining these logic elements. If the system was to be implemented in very large scale integration (VLSI) circuits then a level might be appropriate where the concerns are for physical parameters such as the width of tracks and type of technology. At a somewhat higher level is the machine level which is normally the lowest level available to the computer user. At this level

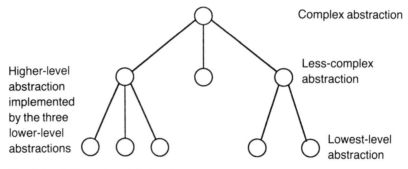

**Fig. 1.1** A hierarchy of abstractions.

bit strings are interpreted as instructions and data. Levels above this are concerned with the operating system, high-level programming languages and applications. One possible hierarchy of levels of abstraction is given in Fig. 1.2. Higher levels have higher complexity than lower levels and each level relies on the level below it to implement its primitive operations. Each level has its own set of primitive components and its own set of design methods to interconnect these primitive components. In addition each level may have its own basic theory which underpins the construction method. For example, the logic level has propositional calculus and Boolean algebra as the basis of the synthesis and analysis of logic circuits. This layered approach is appealing

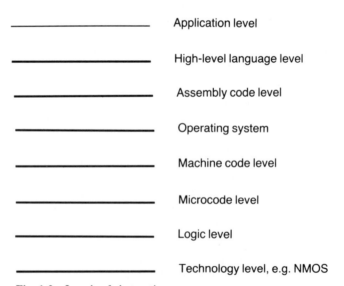

**Fig. 1.2** Levels of abstraction.

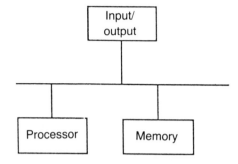

**Fig. 1.3**    Functional block diagram of computer.

since it relegates details of the synthesis and analysis of components to the appropriate level thus giving rise to a hierarchically structured approach.

## 1.1.2    Functional decomposition

Another approach to understanding computers is to adopt a functional decomposition, where the computer structure is split up into functional components and each functional block is considered separately. A typical computer could be split up into the basic functional blocks shown in Fig. 1.3, where, for example, memory is considered to be a functional block. Memory can be further subdivided into different types, such as random access memory (RAM) and read-only memory (ROM), and each of these types considered separately. In effect, this again gives a hierarchical structure, a tree, where each subtree consists of functionally related items. This decomposition is attractive since concerns about physically related components are grouped together and hence are easy to compare.

To illustrate the advantage of the functional decomposition, consider the topic of memory. In functional decomposition this would occupy a large subtree and, in terms of a book, would appear in a single chapter or group of chapters. In the layered approach different aspects of memory would be found in different layers. For example, the implementation of a memory would be found at one of the logic levels, whilst virtual memory would be considered at the operating system level. It would thus seem that the functional approach is the best way to understand computer architecture. However, there are many cases, especially at the lower levels of abstraction, where consideration of an abstraction level rather than separate functions becomes attractive. For example, the topic of logic design would appear as a single entity in the layered approach but would be scattered throughout all the components in the functional approach. Since there is an underlying rationale to logic design it makes sense to consider this as a topic in its own right. Since it depends on the viewpoint as to which is the best approach, a mixture of approaches has been taken in this book, depending on which view of a particular topic the authors wish to present.

## 1.2   Translation and interpretation

Consider, for the moment, the structure of a computer to be a series of abstraction layers. Some method of implementing the highest level abstraction by means of components of a lower level is required. For the following discussion consider just two levels and how to implement components at the higher level in terms of components of the lower level. As will be explained, this principle can be applied several times over to implement a hierarchy of levels.

### 1.2.1   Translation

There are two basic methods of implementing the higher level in terms of the lower. One technique, called **translation**, involves decomposing the higher-level abstraction into a set of lower-level abstractions. Consider, for example, how to make a cup of tea. The higher-level abstraction is 'make a cup of tea' whilst the lower-level abstractions might be 'fill the kettle with water', 'put the kettle on the stove', 'when the kettle boils pour a little water into the pot', etc. Here the action of making a cup of tea has been translated into a set of sub-actions to do the same task. The action of making a cup of tea has been translated into a set of simpler, more specialized actions at the lower level. These lower-level actions could be performed by a simpler device or devices than the higher-level action.

### 1.2.2   Interpretation

An alternative way of implementing the higher-level requirement is to build a high-level machine – in our example a robot to make a cup of tea – out of lower-level components. This higher-level machine understands the abstraction 'make a cup of tea'. This is called **interpretation**.

It appears that these two approaches produce the same result, as indeed they must if they are to implement the higher level abstraction, but they do so in different ways. Consider the case of translation and our tea-making example. The result of the translation is a set of lower-level instructions detailing how to make a cup of tea. This set of instructions may be implemented by a simple device which has only to understand these lower level instructions, not how to make a cup of tea. In the case of interpretation, the objective is to build a machine which just understands the operation 'make a cup of tea'. The machine may be built up of the same primitive operations as before, for example, fill the kettle, but these are hidden and are not provided as operations at this level. In terms of our example we wish to produce a fully automatic teamaker which only understands how to make a cup of tea.

How are these ideas translated into computer architecture implementation? The two methods described above can be used to implement layers of abstraction. Assuming for the moment that the hardware understands machine code, bit patterns, then a higher-level language such as Pascal, a higher-level of abstraction, may be implemented by means of either translation or interpretation. Using translation the high-level programming concepts are transformed into the equivalent machine code which the hardware can then execute. Using interpretation, a Pascal machine would be 'built' out of the hardware and some software, that is, a program would be written to run on the hardware which would imitate the actions required of a Pascal machine. This new machine would understand Pascal so that it would directly execute Pascal programs.

The distinction between translation and interpretation is central to the problem of realizing an architecture. In most computer systems the lower levels of abstraction are realized by interpretation, that is, building a machine using the lower-level primitives, whilst the higher-level abstractions are realized by translation, that is, creating the set of lower-level constructs equivalent to the higher-level abstraction. The basic differences between the two approaches in terms of the user's perception is that translation produces a faster implementation although debugging has to be performed at a lower level, whereas interpretation, although slower, can produce diagnostics more easily. In section 12.6.1, a more detailed example will be given.

## 1.3 Languages and abstract machines

It may appear at first sight that a computer language and a computer architecture do not have very much in common. However, the discussion above has shown that a language and an architecture go together. Given a (computer) language a machine can be built, in hardware or software, to 'understand' it; this is essentially what an interpreter is. Thus a machine is equivalent to a language in the restricted context of computers. Thus the various levels of computer abstractions may be thought of in terms of either languages or machines whichever is the more convenient. For example, a washing machine controller can be considered either in terms of the set of instructions it will obey, such as wash, rinse and spin, or in terms of a machine which has the instructions wash, rinse and spin as part of its instruction set. This does not imply that the design should be implemented in this particular way; only that it is convenient to think about it as such. This ability to consider designs as either languages or machines gives the designer the flexibility to explore the design space in a number of different ways.

## 1.4 Sequentiality, concurrency and distribution

One of the major issues in computer architecture at the present time is the subject of concurrency, especially at the higher levels of abstraction. If two actions occur concurrently then these actions occur 'at the same time', whereas if they occur sequentially then one of them cannot start until the other has finished. Thus concurrent operation implies some overlap of execution. At the lower levels of abstraction, that is, hardware, concurrency exists. In general, electronic components react immediately to a change of one or more of their inputs. Thus if the inputs to more than one component are changed 'at the same time' then the components will react to these changes concurrently. At this level of abstraction there is a considerable amount of concurrency possible in a typical computer. However, most high-level programming languages do not include any constructs for the user to express concurrency in his program; most high-level programming languages are purely sequential and the user may only state the sequence in which his statements are to be performed. Mainly due to the search for ever increasing speed there has recently been an increased interest in concurrency at the higher levels of abstraction. Up until now the increase in performance of computers has been mainly due to technological improvements at the lower levels of abstraction but physical limits are now being approached so that increased performance in the future may depend on improved techniques such as concurrency at the higher levels where many operations may be performed at once.

For a computer system to execute multiple instructions concurrently multiple processors are required. There are many different computer architectures containing multiple processors and there are several different ways of classifying them, some of which will be described later in this book. One classification which has become increasingly important is that of **distributed computing systems**. A distributed computing system is one in which a computation is physically distributed across an interconnected set of computers. In other words a single user's program is run on a co-operating set of computers. The units of distribution may be large or small and the computers may be arranged in one of many different configurations. It is in this area of distributed computing that much of the recent work on computer architecture has been concentrated.

# 1.5   Summary

The process of design is one of hierarchical decomposition. There are many different criteria for the decomposition which give rise to many different approaches to computer architecture. One of the most common decompositions gives rise to a layered approach to architecture where successive layers are built from the primitives provided by the lower levels. Using this approach, computers are built from logic devices which are used to implement a processor which executes programs to implement higher-level machines. A contrasting approach is the functional approach where a computer is thought of as being composed of a set of functional units and the total design is in terms of the interconnection of functional units. Which approach is taken depends on the particular importance placed on facets of the design.

Using the layered approach there are two methods of implementing a higher level in terms of a lower one; translation and interpretation. In a computer architecture the lower levels of abstraction are implemented by interpretation and the upper levels by translation.

Central to current computer architecture discussions are the notions of concurrency. Real concurrency implies that two or more actions overlap in time and hence implies more than one processor. A class of concurrent architectures is known as distributed architectures where processors are physically distributed and interaction between them only takes place by message passing.

# 2

# Introduction to digital logic

## 2.1 Introduction

Digital logic systems are used to process information, and to control plant and machinery in the 'real world'. The use of digital systems and, in particular, computers, has become increasingly widespread over the past few decades, and the rate of expansion shows no signs of slowing down. This has occurred for two simple reasons. First, information can be easily represented and manipulated in binary form, and is easily stored and manipulated using very simple electronic circuits, usually known as gates. Secondly, the ability to fabricate integrated circuits onto silicon chips, containing many hundreds or even thousands of these simple gates, has meant that the cost of a digital logic system has continued to fall in real terms. The obvious example of such a logic system is the small computer, or microcomputer as it is frequently known.

In this chapter the fundamentals of Boolean algebra, or switching theory, are considered, together with the families of gates that are available for implementing logic systems. This chapter provides all the background knowledge necessary for understanding Chapters 3 and 4, which consider the design and implementation of combinatorial and sequential logic. It is assumed that the reader has a basic knowledge of binary codes and binary arithmetic, and some elementary understanding of simple circuit theory, Ohm's law, etc.

## 2.2 Combinatorial and sequential logic

At the highest, or most abstract, level, a digital logic system may be regarded as a black box, as shown in Fig. 2.1. This box has a number of inputs, shown on the left, and a number of outputs, shown on the right. Each input and each output may take only one of two values. These values are referred to as **TRUE** and **FALSE**. When a logic system is implemented with an electronic circuit, voltages are used to represent these values. Usually a low voltage, close to

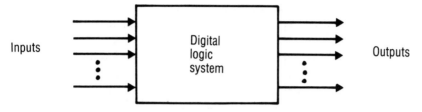

**Fig. 2.1**    Basic digital logic system.

0 V, is used to represent **FALSE**, and a high voltage, usually in the region 5–15 V, is used to represent **TRUE**. The words **HIGH** and **LOW** are frequently used as analogous to **TRUE** and **FALSE**. In the discussion of the algebra of logic, Boolean algebra, in the next section the established practice of using 1 for **TRUE** and 0 for **FALSE** will be employed.

Sometimes the words **ON** and **OFF** are used in logic systems; these words are again analogous to **TRUE** and **FALSE** and arise from the time when logic circuits were implemented with relay switches, a relay being switched either **ON** or **OFF**. It will be shown later that a transistor may be used as a switch, having two stable states which correspond to the transistor being switched either **ON** or **OFF**. Again, these two states are used to represent **TRUE** and **FALSE**.

Digital logic circuits are divided into two distinct types, namely combinatorial logic circuits and sequential logic circuits. However, most real logic systems, such as computers, are a mixture of both combinatorial and sequential logic circuits. A combinatorial circuit is one where the values of the outputs depend only on the present values of the inputs. Combinatorial circuits have no memory, so the outputs cannot depend on the order in which the values of the inputs are changed, or on any previous values of those inputs. The design of combinatorial circuits is discussed in Chapter 3.

A sequential circuit, on the other hand, is one in which the outputs depend not only on the present values of the inputs, but also on the past values of those inputs, i.e. on the history of the circuit. Clearly a sequential circuit requires a memory to store the necessary history of the circuit. In practice, a sequential logic circuit contains combinatorial logic and memory elements, as shown in Fig. 2.2. Such sequential logic systems are often referred to as finite state machines (FSM). Sequential logic circuits are discussed fully in Chapter 4.

## 2.3   Basic logic gates

Figure 2.3 shows the simplest possible combinatorial logic circuit: a single input labelled $A$ and a single output labelled $Z$. The circuit of Fig. 2.3a is

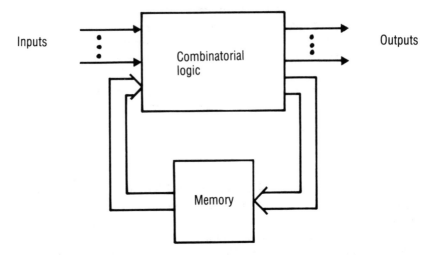

**Fig. 2.2** Block diagram of a sequential logic circuit.

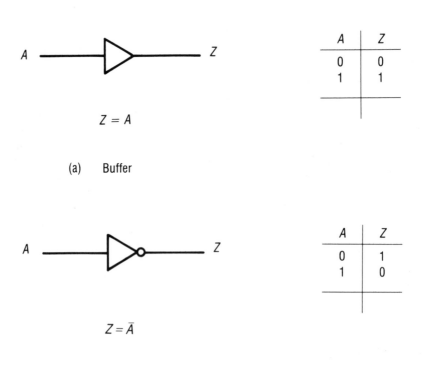

| A | Z |
|---|---|
| 0 | 0 |
| 1 | 1 |

$$Z = A$$

(a)   Buffer

| A | Z |
|---|---|
| 0 | 1 |
| 1 | 0 |

$$Z = \bar{A}$$

(b)   NOT gate

**Fig. 2.3** The basic 1-input logic gates.

known as a buffer. The output $Z$ always has the same logic level as the input, so the Boolean equation defining its behaviour is

$$Z = A$$

and is read as $Z$ equals $A$.

Figure 2.3b is an inverter or **NOT** gate. The value of the output is always the inverse, or complement, of the input. The logic equation is

$$Z = \bar{A}$$

and is read as $Z$ equals **NOT** $A$. The line, or bar, over the $A$ implies **NOT**, in this case **NOT** $A$. The logic symbol of the **NOT** gate is really composed of two parts, a triangle and a circle, or bubble as it is usually called. The triangle means that the element is a buffer and the bubble means that this buffer is actually an inverting buffer so that the element performs the **NOT** function. Note for the present that the bubble may be drawn either on the input to, or the output from, the buffer. The use of the bubble notation will be discussed more fully in section 2.6. The simplicity of the **NOT** gate hides its importance: without the **NOT** gate, the design of many useful digital logic systems would not be possible!

Slightly more complicated are the combinatorial circuits shown in Fig. 2.4, each of which has two inputs, labelled $A$ and $B$, and one output, labelled $Z$. Since each of the inputs $A$ and $B$ can take one of only two possible values, 0 or 1, there are $2^2$ or 4 possible input combinations. Although there are actually 16 logic functions that have two inputs, or variables, there are only five fundamental elements, namely **AND, OR, NAND, NOR** and **EOR**. Figure 2.4 shows the accepted logic symbols of four of these five basic elements, or gates as they are frequently known. Each circuit is defined by a Boolean logic equation and by a **truth table**; both definitions are shown in Fig. 2.4. These gates will now be considered in more detail.

## 2.3.1 The **AND** gate

The output $Z$ is only **TRUE** (i.e. 1) when both the inputs are **TRUE**. The logic equation is

$$Z = A.B$$

where the operator dot symbol (.) means **AND**. The equation is read as $Z$ equals $A$ **AND** $B$. The truth table has three columns, one for each input, $A$ and $B$, and one for the output $Z$ and four rows since there are $2^2 = 4$ possible input combinations of $A$ and $B$. The truth table is usually written using 0s and

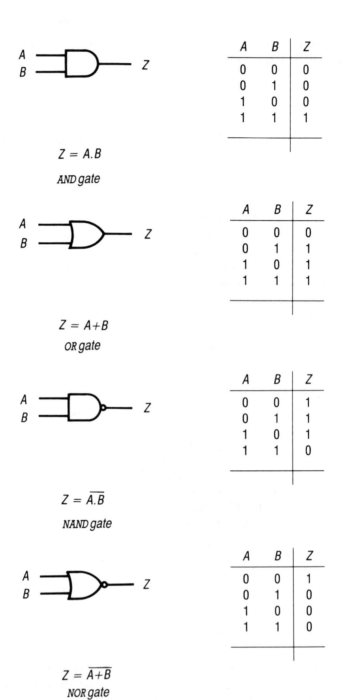

$$Z = A.B$$

*AND gate*

$$Z = A+B$$

*OR gate*

$$Z = \overline{A.B}$$

*NAND gate*

$$Z = \overline{A+B}$$

*NOR gate*

**Fig. 2.4** The basic 2-input logic gates.

1s, although **TRUE** and **FALSE** could equally well be used. The number of inputs can be increased to 3, 4 ... $n$ to give an $n$-input **AND** gate. The generalized logic equation then becomes

$$Z = A.B.C \ldots$$

and the truth table will have $2^n$ rows. The output $Z$ will only be 1 when all the inputs are 1.

### 2.3.2 The **OR** gate

The output of the **OR** gate is **TRUE** when either input $A$ and $B$, or both, are **TRUE**. The logic equation is

$$Z = A + B$$

where the operator + (the plus symbol) means **OR**. The equation is read as $Z$ equals $A$ or $B$. The **OR** gate can be expanded to an $n$-input **OR** gate with the logic equation

$$Z = A + B + C \ldots$$

In this case the output $Z$ will be 1 if any of the inputs is 1.

### 2.3.3 The **NAND** gate

The **NAND** gate performs the function **NOT-AND** and is best thought of as an **AND** gate followed by a **NOT** gate. The truth table is obtained by complementing the output column $Z$ of the **AND** gate. The logic equation is

$$Z = \overline{A.B}$$

and is read as **NOT** ($A$ **AND** $B$). Note the use of the bar over the whole expression to symbolize inverting the whole function. (Do not confuse it with **NOT** $A$ **AND** $B$ which is $Z = \overline{A}.B$, and which has a different action and truth table.)

### 2.3.4 The **NOR** gate

Similarly the **NOR** gate may be thought of as an **OR** gate followed by a **NOT** gate. The logic equation is

$$Z = \overline{A + B}$$

and is read as **NOT** ($A$ **OR** $B$).

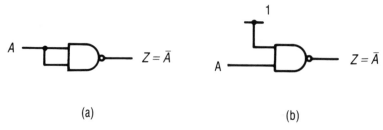

(a)

(b)

**Fig. 2.5** Implementing the **NOT** function with a **NAND** gate.

Both the **NAND** and the **NOR** gates may be expanded to *n*-input, and both gates are of great importance. Although it is useful to think of a **NAND** (**NOR**) gate as a **NOT-AND** (**NOT-OR**) gate, it is designed and implemented directly as a **NAND** (**NOR**) gate. Later it will be shown that all logic functions and systems may be implemented using only **NAND** gates or only **NOR** gates. At present, for example, it should be clear that the **NOT** function can be implemented directly with either a **NAND** gate or a **NOR** state by joining both inputs together. This is shown in Fig. 2.5a for a **NAND** gate. The truth table for the **NAND** and **NOR** functions shows that if both inputs are 0 then the output is 1, while if both inputs are 1 then the output is 0. An alternative way to implement **NOT** with a **NAND** gate is shown in Fig. 2.5b. Here one of the inputs is tied permanently to the logic value 1. Again, inspection of the truth table shows that this performs the **NOT** function.

## 2.3.5 The **EOR** gate

Earlier it was pointed out that there are 16 possible logic functions of two variables that can be generated. So far four of these have been discussed, namely **AND**, **OR**, **NAND** and **NOR**. Of the remaining 12 only one other is commonly implemented, the exclusive-**OR**, **EOR** function. The logic symbol and the truth table for the **EOR** gate are given in Fig. 2.6.

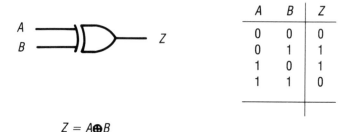

| A | B | Z |
|---|---|---|
| 0 | 0 | 0 |
| 0 | 1 | 1 |
| 1 | 0 | 1 |
| 1 | 1 | 0 |

$Z = A{\oplus}B$

**Fig. 2.6** The exclusive-OR logic gate.

The first three rows of the EOR truth table are identical to those of the OR function. The fourth row is different: if both inputs are logic 1 then the output is logic 0. Thus the output is only 1 if either $A$ or $B$, but not both, are 1. Strictly speaking, the ordinary OR function should be called the inclusive-OR function to distinguish it from the exclusive-OR function.

## 2.4    Example: a 1-bit half adder

Before proceeding with a formal discussion of Boolean algebra, a very simple but widely used combinatorial circuit, the 1-bit half adder shown in black box form in Fig. 2.7, will be considered. The circuit has two 1-bit inputs, $A$ and $B$, and performs binary addition. The circuit generates two outputs, the sum $S$ and the carry $C$.

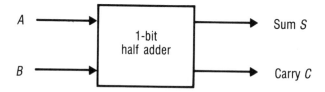

**Fig. 2.7**    The 1-bit adder.

The following truth table shows the relation between the outputs $S$ and $C$ and the inputs $A$ and $B$, for all possible combinations of input values. The truth table has four columns, two for the inputs $A$ and $B$, and two for the outputs $S$ and $C$. There are four rows, one for each of the possible $2^2 = 4$ input combinations.

| A | B | S | C |
|---|---|---|---|
| 0 | 0 | 0 | 0 |
| 0 | 1 | 1 | 0 |
| 1 | 0 | 1 | 0 |
| 1 | 1 | 0 | 1 |

A logic equation for each of the two outputs $S$ and $C$ is now written down in terms of the inputs $A$ and $B$. The procedure for determining these logic equations from the truth table will be discussed in detail in Chapter 3. In this example it leads to

$$S = \bar{A}.B + A.\bar{B}$$
$$\text{and } C = A.B$$

A circuit may be constructed using basic gates to implement a combinatorial circuit that generates $S$ and $C$. In fact, $S$ is just the exclusive-**OR** (**EOR**) of $A$ and $B$, while $C$ is the **AND** of $A$ and $B$, as may be seen by reference to Figs 2.4 and 2.6. The implementation of this simple circuit is shown in Fig. 2.8.

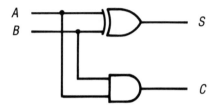

**Fig. 2.8**  The 1-bit adder circuit.

## 2.5  Boolean algebra

As with all sciences, the specification and design of digital logic systems requires a set of basic propositions and rules, i.e. a mathematics. The mathematics we use for digital design is called Boolean algebra, or switching theory, and is based on Boole's work on the algebra of propositions published in 1854. Boolean algebra is also known as propositional calculus, and the form in which it is now used was developed by Shannon in 1938.

### 2.5.1  Propositions and rules of Boolean algebra

The Boolean algebra operators **NOT**, **AND** and **OR** have already been described. The **NOT** operator operates on only a single variable to give its complement, while the **AND** (.) and **OR** (+) operators operate on a pair of variables. There are four basic propositions in Boolean algebra:

1. Commutative proposition

$$A.B = B.A$$
$$A + B = B + A$$

2. Distributive proposition

$$A.(B + C) = A.B + A.C$$
$$A + B.C = (A + B).(A + C)$$

3. Identity proposition

$$A + 0 = A$$
$$A + 1 = 1$$
$$A.1 = A$$
$$A.0 = 0$$

4. Inverse proposition

$$A + \bar{A} = 1$$
$$A.\bar{A} = 0$$

With these propositions a large number of Boolean algebra theorems may be developed. The most important, which will be used where necessary in the text, are:

1. De Morgan's theorem

$$\overline{A + B} = \bar{A}.\bar{B}$$
$$\overline{A.B} = \bar{A} + \bar{B}$$

2. Simplification theorem

$$A + A.B = A$$
$$A + \bar{A}.B = A + B$$

Any of the theorems of Boolean algebra can be proved by evaluating the truth tables for both sides of the equation, and showing that they are equal. This method is demonstrated in the following table for the first of De Morgan's theorems.

| $A$ | $B$ | $A + B$ | $\overline{A + B}$ | $\bar{A}$ | $\bar{B}$ | $\bar{A}.\bar{B}$ |
|---|---|---|---|---|---|---|
| 0 | 0 | 0 | 1 | 1 | 1 | 1 |
| 0 | 1 | 1 | 0 | 1 | 0 | 0 |
| 1 | 0 | 1 | 0 | 0 | 1 | 0 |
| 1 | 1 | 1 | 0 | 0 | 0 | 0 |

Column 4 is identical to column 7, so verifying the theorem. An alternative method is to manipulate the theorem using the propositions and any previously proven theorems, until the new theorem is proved. For example, to prove the first of the simplification theorems

$$A + A.B = A$$

the third identity proposition can be used and $A.1$ substituted for $A$. The left-hand side then becomes

$$A.1 + A.B$$

$A$ is a common factor so this can be rewritten as

$$A.(1 + B)$$

Finally, using the identity proposition $B + 1 = 1$, the left-hand side of the original equation is then just $A.1 = A$, and as this is equal to the right-hand side the proof is completed.

## 2.5.2 Sum-of-products

When designing combinatorial logic systems one logic equation is derived for each output. These equations will have a single logical variable on the left-hand side, the output variable, while the right-hand side will be a Boolean expression of the input variables. The complexity of the right-hand side of each equation will depend on the complexity of the logic function to be implemented. Boolean equations may be written down in many ways. For example, in the 1-bit adder discussed above, the equation for the result $S$ for the binary addition of $A$ and $B$ is

$$S = \bar{A}.B + A.\bar{B}$$

This equation is written down in what is called the sum-of-products form, i.e. in this case a sum $(+)$ of two products $(.)$.

A general Boolean expression of two variables, $f(A,B)$, may be written in a sum-of-products form in the following way:

$$f(A,B) = \bar{A}.\bar{B}.f(0,0) + \bar{A}.B.f(0,1) + A.\bar{B}.f(1,0) + A.B.f(1,1)$$

where each of the terms $f(0,0)$, $f(0,1)$, $f(1,0)$ and $f(1,1)$ can take only the value 0 or 1. Again, for example, in the 1-bit half adder $S = f(A,B)$ and so

$$S = f(A,B) = \bar{A}.\bar{B}.0 + \bar{A}.B.1 + A.\bar{B}.1 + A.B.0$$

i.e. $f(0,0) = 0,$    $f(1,1) = 0$
and $f(0,1) = 1,$    $f(1,0) = 1$

The equation for $f(A,B)$ is said to be in canonical form since it contains all possible combinations of the input variables. Each term is called a minterm, which is a (.) product containing each of the input variables, or its complement, just once.

## 2.6  NAND/NOR logic

The design of combinatorial logic circuits proceeds from the truth table to the logic equations, and then to the implementation. The form of the logic equations used in this text is the sum-of-products form, which could be implemented directly if all the different types of basic logic gate are available. For example, returning to the 1-bit half adder, the logic equation for $S$

$$S = \bar{A}.B + A.\bar{B}$$

could be implemented directly, as in Fig. 2.9, using a mixture of **NOT**, **AND** and **OR** gates (assuming, of course, that an exclusive-**OR** gate is not available). However, such an implementation would be very inefficient since it requires two **AND** gates and one **OR** gate in addition to the two **NOT** gates. This is because gates are implemented in integrated circuits, often called chips, which in general only contain groups of a single type of gate. A much more efficient implementation would result if it were possible to implement the logic equation with just **NAND** gates, or just **NOR** gates. It has already been demonstrated how a **NAND** gate can implement the **NOT** function by joining its inputs together (Fig. 2.5).

De Morgan's theorem states that it is always possible to convert a **NAND** function to a **NOR** function, and vice versa. The theorem will now be aplied to the equation for $S$ to eliminate the **OR** operation, as follows.

First, both sides of the equation are complemented, giving:

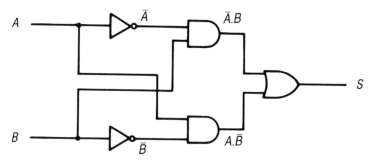

**Fig. 2.9**    1-bit adder circuit using a mixture of **NOT**, **AND**, and **OR** gates.

$$\bar{S} = \overline{\bar{A}.B} + \overline{A.\bar{B}}$$

De Morgan's theorem is now applied to the right-hand side of the equation to change the **OR** function to the **AND** function:

$$\bar{S} = \overline{\overline{\bar{A}.B}} \cdot \overline{\overline{A.\bar{B}}}$$

Finally, both sides of this equation are complemented to leave $S$ on the left-hand side:

$$S = \overline{\overline{\bar{A}.B} \cdot \overline{A.\bar{B}}}$$

$S$ has now been expressed in such a way that it can be entirely implemented with **NAND** gates, as shown in Fig. 2.10a.

It is quite easy to make mistakes in this type of algebraic manipulation; a simpler approach is to use a diagrammatic technique. This technique begins

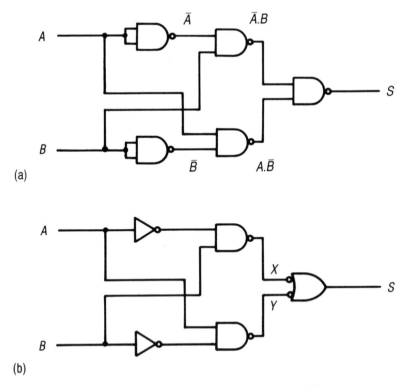

(a)

(b)

**Fig. 2.10** (a) Implementation of 1-bit adder using only **NAND** gates; (b) illustration of the 'bubble' technique.

with the original logic gate diagram of Fig. 2.9; again it is assumed that the circuit will be implemented with only **NAND** gates. The first stage is to identify the two **AND** gates and change them to **NAND** gates by adding bubbles to their outputs. Clearly, this completely changes the logic function of the circuit. To maintain the correct logic function, an inverter, or a second bubble, must be added into each of the lines leading to the **OR** gate. If the bubbles are added at the inputs of the **OR** gates then the logic diagram is as shown in Fig. 2.10b. Although it may not be apparent at first sight, this simplifies the circuit, since the combination of the **OR** gate symbol with the bubbles on the two input lines is actually a **NAND** gate. If the two inputs to the two bubbles at the **OR** gate are labelled $X$ and $Y$ (refer to Fig. 2.10b) then this gate performs the logic function

$$\bar{X} + \bar{Y}$$

which by De Morgan's theorem is just $\overline{X.Y}$, the **NAND** function of $X$ and $Y$. This completes the conversion, since again the original circuit has been converted to one containing only **NAND**s.

Figure 2.11a shows two equivalent ways of drawing a **NAND** gate, following directly from De Morgan's first theorem:

$$\overline{A.B} = \bar{A} + \bar{B}$$

In a similar way, the second of De Morgan's theorems

$$\overline{A + B} = \bar{A}.\bar{B}$$

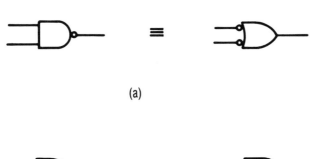

(a)

(b)

**Fig. 2.11**   Equivalent ways of drawing (a) **NAND** and (b) **NOR** gates.

gives two different ways of drawing the **NOR** gate symbol, shown in Fig. 2.11b. The gate symbol which should be used for **NAND** and **NOR** depends on the circumstances. The first **NAND** symbol implies that the output is active low when both the inputs are active high, while the second **NAND** symbol implies that the output is active high when the inputs are active low. Similar arguments apply to the **NOR** gate symbols. The meaning of active high and active low will be discussed in the next section.

The example of logic design described above has shown how implementation using a single type of logic gate, namely **NAND** gates, is possible. The design could equally well have been implemented with only **NOR** gates, and the reader is recommended to try this as an exercise. The idea of being able to move bubbles around in a design, and of adding pairs of bubbles when necessary, is extremely useful, and one which will be used in Chapter 3.

## 2.7   Positive and negative logic

So far it has been assumed that positive logic is being used, i.e. **TRUE** is represented by logic 1 and **FALSE** by logic 0. This leads to the truth table for the **NAND** function:

| $A$ | $B$ | NAND | | $A$ | $B$ | NAND |
|-----|-----|------|---|-----|-----|------|
| $F$ | $F$ | $T$ | | 0 | 0 | 1 |
| $F$ | $T$ | $T$ | | 0 | 1 | 1 |
| $T$ | $F$ | $T$ | | 1 | 0 | 1 |
| $T$ | $T$ | $F$ | | 1 | 1 | 0 |
| (a) | | | | (b) | | |

where (b) is obtained directly from (a) by making the substitutions $F = 0$ and $T = 1$. This is known as positive logic. Any logic scheme could also be implemented using negative logic by making the substitutions $F = 1$ and $T = 0$. Making these substitutions, i.e. $0 = T$ and $1 = F$ in table (b) above gives

| $A$ | $B$ | $Z$ |
|-----|-----|-----|
| $T$ | $T$ | $F$ |
| $T$ | $F$ | $F$ |
| $F$ | $T$ | $F$ |
| $F$ | $F$ | $T$ |

(c)

Examination shows that $Z$ is the **NOR** function. This leads to the conclusion that a positive logic **NAND** gate can also be regarded as a negative logic **NOR** gate. In the same way, if the same substitutions are carried out to a **NOR** gate it becomes clear that a positive logic **NOR** gate can also be regarded as a negative logic **NAND** gate.

## 2.8   Logic implementation

So far the practical implementation of the basic logic gates has not been considered. There are several ways of implementing digital logic systems, including fluidic logic, relay logic and electronic logic gates; only the last will be considered here. The aim of this section is, first, to introduce the concept of using a transistor as a digital switch and, secondly, to discuss families of electronic logic gates. This will be taken to the extent that the reader will feel confident that he can implement simple logic designs by interconnecting logic chips, and have an appreciation of the differences between the logic families available.

### 2.8.1   The field-effect transistor as a switch

Transistors are the basic 'building blocks' of all integrated electronic logic circuits. Although there are two main types of transistor family available, each with several variants, all transistors have the ability to act as a digital switch. It is this capability that is exploited in all digital logic circuits.

Figure 2.12 shows the circuit symbols used for the most widely available transistors, namely the *npn* bipolar transistor and the field-effect transistor (FET). Both devices have three terminals. These are called emitter, base and collector in the bipolar transistor, and source, gate and drain in the FET.

The basic transistor switch circuit using a FET is shown in Fig. 2.13a. Although there are several different types of FET available, only one, the so-called '*n*-channel enhancement mode FET', will be considered in this section. In addition to the FET, the circuit contains a resistor $R_L$, known as a load

**Fig. 2.12**   Bipolar transistor (*npn*) and FET symbols.

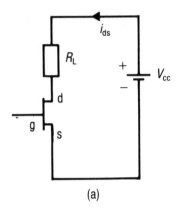

(a)

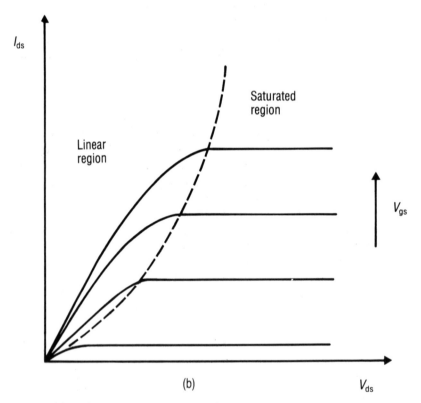

(b)

**Fig. 2.13** (a) Basic FET transistor circuit. (b) Characteristic curves for a typical *n*-channel enhancement mode FET. Each curve is a plot of the drain–source current, $i_{ds}$, as a function of the drain–source voltage, $V_{ds}$, for given values of the gate–source voltage, $V_{gs}$.

resistor, and a battery, whose voltage is labelled $V_{cc}$. A similar circuit applies for the bipolar transistor switch. The battery, resistor $R_L$, drain–source of the FET and the connecting wires form a simple series circuit. No current flows around this circuit, because there is no voltage on the gate, since no connection has been made to the gate, and the transistor is turned off. The drain–source path thus acts like an open switch, and so the drain–source current, $i_{ds}$, is zero. Moreover, because no current flows in this circuit there is no voltage drop across $R_L$ (by Ohm's law) and so the voltage across the drain–source of the FET, $V_{ds}$, is $V_{cc}$ volts. Since no connection was made to the gate, the gate–source voltage $V_{gs} = 0$ V. Note that the voltage differences are defined relative to the source of the FET.

Now consider what happens when a non-zero voltage is applied to the gate relative to the source, i.e. $V_{gs} > 0$. This voltage difference places a positive charge on the gate of the FET. If $V_{gs}$ is greater than a threshold voltage, $V_t$, then the transistor is turned on. There is now a conducting path between the drain and the source which completes the circuit so that a current can now flow around the battery, load resistor, FET circuit, i.e. $i_{ds} > 0$.

The threshold voltage, $V_t$, varies from a few tenths of a volt to a few volts, depending on the design of the FET. Figure 2.13b shows how the drain–source current, $i_{ds}$, varies with the drain–source voltage, $V_{ds}$, for a number of values of the gate–source voltage, $V_{gs}$. Each curve, corresponding to a constant value of $V_{gs}$, falls into two distinct regions, namely the linear region and the saturation region. As $V_{ds}$ is increased from zero, the drain current, $i_{ds}$, initially increases approximately linearly with $V_{ds}$. However, above a certain value of $V_{ds}$ the curve 'flattens out', or saturates, so that $i_{ds}$ remains constant for any further increase in $V_{ds}$. FETs used as digital switches are operated in the saturation region.

This will be achieved if $V_{gs}$ is much greater than the threshold voltage $V_t$, by making $V_{gs} = V_{cc}$, say. The drain–source path then behaves like a closed switch. The resistance of the drain–source path is very small and can be neglected. If this is the case then $V_{ds} = 0$, by Ohm's law, and the voltage drop across the resistor equals $V_{cc}$.

This is the basic FET digital switch, and is redrawn in Fig. 2.14. By convention all voltages are referred to the source terminal of the FET. The input voltage $V_{in}$ is applied to the gate, so $V_{gs} = V_{in}$. The output is taken from the drain terminal, so $V_{out} = V_{ds}$. There are only two possible values for $V_{in}$, either 0 volts or $V_{cc}$. Thus the two following cases are possible:

1. $V_{in} = 0$. The FET is switched off, so $i_{ds} = 0$ and $V_{out} = V_{cc}$.
2. $V_{in} = V_{cc}$. The FET is switched on, so $i_{ds} > 0$, and $V_{out} = 0$. From Ohm's law $i_{ds} = V_{cc}/R_L$.

These two conditions can be expressed as a truth table:

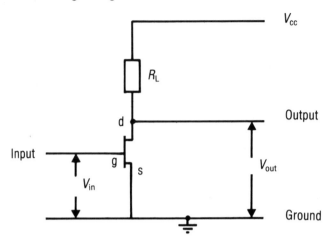

**Fig. 2.14** Basic FET switch circuit.

| $V_{in}$ | $V_{out}$ | or | $V_{in}$ | $V_{out}$ |
|----------|-----------|-----|----------|-----------|
| 0 | $V_{cc}$ | | 0 | 1 |
| $V_{cc}$ | 0 | | 1 | 0 |

where, as usual, 0 represents logic level 0, and $V_{cc}$ logic level 1.

This is clearly the truth table for a **NOT** gate, and so a single FET can be used to implement the **NOT** function.

### 2.8.2 Field-effect transistor **NAND** and **NOR** logic gates

**NAND** and **NOR** logic gates may be constructed very simply from the basic FET switching circuit just described. The circuit of Fig. 2.15 is a 2-input **NAND** gate. The inputs are $A$ and $B$, while the output $Z$ is taken from the junction between the drain of the top FET and the load resistor $R_L$. The $V_{cc}$ power supply and the connecting wires have been omitted for simplicity. There are four possible input conditions. Consider first $A = B = 0$. Both transistors are switched off so no current flows down the chain comprising the load resistor $R_L$ and the two transistors. Thus the output $Z$ is at the supply voltage $V_{cc}$, i.e. $Z = 1$. A similar argument applies for $A = 0$, $B = 1$ and for $A = 1$, $B = 0$. Only for the case $A = B = 1$, when both FETs are turned on, can a current flow so that $Z = 0$. The circuit is clearly that of a **NAND** gate.

Figure 2.16 shows a 2-input **NOR** function constructed from two FETs in parallel. The reader should be able to verify that this circuit does indeed

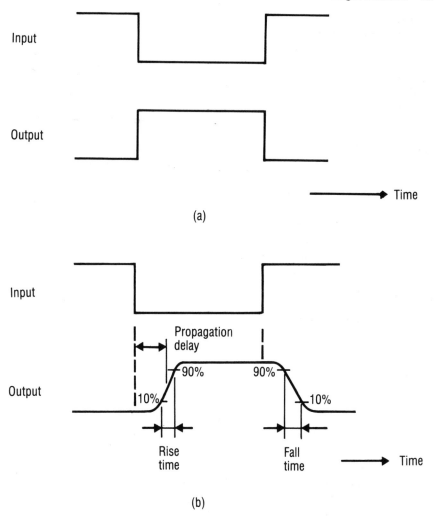

Input

Time

(a)

Input

Propagation delay

90%

90%

10%

10%

Rise time

Fall time

Time

(b)

**Fig. 2.17**   Input and output signals of an (a) ideal and (b) actual **NOT** gate.

transistor logic) and CMOS (complementary metal oxide semiconductor) logic, will now be discussed.

## 2.9.2   Transistor–transistor logic

Although TTL has been available since the 1960s, continuing development effort has produced a number of different families of TTL, listed in Table 2.1, so that it remains a popular choice for building small to medium scale logic systems. The technology used to build TTL circuits is based on bipolar

**Table 2.1**   Characteristics of TTL families of integrated circuits

| Series | Propagation delay (ns) | Power (mW) | Fan-in | Fan-out | Properties |
|--------|------------------------|------------|--------|---------|------------|
| 74XX   | 10 | 10 | 1    | 10   | Standard series |
| 74LXX  | 33 | 1  | 0.25 | 2.5  | Low power consumption but slow |
| 74HXX  | 6  | 22 | 1.25 | 12.5 | High speed but high power consumption |
| 74LSXX | 10 | 2  | 0.25 | 5    | Low power Schottky; compromise between low power and high speed |

transistors. The TTL parameters relevant to users that must be considered are logic levels, fan-out, fan-in, gate propagation delay and power requirements.

## (a)   Logic levels

TTL logic levels have the following voltage ranges:

Output:   Logic 1   2.4–5.0 V
          Logic 0   0–0.4 V
Input:    Logic 1   2.0–5.0 V
          Logic 0   0–0.8 V

The output of a TTL gate for logic level 1 is guaranteed to be greater than 2.4 V. (In practice, it is more likely to be closer to 3.5 V.) However the input to a gate for logic level 1 need only be 2.0 V, i.e. 0.4 V less than the minimum logic level 1 output voltage. This difference is called the noise immunity margin. Consider Fig. 2.18 which shows the output of a **NOT** gate being fed into the input of a second **NOT** gate. Suppose the output of gate $A$ is logic level 1, and is actually the minimum value of 2.4 V. If this output is viewed on an oscilloscope, it may well be seen that the output is not a steady voltage of 2.4 V but comprises two components: the steady level of 2.4 V and a randomly fluctuating noise voltage of perhaps several hundred millivolts. Gate $B$ will still recognize the input to be a logic level 1 provided that the amplitude of the noise voltage does not exceed 0.4 V in this example. Now suppose the output of gate $A$ is logic level 0, and is 0.4 V, i.e. at the top of the logic 0 range. What digital noise can be tolerated on this output? The answer is again a noise amplitude that does not exceed $0.8 - 0.4 = 0.4$ V. Thus TTL is said to have a noise margin of 0.4 V.

Finally, note that voltages in the range 0.8–2.0 V are not defined and must not occur. The output of a gate whose input lies in this range is undefined.

**Fig. 2.18** Noise immunity example.

## (b) Fan-out

The current-driving capabilities of TTL logic will now be discussed. Consider the TTL **NOT** gate shown in Fig. 2.19a. The output is shown driving a load to ground which is represented by the resistor $R$. Let the input to the gate be logic level 0 so the output is logic level 1. The symbol for the output high voltage used in TTL data sheets is $V_{OH}$ and the output current flowing through the resistor $R$ to ground is $I_{OH}$. The quantitites $V_{OH}$, $I_{OH}$ and $R$ are related by Ohm's law:

$$I_{OH} = V_{OH}/R$$

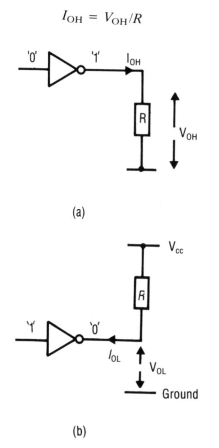

(a)

(b)

**Fig. 2.19** Definition of TTL (a) source and (b) sink currents.

Suppose $R$ is initially 'large', i.e. several thousands of ohms or more, and is then progressively decreased. The above equation shows that $I_{OH}$ will increase as this happens. However, as $I_{OH}$ increases it is found that $V_{OH}$ starts to decrease. This is allowable of course, provided that it does not fall below 2.4 V. $I_{OH}$ is known as the source current, and the maximum value allowed is $-400\,\mu A$. The negative sign is used by convention to mean that the current is flowing out of the gate. When the maximum source current is drawn, $V_{OH}$ will still be above (although perhaps only just) the minimum value of 2.4 V.

Now consider the situation shown in Fig. 2.19b where the load $R$ is connected between the output of the gate and the TTL power supply, nominally +5 V. The gate input is now logic level 1 so the output is logic level 0. Current will flow from the power supply through the load resistor $R$ and into the gate. This current is known as the output low current $I_{OL}$, and is usually referred to as the sink current. If the output low voltage is $V_{OL}$ then the voltage drop across the load resistor is $V_{cc} - V_{OL}$. Applying Ohm's law to $R$ gives:

$$I_{OL} = \frac{V_{cc} - V_{OL}}{R}$$

Again if $R$ is initially 'large' and then progressively decreased, $I_{OL}$ will increase. However, this time as $I_{OL}$ increases $V_{OL}$ begins to rise above 0 V. Eventually it reaches the maximum TTL value allowed of 0.4 V. The maximum sink current $I_{OL}$ is (+)16 mA. Note that the maximum sink current is much greater than the maximum source current.

Fan-out is the maximum number of gates whose inputs may all be connected to the output of a single gate, i.e. it is the maximum number of gates that the output from a single TTL gate will drive.

### (c)   Fan-in

In the same way as discussed above for output currents, the input current requirements of TTL gates can be considered. It is important to realize that for a TTL gate to work some current must flow into the input circuit of the gate. Consider again the two interconnected **NOT** gates shown in Fig. 2.18. If the input to gate $A$ is logic level 1 then its output will be logic 0. The input to gate $B$ is thus logic 0, and its output, logic 1. The input circuit of gate $B$ provides a load to the output of gate $A$ with the result that a current flows out of gate $B$ into gate $A$. This current is called the input low current $I_{IL}$, and for a standard TTL gate has a value less than 1.6 mA. Now suppose the input to gate $A$ is changed to logic 0. Its output is logic 1 so that now a source current will flow out of $A$ and into the input circuit of $B$. This current is the input high current $I_{IH}$, and is less than $40\,\mu A$ for standard TTL. Comparing these input currents with the output drive current capabilities of standard TTL we see that the standard TTL fan-out is 10.

By definition a standard TTL gate has a fan-in of 1. Figure 2.5 showed the two ways in which a **NAND** gate can be used as an inverter. The circuits differ in that Fig. 2.5a has a fan-in of 2, since the preceding gate must drive both the inputs, while Fig. 2.5b has a fan-in of 1. For this reason the second circuit is usually preferred.

Table 2.1 shows the fan-in and fan-out of the various TTL families, and answers questions of the type 'Can a standard 7400 **NAND** gate drive seven Schottky 74S gates?'

### (d)   Speed versus power

In the introduction to logic families it was argued that the ideal gate should consume no power, and have zero propagation delay. In practice, neither of these requirements can be met, and a trade-off must always be made between them. For example, Table 2.1 shows that a low power TTL gate consumes only 10% of the power of a standard TTL gate, but is about three times slower. A widely used compromise at present is the low power Schottky TTL series of TTL integrated circuits, which have about the same speed as standard TTL but consume only about 20% of the power.

## 2.9.3   Complementary metal oxide semiconductor logic

### (a)   Introduction

The second logic family widely used for implementing digital logic is complemetary metal oxide semiconductor logic, CMOS. Figure 2.20 shows the basic

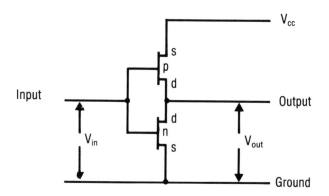

**Fig. 2.20**   Basic CMOS **NOT** gate.

CMOS inverter circuit, or **NOT** gate. Although the circuit may look strange at first sight, it is conceptually very simple. It consists of only two FET transistors, connected in series between the logic power supply. The bottom transistor is an $n$-channel FET similar to the one discussed above in section 2.8.1, while the top transistor is a $p$-channel FET. The main difference between an $n$-channel and a $p$-channel FET is that the $p$-channel FET is turned on when the gate voltage is more negative than the source voltage (i.e. $V_{gs} < 0$) and is turned off when $V_{gs} = 0$.

The arrangement of the transistors in Fig. 2.20 is often referred to as 'push–pull'. The input is applied to the gates of both transistors, which are joined together. The power supply lines are labelled $V_{cc}$ and ground, although frequently $V_{dd}$ is used in place of $V_{cc}$, and $V_{ss}$ in place of ground. Unlike TTL the supply voltage $V_{cc}$ can be varied between +3 and +15 V, or even higher in the case of some CMOS family circuits.

To see how this circuit works consider the two possible logic values that $V_{in}$ can take.

1. $V_{in} = 0$ V, corresponding to logic 0. The bottom transistor is switched off, while the top transistor is switched on. The ratio of the off/on source–drain resistance of an FET is very large, and for our purposes may be assumed infinite. Thus there is effectively a short-circuit path between $V_{cc}$ and $V_{out}$, and an open-circuit path between ground and $V_{out}$. Thus $V_{out} = V_{cc}$.
2. $V_{in} = V_{cc}$, corresponding to logic 1. The bottom transistor is switched on, the top transistor is off, so $V_{out}$ is effectively connected to ground, i.e. $V_{out} = 0$.

The circuit thus acts as a **NOT** gate, and is the fundamental building block used in CMOS circuits. Note that only one transistor is on in both logic states, so in the quiescent state no current flows and hence the power dissipation is zero.

There are a number of CMOS families available, the two main series being the 4000B and the 74Cxx. These two series are completely electrically compatible. In addition, the 74Cxx series is functionally and pin compatible with the 74 series of TTL.

## (b) Logic levels

Figure 2.21 shows a typical transfer characteristic or curve of a CMOS **NOT** gate, i.e. a plot of $V_{out}$ against $V_{in}$. The output changes state when $V_{in}$ is approximately $\frac{1}{2}V_{cc}$. When used as a logic element, input voltages between $0.3V_{cc}$ and $0.7V_{cc}$ are not allowed, i.e. the output state will be undefined. Voltages below $0.3V_{cc}$ are valid logic 0 levels, while voltages above $0.7V_{cc}$ are valid logic 1 levels. The noise immunity of both logic levels is thus 30% of $V_{cc}$.

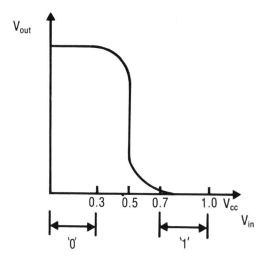

**Fig. 2.21**  Typical transfer characteristic of a CMOS **NOT** gate.

This is considerably greater than the 0.4 V noise immunity of TTL, and has advantages in many applications.

### (c)  Fan-out

Because the transistors used in a CMOS gate are FETs, CMOS circuits have negligible current requirements. This is because the current flowing in the gate circuit of a FET is very small, and can usually be neglected. Thus the output from a CMOS gate can drive any number of CMOS gates in parallel, i.e. the fan-out is theoretically infinite. However, in practice this is not quite true, as is now explained.

The input gate of a FET behaves like a capacitor: when the logic level of a gate is changed from 0 to 1, current flows into the gate capacitance, charging the gate until its voltage equals $V_{cc}$, and conversely when the level is changed from 1 to 0 current has to flow out of the gate capacitance. Consider the circuit shown in Fig. 2.22 where the output of the first CMOS **NOT** gate is used to drive a second **NOT** gate. Assume the input to the first gate is logic 1, so that its output is 0. Transistors $n_1$ and $p_2$ are switched on, while $n_2$ and $p_1$ are off, so that the gate of the second **NOT** gate is at 0 V. Changing the logic level at gate 1 from 1 to 0 switches $n_1$ off and $p_1$ on. The gate of the second FET is now connected to the supply voltages $V_{cc}$ through $p_1$, which has a low effective resistance, $R_{eff}$ say. For the 4000 series of CMOS circuits, $R_{eff}$ is about 500 Ω. Current now flows through $R_{eff}$ and charges the effective capacitance, $C_{eff}$ say, of the second FET's gate. The voltage on the gate $V_g$ will then increase with time according to the equation:

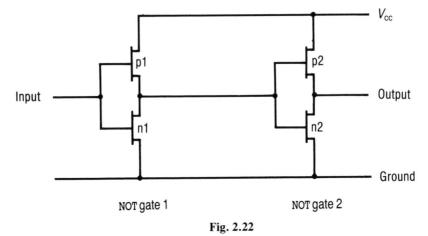

NOT gate 1          NOT gate 2

**Fig. 2.22**

$$V_g = V_{cc}[1 - \exp(-t/R_{eff}C_{eff})]$$

Thus $V_g$ increases in an exponential fashion towards $V_{cc}$ with a time constant $RC$. The value of $C$ is of the order 5 pF, so $R_{eff}C_{eff} = 500 \times 5 \times 10^{-12} = 2.5$ ns. If, however, $n$ more gates are added in parallel with the second gate, the effect is to multiply $C_{eff}$ by $n$, thus increasing the charge/discharge time. It is this effect which in practice limits the fan-out in a real system.

The majority of CMOS chips are designed so that they can drive a 74LS load directly, i.e. they have a maximum current-driving capability of 0.4 mA source and 4 mA sink currents. There are also CMOS buffers available, such as the 4049 inverting and 4050 non-inverting buffer, which can drive two 74xx TTL series loads or eight 74LSxx series loads directly.

### (d) Fan-in

This term is not really applicable to CMOS circuits, since effectively no gate current is required.

Although outside the scope of this book, the interfacing between different logic families, such as TTL and CMOS, is a very important subject. See, for example, Horowitz and Hill in the bibliography.

### (e) Speed versus power

The maximum speed at which a CMOS circuit can be switched is complicated by the fact that it depends not only on the capacitance of the load being driven, but also on the supply voltage $V_{cc}$. Basically, as $V_{cc}$ increases, the gate delay for a given load decreases.

The quiescent power consumption of a CMOS gate is very small, since one of the two gates is always off, and is typically much less than $1\mu$W at $V_{cc} = 5$ V. However, when the gate is being switched, current is required to charge the load that the gate is driving (usually the gate of another FET of course), and power is dissipated while this occurs. The power consumption is proportional to the switching frequency $f$ and is given by the equation

$$P_{ac} = C_{eff} \times V^2_{cc} \times f$$

where $C_{eff}$ is the load capacitance being driven. The subscript ac is used to differentiate the switching from the quiescent power consumption. If we take $C_{eff} = 5$ pF and $f = 100$ kHz then $P_{ac} = 5 \times 10^{-12} \times 25 \times 10^5 = 0.0125$ mW for $V_{cc} = 5$ V. This will be increased by the factor 225/25, or nearly 10 times, if $V_{cc} = 15$ V.

In conclusion, the minimum value of $V_{cc}$ should be selected to minimize the power consumption, at the required maximum switching frequency that will be used.

### 2.9.4   Comparison of transistor–transistor and complementary metal oxide semiconductor logic

Both TTL and CMOS circuits are widely available from many semiconductor manufacturers, and are extensively used in the design of small to medium sized digital logic systems.

The main advantage of TTL is that it is fast, with a maximum switching frequency of up to about 50 MHz. TTL can also sink a relatively large current of up to 16 mA which is sufficient, for example, to illuminate a light-emitting diode (LED). The chief disadvantages of TTL are its relatively high power consumption (to the extent that TTL MSI chips often run very hot) and its low noise immunity.

Compared with TTL, CMOS chips use very little quiescent power and have a much higher noise immunity, but also have a lower maximum switching frequency of about 1–10 MHz.

Although there is continuing development work in both TTL and CMOS, with the net result that TTL chips are using less power, while CMOS chips are getting faster, the trend is towards implementing logic systems with CMOS.

## 2.10   Summary

The basics of digital logic have been discussed in the first half of this chapter. After an introduction to the basic logic gates, **NOT, AND, OR, NAND, NOR** and **EOR**, which form the 'basic building block' of digital logic systems, the necessary mathematics of logic systems, Boolean algebra, was given. An understanding of this algebra, and in particular the use of the basic propositions and De Morgan's theorem, are the basic tools of the digital logic engineer.

The implementation of digital logic systems, with emphasis on the two most popular logic families available, namely TTL and CMOS, were discussed from the user's point of view in the second half of the chapter.

## Exercises

2.1 Simplify the following expressions algebraically:

$$\bar{A}.\bar{B} + A.B + \bar{A}.B$$
$$\bar{A}.B.C + A.\bar{B}.C + A.B.\bar{C} + A.B.C$$

2.2 In section 2.6 it was shown how to implement a 1-bit adder using only **NAND** gates by (a) applying de Morgan's theorem, and (b) using the 'bubble' technique. Using both techniques implement the 1-bit adder using only **NOR** gates.

2.3 Convert the following circuit to one only using **NAND** gates:

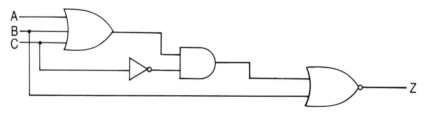

2.4 Using Boolean algebra find a simpler circuit with the same function as that given below:

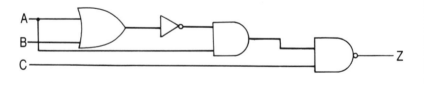

# 3

# Combinatorial logic design

## 3.1 Introduction

A combinatorial logic circuit, as shown in Fig. 3.1, is one whose outputs are dependent only on the inputs. A set of Boolean equations expressing the relationship between the $n$ inputs and each output may be written in the form:

$$\text{Output}_j = f(i_1, i_2 \ldots i_n).$$

The function of the combinatorial circuit is totally specified by these $m$-equations, one for each output. At this point it will be assumed that the outputs respond immediately to any change in an input signal. In practice this is not quite true. Combinatorial circuits are implemented with logic gates and since each gate has a small propagation time, there will inevitably be a small delay between an output signal changing as a result of a change of one or more of the inputs. In a complex combinatorial circuit containing many gates this delay must be taken into account when designing a system.

## 3.2 Problem specification

All circuit design begins with a specification of the problem. It is necessary to appreciate that, at this stage, the specification will almost certainly be incomplete and may even be vague. Before the circuit can be designed or implemented, requirements must be completely understood and the specification must be complete without any ambiguities. Experienced designers know that specification is often the most difficult stage of a project, because it involves persuading the customer to state exactly what his requirements are, and then translating them into an unambiguous and complete specification.

In the case of combinatorial circuits the specification of a circuit should be

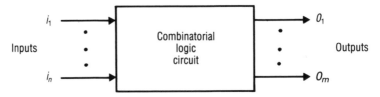

**Fig. 3.1**   Typical combinatorial logic circuit.

written in the form of either a truth table or a set of Boolean logic equations.
The following design procedure should be adopted:

1. list the outputs required;
2. list the inputs available, or required;
3. state the functions required to obtain the outputs from the available inputs;
4. for each output draw a truth table.

All possible input combinations must be shown on this truth table, including
those labelled 'don't care' or 'can't normally occur'. They are usually marked
with a cross. The table should have one column for each input, one column
for each output, and $2^n$ rows, where $n$ is the number of inputs, since $2^n$ is the
total number of possible input combinations.

Truth tables must be completely filled in, since 'can't normally occur' input
conditions may arise under unusual or fault conditions. Such inputs must be
properly considered so that the combinatorial circuit always produces a known
output for every possible combination of the input signals.

The next stage in the design process is implementation. If the design is a
simple one then this is done directly, using either suitable gates or an MSI
chip. For more complex designs the implementation is preceded by a further
stage, called minimization or reduction, in which techniques are applied to
eliminate any redundant terms in the design, so that an implementation can
be achieved with the minimum number of gates. Before outlining minimization
techniques, two design examples, of a parity generator and of a 7-segment
decoder, will be presented.

## 3.3   Design example: a parity generator

### 3.3.1   Description

Data transmitted over long distances are prone to corruption, i.e. individual
bits may be lost or changed, and it is essential to know when such corruption
has occurred. Many techniques, of varying degrees of sophistication, exist,
the simplest being to add an additional bit at the sending end, to make the

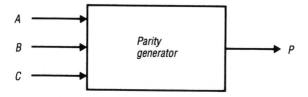

**Fig. 3.2**   Block diagram of parity generator circuit.

number of 1-bits in the pattern even or odd, and to check this bit at the receiving end. This extra bit is known as a parity bit. A single parity bit transmitted with a group of data bits allows the detection of a single-bit error, i.e. a 0 corrupted to a 1 or vice versa.

In this example, a circuit is required to accept a 3-bit binary number and to generate an odd parity bit $P$. Figure 3.2 shows a block diagram of the system required. If the number of 1s in the data is odd, $P = 0$, while if the number of 1s is even, $P = 1$.

### 3.3.2   Outputs

The circuit has a single output $P$.

### 3.3.3   Inputs

The three inputs are labelled $A$, $B$ and $C$.

### 3.3.4   Truth table

The truth table can be written down immediately, as follows:

| Input | A | B | C | P |
|-------|---|---|---|---|
| 0 | 0 | 0 | 0 | 1 |
| 1 | 0 | 0 | 1 | 0 |
| 2 | 0 | 1 | 0 | 0 |
| 3 | 0 | 1 | 1 | 1 |
| 4 | 1 | 0 | 0 | 0 |
| 5 | 1 | 0 | 1 | 1 |
| 6 | 1 | 1 | 0 | 1 |
| 7 | 1 | 1 | 1 | 0 |

### 3.3.5 Boolean equation

A logic equation is now written down in sum-of-products form for the output $P$ in terms of the inputs $A$, $B$ and $C$. This is done by identifying the rows in the truth table for which $P$ is 1. These are rows 1, 4, 6 and 7. The input logic combinations of $A$, $B$ and $C$ corresponding to these rows are 000, 011, 101 and 110. The logic equation for $P$ is then the sum of these products, i.e.:

$$P = \bar{A}.\bar{B}.\bar{C} + \bar{A}.B.C + A.\bar{B}.C + A.B.\bar{C}$$

This equation may be rewritten in the shorthand notation

$$P = 0 + 3 + 5 + 6$$

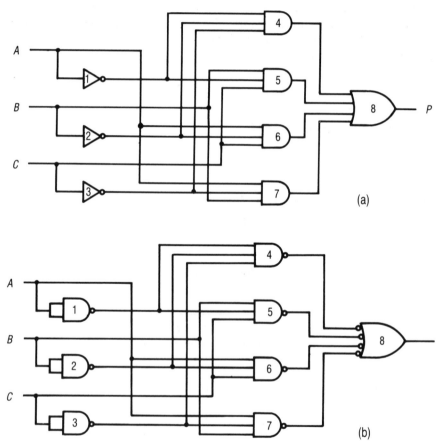

**Fig. 3.3** Implementation of parity generator circuit using (a) basic gates; (b) only NAND gates.

where the numbers correspond to the appropriate input values that give $P = 1$. Note that there are four product terms, since there are four input combinations that give $P = 1$.

## 3.3.6   Implementation

$P$ can be implemented directly, using a combination of **NOT**, **AND** and **OR** gates, as shown in Fig. 3.3a. Although this implementation is straightforward, it is not ideal since it uses three different types of gate. Moreover, since only three 3-input **AND** gates are normally available in a single integrated circuit, two such packages must be used to give the necessary four **AND** gates.

   A number of simplifications can be made to this circuit. In Chapter 2 it was shown that all combinatorial circuits can be implemented with either **NAND** or **NOR** gates. Here the implementation of the above circuit using only **NAND** gates is considered. This may be done either by applying De Morgan's theorem directly to the equation for $P$ to change the **OR** terms into **AND** terms, or equivalently by applying the graphical technique, discussed in Chapter 2, to Fig. 3.3a. The inverting gates 1, 2 and 3 can be implemented with $n$-input **NAND** gates, with the $n$-inputs tied together. Using the graphical technique, the **AND** gates may be converted to **NAND** gates by adding 'bubbles' to each of the gate outputs. However, to keep the function of the circuit the same 'bubbles' must then be added at the other ends of the output lines from gates 4, 5, 6 and 7. Gate 8 then becomes a 4-input **OR** gate with negative true input logic, which is just a 4-input **NAND** gate with normal positive true logic. The final circuit can thus be implemented using only **NAND** gates, and is shown in Fig. 3.3b.

## 3.4   Design example: a 7-segment decimal decoder

### 3.4.1   Description

A frequently used circuit is the 7-segment decoder used to drive 7-segment LED or LCD displays (Fig. 3.4). Although this function is available as an MSI chip, its design and implementation using standard gates are described here. The function of the decoder is to accept four bits of data containing the binary code of the number to be displayed (i.e. 0 to 9), and to generate the appropriate outputs to drive the seven segments of the display. Figure 3.4 shows the black box representation of the circuit required together with the conventional labelling of the segments of the display. For example, to display the digit 4, the segments $b$, $c$, $f$ and $g$ are turned on, i.e. logic 1, while the remaining segments $a$, $d$ and $e$ are turned off, i.e. logic 0.

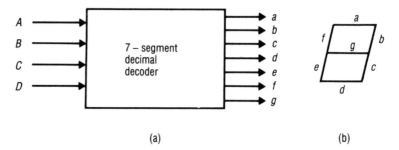

(a)                                                     (b)

**Fig. 3.4**  (a) Block diagram of 7-segment decimal decoder; (b) labelling of segments.

## 3.4.2  Truth table

The truth table of the combinatorial circuit required can be written down directly from an inspection of Fig. 3.4b, as follows:

| Decimal number | Binary representation | | | | Segments | | | | | | |
|---|---|---|---|---|---|---|---|---|---|---|---|
| | $A$ | $B$ | $C$ | $D$ | $a$ | $b$ | $c$ | $d$ | $e$ | $f$ | $g$ |
| 0 | 0 | 0 | 0 | 0 | 1 | 1 | 1 | 1 | 1 | 1 | 0 |
| 1 | 0 | 0 | 0 | 1 | 0 | 1 | 1 | 0 | 0 | 0 | 0 |
| 2 | 0 | 0 | 1 | 0 | 1 | 1 | 0 | 1 | 1 | 0 | 1 |
| 3 | 0 | 0 | 1 | 1 | 1 | 1 | 1 | 1 | 0 | 0 | 1 |
| 4 | 0 | 1 | 0 | 0 | 0 | 1 | 1 | 0 | 0 | 1 | 1 |
| 5 | 0 | 1 | 0 | 1 | 1 | 0 | 1 | 1 | 0 | 1 | 1 |
| 6 | 0 | 1 | 1 | 0 | 0 | 0 | 1 | 1 | 1 | 1 | 1 |
| 7 | 0 | 1 | 1 | 1 | 1 | 1 | 1 | 0 | 0 | 0 | 0 |
| 8 | 1 | 0 | 0 | 0 | 1 | 1 | 1 | 1 | 1 | 1 | 1 |
| 9 | 1 | 0 | 0 | 1 | 1 | 1 | 1 | 0 | 0 | 1 | 1 |

The main difference between this example and the previous one is that there are several outputs, instead of just one. However, as these outputs are independent, a Boolean equation may be written down for each output, $a$ to $g$, in sum-of-products form directly from an inspection of the truth table. For example, the Boolean equation for $a$ is:

$$a = \bar{A}.\bar{B}.\bar{C}.\bar{D} + \bar{A}.\bar{B}.C.\bar{D} + \bar{A}.\bar{B}.C.D + \bar{A}.B.\bar{C}.D + \bar{A}.B.C.D + A.\bar{B}.\bar{C}.\bar{D} + A.\bar{B}.\bar{C}.D$$

or in shorthand notation:

$$a = 0 + 2 + 3 + 5 + 7 + 8 + 9$$

Similarly for the other segments:

$$b = 0 + 1 + 2 + 3 + 4 + 7 + 8 + 9$$
$$c = 0 + 1 + 3 + 4 + 5 + 6 + 7 + 8 + 9$$
$$d = 0 + 2 + 3 + 5 + 6 + 8$$
$$e = 0 + 2 + 6 + 8$$
$$f = 0 + 4 + 5 + 6 + 8 + 9$$
$$g = 2 + 3 + 4 + 5 + 6 + 8 + 9$$

### 3.4.3   Implementation

Clearly it would be perfectly possible at this stage to implement the seven circuits required to drive the segments using **NAND** or **NOR** gates, in a similar fashion to the previous example. However, the circuit will be cumbersome, containing a large number of gates, many of which are redundant. In the next section, methods to minimize the number of gates required to implement a given logic function are discussed and these methods are applied to the implementation of the current example.

## 3.5   Minimization of Boolean functions

The aim of minimization is to simplify Boolean expressions and to eliminate any redundant terms, using the rules of Boolean algebra. The resulting expression will usually have fewer terms. In addition, each of the remaining terms will often have fewer variables, which leads in turn to a simpler implementation with either fewer or simpler gates. It is rarely worthwhile to take this process to the extreme, that is, to minimize the amount of logic required. This is particularly the case in designs that are to be implemented with larger-scale integration, where the cost of using extra gates is minimal, and where the cost in design time of minimization will often outweigh the savings in hardware.

Consider the Boolean equation for driving segment $a$ of a 7-segment display:

$$a = \bar{A}.\bar{B}.\bar{C}.\bar{D} + \bar{A}.\bar{B}.C.\bar{D} + \bar{A}.B.C.D + \bar{A}.B.\bar{C}.D + \bar{A}.B.C.D +$$
$$A.\bar{B}.\bar{C}.\bar{D} + A.\bar{B}.\bar{C}.D$$

In reducing a Boolean expression, one aim is to combine terms with common factors to give expressions of the form $X + \bar{X}$, which reduce to 1. For example, $\bar{A}.\bar{B}.C$ is a common factor in both terms 2 and 3, and so can be combined to give

$$\bar{A}.\bar{B}.C.(\bar{D} + D) = \bar{A}.\bar{B}.C$$

Similarly, terms 8 and 9 can be combined to give $A.\bar{B}.\bar{C}$, leading to

$$a = \bar{A}.\bar{B}.\bar{C}.\bar{D} + \bar{A}.\bar{B}.C + \bar{A}.B.\bar{C}.D + \bar{A}.B.C.D + A.\bar{B}.\bar{C}$$

Can this expression be simplified further? Has it been reduced in such a way that the simplest implementation is given? These questions are difficult to answer even when there are only four variables, as in the present example, and become even more so when the number is increased. Moreover, any of the 'don't care' terms can always be added to the Boolean equation if it leads to a further simplification, but it is often quite difficult to see which ones, if any, to add to do this. The graphical technique discussed in the next section allows this to be done in a straightforward manner.

### 3.5.1   Use of Karnaugh maps

A Karnaugh map or K-map is a diagram on which the sums-of-products of a Boolean expression are plotted, and which allows the elimination and reduction of terms to be made visually. A K-map for $n$ variables contains $2^n$ squares, so that every combination of the input variables is shown. K-maps for two, three and four variables are shown in Fig. 3.5. The squares are labelled so that only one variable changes (e.g. from $A$ to $\bar{A}$ or vice versa) on going from one square to the next horizontally or vertically. This coding (known as a Gray code) makes the identification of terms which can be combined fairly obvious, as will now be demonstrated. Note that the square at the top left is effectively adjacent to the square at the top right: in the 4-variable map these squares are $\bar{A}.\bar{B}.\bar{C}.\bar{D}$ and $A.\bar{B}.\bar{C}.\bar{D}$, that is, they differ only in the variable $A$. In the same way, the square at the top left is also adjacent to the square at the bottom left, since only variable $C$ differs. The map may thus be thought of as being wrapped ('around cylinders') both vertically and horizontally. It is helpful to write the shorthand number corresponding to the variable combination in each square. This enables the K-map to be filled in easily from the truth table.

It should be emphasized that there is one K-map for each Boolean output variable in a design. The procedure for filling in the K-map and then using it to reduce a Boolean expression to its simplest form is as follows.

### (a)   Step 1

A 1 is written into each square of the map corresponding to each term in the original Boolean expression, or to each row of the truth table for which the output is a 1 value. For example, Fig. 3.6a shows the 4-variable K-map for

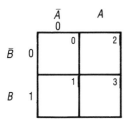

| Square | A | B |
|--------|---|---|
| 0 | 0 | 0 |
| 1 | 0 | 1 |
| 2 | 1 | 0 |
| 3 | 1 | 1 |

(a)

| Square | A | B | C |
|--------|---|---|---|
| 0 | 0 | 0 | 0 |
| 1 | 0 | 0 | 1 |
| 2 | 0 | 1 | 0 |
| 3 | 0 | 1 | 1 |
| 4 | 1 | 0 | 0 |
| 5 | 1 | 0 | 1 |
| 6 | 1 | 1 | 0 |
| 7 | 1 | 1 | 1 |

(b)

| Square | A | B | C | D |
|--------|---|---|---|---|
| 0 | 0 | 0 | 0 | 0 |
| 1 | 0 | 0 | 0 | 1 |
| 2 | 0 | 0 | 1 | 0 |
| 3 | 0 | 0 | 1 | 1 |
| 4 | 0 | 1 | 0 | 0 |
| 5 | 0 | 1 | 0 | 1 |
| 6 | 0 | 1 | 1 | 0 |
| 7 | 0 | 1 | 1 | 1 |
| 8 | 1 | 0 | 0 | 0 |
| 9 | 1 | 0 | 0 | 1 |
| 10 | 1 | 0 | 1 | 0 |
| 11 | 1 | 0 | 1 | 1 |
| 12 | 1 | 1 | 0 | 0 |
| 13 | 1 | 1 | 0 | 1 |
| 14 | 1 | 1 | 1 | 0 |
| 15 | 1 | 1 | 1 | 1 |

(c)

**Fig. 3.5** K-maps for (a) two; (b) three; and (c) four variables.

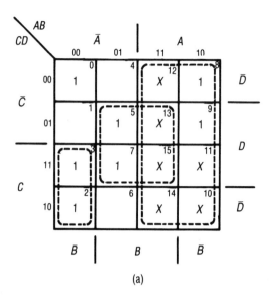

(a)

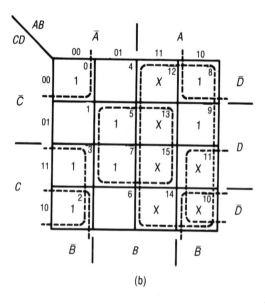

(b)

**Fig. 3.6** K-map for the *a*-segment of the decimal decoder: (a) shows an initial attempt at combining terms, while in (b) the full combination of terms is shown.

segment $a$ of the 7-segment decoder. The 'don't care' terms are then represented by writing a cross in the appropriate squares. In this example a cross is placed in squares 10 to 15. Note that 0s are represented by blank squares.

## (b)  Step 2

Adjacent squares containing 1s, or 1s and crosses, are then combined. Squares can only be combined in groups of powers of two, for example, 2, 4, 8, 16, etc. Each group must be a square or rectangle with sides which are a power of two.

There are three basic rules that must be followed when combining squares:

1. every square containing a 1 must be included in at least one group;
2. each group should be as large as possible; and
3. 1s must not be included in more than one group unless they increase the size of both groups.

It is usually easiest to start in the middle of the K-map. For example, in Fig. 3.6a squares 5, 7, 13 and 15 can be combined. This is shown by drawing a dotted line around them. Combining these four squares means that terms 5 ($\bar{A}.B.\bar{C}.D$) and 7 ($\bar{A}.B.C.D$) are replaced by the much simpler term $B.D$. This is because the four squares cover the regions $A$ and $\bar{A}$, $C$ and $\bar{C}$, but only $B$ and $D$ (i.e. the regions $\bar{B}$ and $\bar{D}$ are not covered). Without the K-map the common factor $\bar{A}.B.D$ would probably have been identified easily but it would have been more difficult to identify the 'don't care' terms which allow the removal of $A$.

In a similar way, terms 8–15 inclusive can be combined to give $A$. The 1s in squares 0, 2 and 3 are then left. A first attempt might be to combine terms 2 and 3 to give $\bar{A}.\bar{B}.C$ and to leave term 0.

The expression for $a$ then reduces to:

$$a = B.D + A + \bar{A}.\bar{B}.C + \bar{A}.\bar{B}.\bar{C}.\bar{D}$$

However, the fact that the K-map is wrapped, i.e. square 0 is also adjacent to squares 8 and 2, has not been used. With this fact terms 0, 2, 8 and 10 can be combined to give $\bar{B}.\bar{D}$, so that $a$ reduces to:

$$a = B.D + A + \bar{A}.\bar{B}.C + \bar{B}.\bar{D}$$

Terms 2 and 3 are adjacent to terms 10 and 11, and so can be combined to eliminate $\bar{A}$ from the third component in the equation for $a$. The final combination of terms in the K-map is shown in Fig. 3.6b, and gives:

$$a = B.D + A + \bar{B}.C + \bar{B}.\bar{D}$$

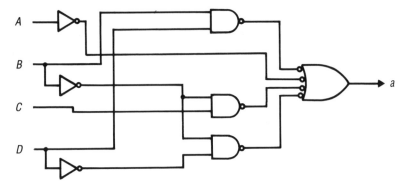

**Fig. 3.7** NAND gate implementation of *a*-segment decoder.

This is quite startling since the original equation for *a* has been minimized from seven 4-variable terms to three 2-variable terms and one 1-variable term, with a consequent drastic reduction in the number and size of gates required for the implementation. Figure 3.7 shows a **NAND** gate implementation of this equation. Note also that there is often not a unique solution to the process of combining terms on a K-map. In the present example there is one other solution that has the same number of terms. Its detection is left as an exercise for the reader.

So far only the equation for the *a* segment has been considered. The question now arises as to what happens when multiple outputs occur, as in this example. Figure 3.8 shows the seven K-maps for the decoding required for segments *a–g*. Although these maps can be treated independently, using the rules discussed above to combine terms, it is better to try to identify common groupings which occur in as many of the maps as possible, since this will lead to as much common hardware in the final implementation as possible. A simple way to identify common groupings is to draw the maps on see-through film so that they can be overlapped.

The K-map technique is useful and relatively easy to use for combinatorial designs that have a maximum of about six variables. Designs with more variables should be minimized using computational methods amenable to computer solution, such as the Quine-McClusky method (see Lewin, for example, in the bibliography). Computer-aided design (CAD) tools are available which will minimize the amount of logic required for circuit implementation.

## 3.6  Medium scale integrated functions

A glance through a TTL or CMOS data handbook will show that in addition to the standard gates, such as **NOT**, **NOR** and **NAND**, there are a large number

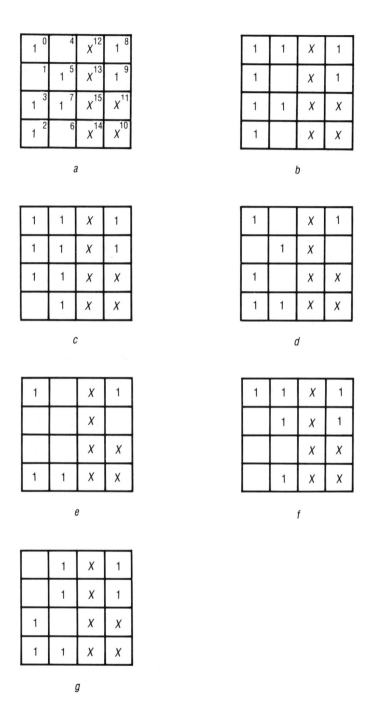

**Fig. 3.8** K-maps for the seven segments of the decoder.

of special-purpose combinatorial circuits available. These circuits are medium scale integrated (MSI) circuits containing up to 100 gates per chip. They are available for functions for which the semiconductor manufacturers have identified large markets. Such circuits include arithmetic functions, binary adders and multipliers, decoders (used extensively in display functions and in address selection of memory registers within a computer), multiplexers to enable selection between a number of possible data streams, bus drivers and receivers (also used extensively in computers).

In this section those MSI circuits that will be used in the construction of computer circuits in the later chapters are discussed.

## 3.6.1 Demultiplexers and decoders

A demultiplexer is a circuit that has one input line, and several possible output lines, $N$ (a power of two), as shown in Fig. 3.9. The input is connected to one of the output lines, depending on the code bits that are supplied on the select lines, and so acts in exactly the same way as a switch. These select lines are often referred to as address lines, since the code word or address on them is used to select, or address, one of the output lines. $M$ address lines are required, where $N = 2^M$.

A decoder is very similar with the exception that there is no input line. The address on the select lines is decoded to select one of the $N$ possible output lines. An example is the 2-line to 4-line TTL decoder shown in Fig. 3.10. One of the output lines, $Y_0$ to $Y_3$ is selected and set low, depending on the code supplied on the two select or address inputs, $A_0$ and $A_1$. The bubbles on the outputs indicate that they are active low. In addition there is an enable input $G$ which is also active low. The truth table for this decoder, with x representing 'don't care' values, is as follows:

| Enable | Select | | Outputs | | | |
|---|---|---|---|---|---|---|
| $G$ | $A_1$ | $A_0$ | $Y_0$ | $Y_1$ | $Y_2$ | $Y_3$ |
| 1 | x | x | 1 | 1 | 1 | 1 |
| 0 | 0 | 0 | 0 | 1 | 1 | 1 |
| 0 | 0 | 1 | 1 | 0 | 1 | 1 |
| 0 | 1 | 0 | 1 | 1 | 0 | 1 |
| 0 | 1 | 1 | 1 | 1 | 1 | 0 |

If $G = 1$ none of the outputs is selected, while if $G = 0$ just one of the outputs is selected, i.e. taken low. Although this function could be implemented easily with three 3-input **NAND** gates, it is required so often that it is available as a MSI chip, the TTL 74139 decoder. The 74139 contains two

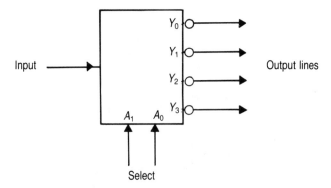

Fig. 3.9 Demultiplexer (1-line to 4-line).

2-line to 4-line decoders in a single chip. (In the data sheet of this decoder the select lines are labelled $A$ and $B$, but $A_0$ and $A_1$ will be used here to avoid confusion with $A$ and $B$ used in the 7-segment decoder.)

Decoders are available in the following sizes: 2-line to 4-line (two to a package), 3-line to 8-line, 4-line to 10-line (decimal decoder) and 4-line to 16-line. The use of a 2-line to 4-line decoder to select between different memory chips in a microcomputer system is discussed in Chapter 9.

## 3.6.2 Multiplexers

A multiplexer performs the opposite function to a decoder/demultiplexer switch; it connects one of a given number of input lines to a single output line. Figure 3.11 shows a 4-line to 1-line multiplexer. The input lines are $D_0$ to $D_3$, $Y$ is the output line and $A_0$ and $A_1$ the select or address lines. The truth table is as follows:

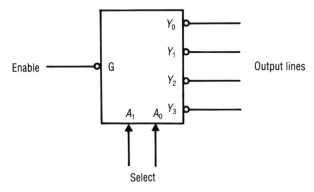

Fig. 3.10 2-line to 4-line decoder.

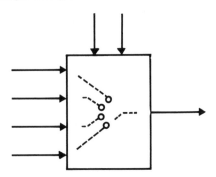

**Fig. 3.11** Multiplexer (4-line to 1-line).

| $A_1$ | $A_0$ | $Y$ |
|-------|-------|-----|
| 0 | 0 | $D_0$ |
| 0 | 1 | $D_1$ |
| 1 | 0 | $D_2$ |
| 1 | 1 | $D_3$ |

In addition most multiplexers contain an enable input. The logic equation for this multiplexer is:

$$Y = \bar{A}_1.\bar{A}_0.D_0 + \bar{A}_1.A_0.D_1 + A_1.\bar{A}_0.D_2 + A_1.A_0.D_3$$

Thus to select input $D_1$, for example, select code $A_1 = 0$, $A_0 = 1$ is required.

In addition to their use as data selectors, multiplexers are frequently used to simplify the generation of logic functions. This is most easily explained by considering an example; the 7-segment decimal decoder discussed earlier will be used. The equation for the $a$ segment is

$$a = \bar{A}.\bar{B}.\bar{C}.\bar{D} + \bar{A}.\bar{B}.C.\bar{D} + \bar{A}.\bar{B}.C.D + \bar{A}.B.\bar{C}.D + \bar{A}.B.C.D + A.\bar{B}.\bar{C}.\bar{D} + A.\bar{B}.\bar{C}.D$$

The simplest implementation is to use a multiplexer which has the same number of select lines as variables. In this example this means a 16-line to 1-line multiplexer with four select lines, as shown in Fig. 3.12a. The variables $A$, $B$, $C$ and $D$ are connected to the select lines $A_3$, $A_2$, $A_1$ and $A_0$, while the data lines $D_0$ to $D_{15}$ are connected to either logic level 0 or logic level 1 as appropriate, so that the output of the multiplexer, $a$, is 1 for terms 0, 2, 3, 5, 7, 8 and 9, and 0 for terms 1, 4 and 6, and 'don't care', x, for terms 10 to 15. In most implementations the 'don't care' terms will be connected to logic 0.

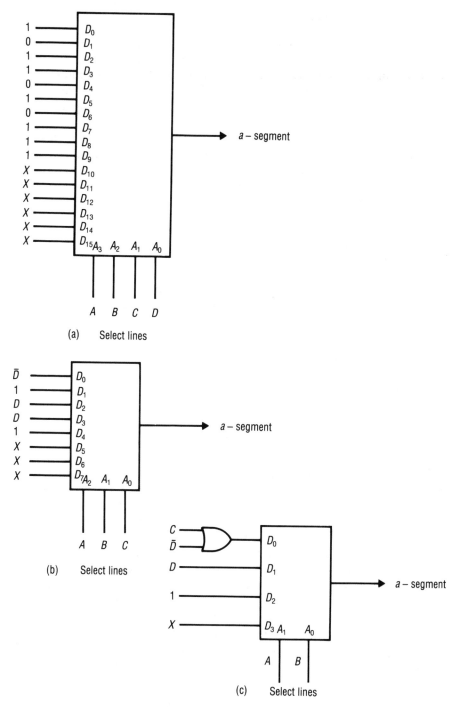

**Fig. 3.12** Multiplexer implementation for the *a*-segment of the decimal decoder.

Although this solution is simple, and works, it uses a large multiplexer, so the question arises as to whether a smaller multiplexer can be used. An 8-line to 1-line multiplexer with three select lines can be used but only three of the four variables can be applied to the select lines; $A$, $B$ and $C$ are chosen arbitrarily, as shown in Fig. 3.12b. The fourth variable $D$ is now applied to the data lines, where appropriate, so that again $a$ is generated at the multiplexer output. Consider the first term in the Boolean equation for $a$, $\bar{A}.\bar{B}.\bar{C}.\bar{D}$. When $\bar{A}$, $\bar{B}$ and $\bar{C}$ are applied to the multiplexer select lines, data line $D_0$ is connected to the output, and so to generate the correct logic level $\bar{D}$ must be connected to $D_0$. The second and third terms of $a$ contain the common factor $\bar{A}.\bar{B}.C$, and so reduce to:

$$\bar{A}.\bar{B}.C.(\bar{D} + D) = \bar{A}.\bar{B}.C$$

by the inverse proposition discussed in Chapter 2.

Now $\bar{A}.\bar{B}.C$ selects data line $D_4$, and so this must be connected to logic level 1. Continuing in this way the data line connections required to generate $a$ with this multiplexer are:

Data line $D_0 = \bar{D}$ for $ABC = 000$
Data line $D_1 = 1$ for $ABC = 001$
Data line $D_2 = D$ for $ABC = 010$
Data line $D_3 = D$ for $ABC = 011$
Data line $D_4 = 1$ for $ABC = 100$
Data lines $D_5$, $D_6$ and $D_7$ are 'don't care'.

However, this is still not the minimum size of multiplexer necessary in this example. It turns out that a multiplexer is required which has $n$ select lines, where $n$ is half the number of variables (rounded up to a power of 2 when necessary). In this case $n = 2$, so that a 4-line to 1-line multiplexer having two select lines is the minimum size required. Two of the variables are applied to the multiplexer select lines, while the remaining variables, known as the residues, are applied to the data lines. The choice of which variables to apply to the select lines is arbitrary (but see below). The data line connections are then worked out either by following the method used above in the 3-line to 1-line multiplexer case, or by using a modified K-map technique, as follows.

There are six possible variations of control variable, namely $AB$, $AC$, $AD$, $BC$, $BD$ or $CD$. In this example, arbitrarily choose $AB$. The K-map for the $a$ segment is redrawn in Fig. 3.13. The residue functions are functions of the variables $C$ and $D$, and comprise the functions shown in the vertical columns of the K-map. Because of this, terms may now only be combined in each vertical column, as shown in Fig. 3.13. The residue functions are:

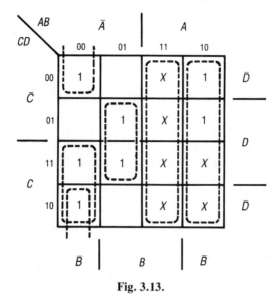

**Fig. 3.13.**

$D_0 = C + \bar{D}$ for $AB = 00$
$D_1 = D$ for $AB = 01$
$D_2 = 1$ for $AB = 10$
$D_3 = X$ for $AB = 11$

The implementation is shown in Fig. 3.12c. Note its simplicity, with only two chips being required. Repeating the example with $C$ and $D$ as the control variables is left as an exercise for the reader. The choice of control variables should be made, by trial and error, to give the simplest residue functions. Circuits for the other segments of the decoder may be obtained in a similar manner.

## 3.7 Programmable logic arrays

Several examples have been given in the text of combinatorial functions expressed as sum-of-products equations. These equations may be implemented directly by forming the product terms of the inputs, or their complements where necessary, using **AND** gates, and then combining the outputs with an **OR** gate.

A programmable logic array (PLA) is a special-purpose LSI (large scale integrated) chip designed so that sum-of-products expressions can be implemented directly. A simple PLA is shown in Fig. 3.14. It has four inputs, $A$, $B$,

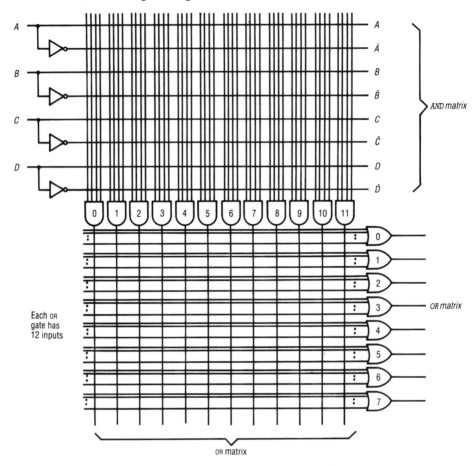

**Fig. 3.14** A simple PLA, having four inputs, twelve product terms and eight outputs.

$C$ and $D$, and the complement of each input is formed internally so that there are eight input signals available. In addition there are 12 **AND** gates, each having four inputs. These inputs are the vertical lines in Fig. 3.14. The **AND** gates are used to form the product terms, the horizontal and vertical lines effectively forming the **AND** matrix. At each of the intersections in this matrix there is an optional link. These links are actually transistors but are thought of, and usually referred to, as fuses. In this example PLA, up to 12 product terms, each having up to four inputs, may be formed. The matrix at the bottom is the **OR** matrix, which is connected to the output **OR** gates. This PLA has eight outputs so there are eight **OR** gates. Each of these **OR** gates has 12 input lines, one from each of the **AND** gates. Again, connections are made

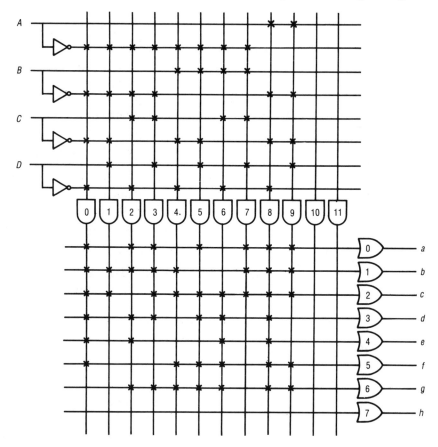

**Fig. 3.15** PLA implementation of the decimal decoder.

where required between the vertical outputs from the **AND** gates and the horizontal input lines to the **OR** gates.

Initially all the 'fuses' are intact, so all possible connections are made. The logic function required is 'placed' in the PLA by blowing those 'fuses' where links are not required. This is done either during manufacture or, in the case of a field-programmable logic array (FPLA), by using a special-purpose programmer.

As an example, a PLA implementation of the 7-segment decoder is considered. The starting point is the truth table discussed in section 3.4. There are seven outputs, $a$ to $g$, so only seven of the eight PLA outputs are required. There are ten product terms corresponding to the ten possible input values 0 to 9, so ten **AND** gates of the PLA are used. Figure 3.15 is a slightly simplified redrawing of the PLA of Fig. 3.14, in which the crosses correspond to the connections required to implement all seven decimal decoder outputs, *a* to *g*. Note that the absence of a cross where a horizontal and vertical line meet means that there is no connection.

In practice, PLAs are manufactured in standard sizes, the smallest being a 14-input, 48 product term, 8-output chip. In general, minimization techniques are unnecessary when using PLAs unless the number of initial product terms exceeds the number of product terms in the PLA being considered.

A recent development is the introduction of electrically programmable logic devices (EPLD). An EPLD contains a PLA, as described above, and a number of user-programmable macrocells, one for each output. These macrocells allow the outputs to be programmed into a number of different configurations, allowing both combinatorial and sequential circuits to be implemented with the same device. A typical EPLD is the EP600 from Altera Corporation. It has 20 inputs, 16 outputs each with its own macrocell, and allows up to 160 product terms to be generated. The main advantages of EPLDs is that they are easily and quickly programmed, and can be erased using ultraviolet light in the same way as an EPROM. A wide range of EPLDs is available, together with computer-aided design software that runs on standard personal computers.

## 3.8 Read-only memories

The programmable array discussed in the last section can be regarded as a memory. When a binary pattern is applied to the input lines, an output is obtained on the output lines which is determined by the links made in the **AND** and **OR** matrices of the PLA. The input lines are effectively address lines and the outputs are data lines on which data, which have been previously stored in the PLA, appear.

However, PLAs can only be used to form a limited number of product terms. For example, the small FPLA mentioned with 14 inputs only has 48 product terms, so that only 48 data words may be stored in it. This is a very small subset of the total number of products that can be formed from 14 variables, which is $2^{14} = 16\,384$. A read-only memory (ROM) differs from a PLA in that all product terms are generated. Although functionally very similar to a PLA, a ROM is usually thought of in a rather different manner. It is a device in which sets of data called words are stored. Figure 3.16 shows a schematic diagram of a small ROM. It has five inputs, the address lines, labelled $A_0$ to $A_4$, and four outputs called data lines, labelled $D_0$ to $D_3$. Since five address lines can select $2^5 = 32$ different 'places', or memory locations, the ROM contains 32 memory locations. In each of these, a 4-bit data word is stored. When a 5-bit address is placed on the address lines, the contents of the memory location addressed are placed on the data lines. The ROM shown is

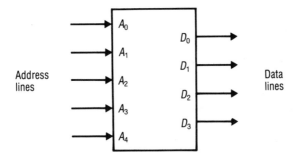

**Fig. 3.16**   A 32 × 4 read-only memory (ROM).

said to be of size 32 × 4 since it stores 32 words, each having a length of four-bits. In general, a ROM with $M$ address lines has $2^M \times N$ bits.

Memories are one of the most important components of a computer system, and they will be discussed in more detail in Chapter 6.

## 3.9   Summary

The specification, design and implementation of combinatorial logic circuits has been discussed in detail in this chapter. The specification is best written down in the form of a truth table which shows the value of each of the circuit outputs for each possible combination of the circuit inputs. This truth table must be complete, and should be thoroughly checked before the design continues. The method that is to be used for the implementation then has to be decided. Possible methods include using basic gates for relatively simple circuits, and PLAs and ROMs for more complicated circuits. If a gate implementation is to be used, a Boolean logic equation should be written down for each output in the sum-of-products form. If appropriate, these equations should be minimized using the K-map technique. The resulting equations should then be converted into **NAND** or **NOR** form, using either De Morgan's theorem or the graphical 'bubble' technique, and a circuit diagram of the implementation drawn.

The choice between a PLA or ROM implementation usually depends on the number of product terms of the inputs required. If this is small compared to the total number of product terms that can be generated from the inputs, then a PLA implementation will usually be the most efficient. Conversely, if most of the product terms are required, then a ROM implementation will be the obvious choice. In either case, the size of the PLA or ROM necessary for the implementation must be chosen, and the programming of the truth table into the PLA or ROM carried out.

## Exercises

3.1 Design a combinatorial circuit that has as input a decimal number in the range 0–7, represented in binary, and outputs the binary equivalent of the square of the input. The circuit implementation should use only **NAND** gates.

3.2 Minimize the logic function

$$f = A.\bar{B}.\bar{C} + \bar{A}.B.\bar{C} + A.B.C + A.B.\bar{C}$$

using the K-map technique, and then show how it may be implemented using (a) **NAND** gates, and (b) a 4-line to 1-line multiplexer.

3.3 The majority function $M(a,b,c)$ of the three Boolean inputs $a$, $b$ and $c$ is logic-1 if two or more of the inputs are logic-1, and logic-0 otherwise. Design a circuit that implements the majority function. How would you extend it to four or more inputs?

3.4 In section 3.5 the implementation of the circuit required for the $a$-segment of a 7-segment decoder was discussed. Design the circuits required for the other six segments ($b$ to $g$). You should attempt to minimize the functions in such a way that the six circuits share as much common logic as possible, to keep the number of gates required to a minimum.

3.5 Design a PLA circuit that has as input a decimal digit (0–9) represented in binary-coded decimal (BCD), and outputs the input multiplied by 5, as two BCD digits. (Refer to Chapter 10 for a definition of BCD).

# 4

# Sequential logic design

## 4.1   Introduction

In the previous chapter, circuits whose outputs are a function of the inputs only were discussed. However, in many digital designs there is a need for logic circuits whose outputs depend not only on the present inputs, but also on the past history, or sequence of actions, of the circuit. In other words, the concept of time has to be introduced, and memory circuits are required to store information about the past history of the circuit. Such circuits are known as sequential logic circuits, because they follow a predetermined sequence.

There are numerous examples of sequential circuits, one of the most widely met being the traffic light controller. The controller may be regarded as usual as a black box, as shown in Fig. 4.1. There are three outputs, labelled red, yellow and green, to drive the three lights, and a single input labelled clock. A light will be turned on if there is a logic 1 on its respective output line.

Fundamental to the design of sequential circuits is the concept of internal states, or states for short. At the beginning of the design procedure for a sequential circuit, the total number of internal states that are required must be determined. Each of these internal states is given a symbol, and it is very helpful (and usually essential) to draw a state diagram which shows the internal states and the transitions between them. The simple traffic light controller requires for states, labelled $S_0$, $S_1$, $S_2$ and $S_3$. The state diagram is shown in Fig. 4.2. Each state is shown by a circle, in which the state designation is written. The lines drawn from one state to another show the transition between states. The direction is indicated by an arrow, and the input signal (or input signal combinations) that gives rise to each transition is indicated above the arrow. In Fig. 4.2 each transition between states is initiated by a clock signal, $c$, as there are no other input signals in this simple example. Those outputs which are turned on in a given state are shown either alongside,

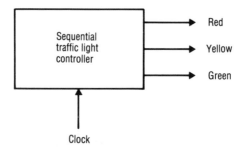

**Fig. 4.1** Traffic light controller.

or inside, the state circles. For example, in state $S_1$ red and yellow are on (logic level 1), while green is off (logic level 0).

## 4.2 Synchronous and asynchronous sequential circuits

There are two different types of sequential circuit, namely synchronous and asynchronous. In an asynchronous circuit there is no clock, and transitions between states are initiated by changes in the appropriate input signals. Asynchronous circuits are also known as event-driven circuits. In a synchronous circuit, transitions between states are initiated by a pulse from a single clock. It is assumed that any changes in the input signals occur between clock pulses, so that the input signals are stable when a clock pulse is applied. Synchronous circuits are easier for the beginner to design, and so the discussion will be restricted to their design.

Figure 4.3 shows two typical clock signals. The first (Fig. 4.3a) is a repetitive signal, derived from an oscillator circuit, and has a constant frequency, $f$, say. At any instant in time, its value is either 0 or $V_H$, where $V_H$ is the voltage that corresponds to logic level 1 for the logic family being used to implement the sequential design. The period $T$ of this clock signal is related to its

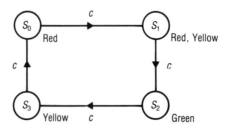

**Fig. 4.2** State diagram for simple traffic light controller.

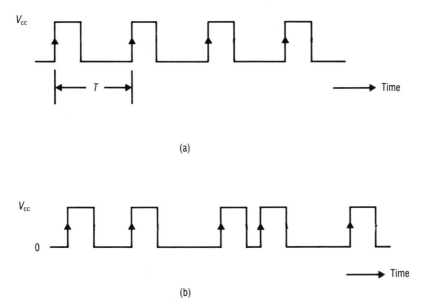

(a)

(b)

**Fig. 4.3**  Typical clock signals used to clock synchronous logic circuits: (a) is a repetitive clock with a constant frequency 1/T; (b) is a pulsed clock signal.

frequency by $T = 1/f$. The second clock signal (Fig. 4.3b), although repetitive, does not have a constant frequency. It is often referred to as a pulsed clock, the pulses being generated either at random intervals in time, or in response to a change in one or more input signals to a sequential circuit.

A synchronous circuit is designed to change state either when the clock goes from low to high, a positive transition, or when the clock goes from high to low, a negative transition. The arrows in Fig. 4.3 indicate the positive transitions of the clock.

## 4.3  State diagrams and state variables

In the previous section the concept of the internal states of a sequential circuit was introduced. This idea will now be developed more fully by reference to the state diagram of the simple traffic light controller shown in Fig. 4.2. Note that there are no inputs, except for the clock which is not considered as a normal input, since all sequential circuits must have a clock; indeed, it is not normally shown on a state diagram.

Drawing the state diagram is the first stage of sequential logic design and, having checked that it agrees with the specification for the sequential logic system required, the next is to write down a *state table*. The state table contains the same information as the state diagram but in a form that is more readily usable for the circuit implementation. For simple circuits it is possible to write down the state table directly from the specification. However, this is not advisable for the beginner since the drawing of a state diagram is a very good check of the specification, and should show up any ambiguities therein.

The state table for the simple traffic light controller is given in Table 4.1. It contains a row for each state of the circuit and a column for every possible combination of input signals, so that if there are $n$ input signals there are $2^n$ columns. In this example there are no input signals, apart from the clock signal ($n = 0$ and $2^0 = 1$) so only one column is required.

**Table 4.1**   State table for the simple traffic light controller

| Present state | Next state |
| --- | --- |
| $S_0$ | $S_1$ |
| $S_1$ | $S_2$ |
| $S_2$ | $S_3$ |
| $S_3$ | $S_0$ |

The implementation of this state diagram will be considered later in the chapter.

As a second example consider a combination door lock which has three buttons, labelled $a$, $b$ and $c$. The buttons are of the momentary type (i.e. contact is only made when they are pushed). They must be pushed in the order $b$, $a$, $c$ for the door to open. It is further assumed that a clock pulse, similar to that shown in Fig. 4.3b, is generated whenever a button, or combination of buttons, is pushed. A black box diagram of the system is shown in Fig. 4.4. In addition to the three input signals there is a single output, labelled open, and of course the clock signal.

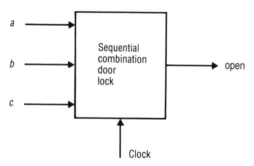

**Fig. 4.4**   Combination door lock.

A first attempt at the state diagram for the combination door lock is shown in Fig. 4.5a, and shows what happens when the buttons are pushed in the correct sequence. Initially the system is in the idle state $S_0$, with open $= 0$. Pushing button $b$ causes the transition from $S_0$ and $S_1$ on the next clock pulse. In state $S_1$, open $= 0$. In a similar way the system goes from state $S_1$ to $S_2$ when button $a$ is pushed, and then finally from $S_2$ to $S_3$ when button $c$ is pushed. The value of the output open becomes 1 when state $S_3$ is entered.

Drawing this state diagram shows that at least four states are required. However, the state diagram is not complete, since at present it only shows what happens when the buttons are pushed in the correct order. To be complete it must show what happens for all *possible* combinations of the inputs, in *each* state. For example, if the system is in state $S_0$ and buttons $a$ or $c$ are pushed, it will be assumed that the system must remain in state $S_0$. This is shown in Fig. 4.5b by the 'arc' around the circle of state $S_0$, labelled $a,c$. Now consider what should happen if the system is in state $S_1$ and either $b$ or $c$ is depressed. There are two possibilities: either the system remains in state $S_1$, or the system should return to the idle state $S_0$, and wait for button $b$ to be pushed again. A similar decision must be made for state $S_2$, if either $a$ or $b$ are pushed. The specification must state these requirements fully. The state diagram of Fig. 4.5b assumes that the system is to return to the idle state $S_0$ if the wrong buttons are pushed in any of states $S_0$, $S_1$ or $S_2$. This state diagram is now complete, since it shows what happens under all possible input sequences for each state.

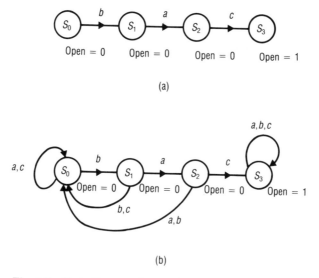

Fig. 4.5   State diagrams for combination door locks.

As in the previous example, the next step is to draw a state table. It will have four rows, corresponding to the four states, and $2^3 = 8$ columns, corresponding to all the possible combinations of the input signals. This may seem strange at first since only three columns might be expected, corresponding to the three possible inputs $a$, $b$ or $c$. However, this is not the case since it is possible for two, or even all three, buttons to be pushed simultaneously. Each column of the state table must be filled in to show unambiguously what the next state will be for each possible combination of the inputs. Thus the specification is not complete at present; it must state what happens if buttons are pushed simultaneously. In this example it will be assumed that the system is required to return to the idle state $S_0$. The completed state table is shown in Table 4.2. Note that most entries in the first three rows are $S_0$, while in the fourth row every entry is $S_3$, since once the system is in this state and the door is open it is irrelevant whether any more buttons are pushed. In practice there will also be a *reset* signal which returns the system to state $S_0$ when the door is closed.

**Table 4.2** State table for the combination door lock

| Present state | Next state | | | | | | | |
|---|---|---|---|---|---|---|---|---|
| | abc 000 | abc 001 | abc 010 | abc 011 | abc 100 | abc 101 | abc 110 | abc 111 |
| $S_0$ | $S_0$ | $S_0$ | $S_1$ | $S_0$ | $S_0$ | $S_0$ | $S_0$ | $S_0$ |
| $S_1$ | $S_0$ | $S_0$ | $S_0$ | $S_0$ | $S_2$ | $S_0$ | $S_0$ | $S_0$ |
| $S_2$ | $S_0$ | $S_3$ | $S_0$ | $S_0$ | $S_0$ | $S_0$ | $S_0$ | $S_0$ |
| $S_3$ | $S_3$ | $S_3$ | $S_3$ | $S_3$ | $S_3$ | $S_3$ | $S_3$ | $S_3$ |

Note that every position in the state table must be completed. If this cannot be done then the specification is either incomplete or ambiguous. The major part of the system design has now been achieved.

In every sequential logic system each state is defined by a set of logic signals called *state variables*. If the system can only exist in one of two states then only one state variable, $A$ say, is required, since $A = 0$ can be used to correspond to one state, and $A = 1$ to the other state. Similarly, $n$ state variables can be used to represent $2^n$ states. A sequential logic system which has $m$ states requires $n$ state variables such that:

$$2^n \geqslant m > 2^{n-1}$$

Thus in the combination lock example above, two state variables are required, i.e. $n = 2$, since $2^2 = 4$ gives four states, which is exactly the number required.

However, for a system with five states, say, three state variables would be necessary. However, since $2^3 = 8$ there would be $8 - 5 = 3$ unused states. These unused states must always be shown on the state table.

The final step in the design process is the implementation which is essentially a straightforward mechanical exercise, following a simple 'recipe'. However, before considering this, storage, or memory, elements will be discussed.

## 4.4  Memory elements

The aim of this section is to show how a simple flip-flop, a storage element for one bit, can be built from gates.

### 4.4.1  The set–reset latch

Figure 4.6 shows the set–reset, SR, latch built from two **NOR** gates. There are two inputs, $S$ and $R$, and two outputs, $Q$ and $Q'$. Note the feedback paths from $Q$ to the input of gate 1, and from $Q'$ to the input of gate 2. These paths mean that the outputs $Q$ and $Q'$ depend not only on the inputs $S$ and $R$, but also on the previous values of the outputs. Thus the circuit is not a combinational one, according to the definition given in Chapter 2, but is a sequential logic element.

The Boolean logic equations describing the behaviour of the SR flip-flop are:

$$Q = \overline{R + Q'}$$

and

$$Q' = \overline{S + Q}$$

There are four possible combinations of the input signals $S$ and $R$, namely $SR$ = 00, 01, 10, 11. These will now be considered in turn.

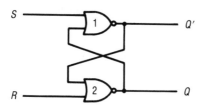

**Fig. 4.6**  The set–reset flip-flop implemented with **NOR** gates.

1. $S = 0$, $R = 0$. The logic equations reduce to:

$$Q = \overline{Q'}$$
$$\overline{Q'} = Q.$$

The outputs are different and stable with either $Q = 0$ or $Q = 1$. Which of these two states the circuit is in depends on the previous values of $S$ and $R$, i.e. just before they were taken to logic 0.

2. $S = 0$, $R = 1$. The logic equations are:

$$Q = \overline{1 + Q'} = \overline{1} = 0$$
$$Q' = \overline{0 + Q} = \overline{Q} = 1$$

This input condition, known as reset, forces $Q = 0$ and $Q' = 1$ (i.e. $Q' = \bar{Q}$).

3. $S = 1$, $R = 0$. The logic equations are:

$$Q' = \overline{1 + Q} = \overline{1} = 0$$
$$Q = \overline{0 + Q'} = \overline{Q'} = 1$$

This is the case opposite to 2, forcing the output to the set condition, $Q = 1$, and $Q' = 0$ (i.e. $Q' = \bar{Q}$ again).

4. $S = 1$, $R = 1$. This case differs from the previous ones in that both outputs assume the same logic state, 0, since:

$$Q = \overline{1 + Q'} = \overline{1} = 0$$
$$Q' = \overline{1 + Q} = \overline{1} = 0$$

Although the outputs are stable, the operation of the circuit in this case becomes uncertain when $S$ and $R$ are changed simultaneously to 0. It is impossible to predict whether $Q$ will remain at 0 or become 1 (and vice versa for $Q'$). Because of this, the case $S = R = 1$ is said to be indeterminate and is not usually allowed to occur.

Figure 4.7 shows a clocked version of the SR flip-flop in which the inputs $S$ and $R$ are ANDed with the clock signal. When the clock signal is 0 the outputs of both AND gates are 0, i.e. $S' = R' = 0$, corresponding to case 1 discussed above. A new value is placed in the flip-flop by first setting up the $S$ and $R$ inputs to the desired values and then applying a clock pulse. When this clock pulse is logic 1, $S' = S$ and $R' = R$, so the latch assumes the new required

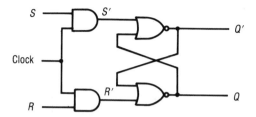

**Fig. 4.7** The clocked set–reset latch.

state. This state is then held when the clock pulse returns to 0. Table 4.3 shows the state table for the clocked SR latch. The column labelled $Q_{t+1}$ is the value taken by the $Q$ output after the next clock pulse has occurred.

**Table 4.3** State table for the clocked SR

| S | R | $Q_{t+1}$ | Comments |
|---|---|---|---|
| 0 | 0 | $Q_t$ | No change |
| 0 | 1 | 0 | Reset |
| 1 | 0 | 1 | Set |
| 1 | 1 | x | Indeterminate |

## 4.4.2 The D-type latch

One of the simplest memory elements available as an integrated circuit is the D-type latch as shown in Fig. 4.8(a). This element is able to store a single bit of information, and so is often referred to as a 1-bit memory. It is actually a special case of the SR latch, in which the reset input is always the complement of the set input, i.e. $R = \bar{S}$. Its state table is given in Table 4.4.

**Table 4.4** State table of the D-type flip-flop

| D | $Q_{t+1}$ |
|---|---|
| 0 | 0 |
| 1 | 1 |

There are two inputs, labelled data, $D$, and clock, $C$, respectively, and two outputs labelled $Q$ and $\bar{Q}$. The $\bar{Q}$ output is always the complement of the $Q$ output. The output $Q$ follows the input $D$, so long as the clock is at logic level 1.

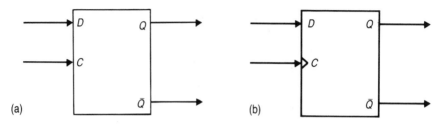

**Fig. 4.8** D-type (a) latch and (b) flip-flop.

The output $Q$ is 'frozen' with the value of $D$ at the instant the clock is taken to logic level 0, that is, the latch stores the value that was on the $D$ input. Note that in both the clocked SR latch and the D-type latch the outputs will respond to any changes in the input signals, so long as the clock signal remains at logic level 1. This can give rise to a number of problems, which are beyond the scope of this book. They can, however, be solved by using a modified form of latch, which is **edge-triggered**. The next section discusses a D-type edge-triggered memory element, which is often referred to as a D-type flip-flop.

### 4.4.3   The D-type edge-triggered flip-flop

The function of the D-type flip-flop is very similar to that of the D-type latch, with the exception that the value stored is the logic level of the D input at the moment when the clock input $C$ is taken from logic level 0 to logic level 1. The small triangle next to the $C$ input indicates that the device is edge-triggered. The output $Q$ is always equal to the logic state of $D$ when the clock transition 0 to 1 occurs.

The action of the D-type flip-flop is illustrated in Fig. 4.9. The positive transitions of the clock occur at times $t_1$, $t_2$, $t_3$, etc., while the logic level of the D-input is changed from 0 to 1 sometime after $t_1$ but before $t_2$. However, since the next clock transition is not until $t_2$ the flip-flop does not store, and the outputs $Q$ and $\bar{Q}$ do not reflect the changed state of the D-input, until time $t_2$. Similarly, although the D-input is changed back from 1 to 0 during the interval $t_3$–$t_4$, the flip-flop does not respond to this change until the next clock pulse at time $t_4$.

D-type flip-flops such as this are available in both the TTL and CMOS logic families.

### 4.4.4   The JK-type flip-flop

The JK flip-flop is shown in Fig. 4.10. It has two inputs labelled $J$ and $K$ as well as an edge-triggered clock input $C$, and two outputs $Q$ and $\bar{Q}$. Again, $\bar{Q}$ is

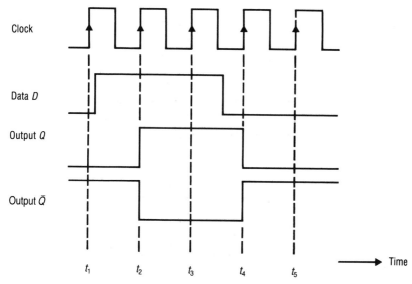

**Fig. 4.9**  D-type flip-flop timing diagram.

always the complement of $Q$. The operation of the JK flip-flop is summarized
in the state table shown in Table 4.5.

**Table 4.5**  State table of a
JK flip-flop

| $J$ | $K$ | $Q_{t+1}$ |
|---|---|---|
| 0 | 0 | $Q_t$ |
| 0 | 1 | 0 |
| 1 | 0 | 1 |
| 1 | 1 | $\overline{Q_t}$ |

The column labelled $Q_{t+1}$ is the value that the $Q$ output assumes after the
next 0–1 clock transition has occurred. The JK flip-flop has four possible
operations, and so is considerably more flexible than the D-type flip-flop,
which has only two operations. The operations are:

1. $J = 0$, $K = 0$. The $Q$ output is unchanged from its present state, i.e.
   $Q_{t+1} = Q_t$.
2. $J = 0$, $K = 1$. This is the **reset** condition: the $Q$ output is reset to 0,
   irrespective of the present state of the output.
3. $J = 1$, $K = 0$. This is the **set** condition; the $Q$ output is set to 1.
4. $J = 1$, $K = 1$. The $Q$ output assumes the opposite state to its present one,
   i.e. $Q_{t+1} = \overline{Q_t}$. This is known as the **toggle** condition.

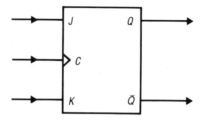

**Fig. 4.10** The JK flip-flop.

**Table 4.6** JK flip-flop state change table

| Original state | New state | J | K |
|:---:|:---:|:---:|:---:|
| 0 | 0 | 0 | x |
| 0 | 1 | 1 | x |
| 1 | 0 | x | 1 |
| 1 | 1 | x | 0 |

x = 'don't care'

In the implementation of sequential logic using JK flip-flops the following question is asked repeatedly: what values of $J$ and $K$ are required for the next state to be either a 0 or a 1 given that the present state is known? The answer is given by the truth table. For example, suppose that the present state is 0 and the output required after the next clock transition is 1. This will be achieved either with $J = 1$ and $K = 0$ (the set condition), or with $J = 1$ and $K = 1$ (the toggle condition). Thus $J$ must be 1 while $K$ can be either 0 or 1, i.e. it is a 'don't care' value. In this way the $J$ and $K$ inputs required for given output state changes may be worked out. They are summarized in Table 4.6.

## 4.5 Implementing sequential logic systems with D-type flip-flops

In this section, we examine the implementation using D-type flip-flops of the two examples discussed so far, namely the traffic light controller and the combination door lock.

### 4.5.1 Traffic light controller

The design proceeds by referring to the state table for the traffic light controller, Table 4.1. Since there are four states, labelled $S_0$ to $S_3$, two state

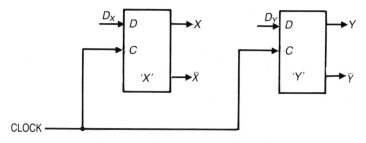

**Fig. 4.11**   Traffic light controller.

variables are required, $X$ and $Y$, say. Each state variable is implemented with a D-type flip-flop, so in this example two flip-flops are used. Both the inputs and the outputs of the flip-flops are labelled with the suffixes $X$ and $Y$, respectively, as shown in Fig. 4.11. The clock inputs are connected together, and are driven from a single clock source. There are now two remaining problems, both involving combinatorial logic, namely the interconnections required to the $D$ inputs of each flip-flop, and the logic required to generate the red, green and yellow output signals from the state variables $X$ and $Y$. The interconnections required to the $D$ inputs of the flip-flops are found by slightly modifying the state table. This table for the traffic light controller is shown in Table 4.7. The states are now shown by their state variables; the assignment of each variable combination is up to the designer but it is simplest, at least initially, to follow the normal binary sequence. Thus $S_0$ is represented by $Y = 0$, $X = 0$, $S_1$ by $Y = 0$, $X = 1$, $S_2$ by $Y = 1$, $X = 0$ and $S_3$ by $Y = 1$, $X = 1$. Note, however, that the choice of state variables may alter the amount of hardware required to implement the necessary combinatorial logic.

**Table 4.7**   Modified state table for the traffic light controller

| Present state | | Next state | |
|---|---|---|---|
| $Y$ | $X$ | $Y'$ | $X'$ |
| 0 | 0 | 0 | 1 |
| 0 | 1 | 1 | 0 |
| 1 | 0 | 1 | 1 |
| 1 | 1 | 0 | 0 |

The symbols $X'$ and $Y'$ represent the values of $X$ and $Y$ at the **next** clock pulse, that is, the next state. Consider the first row of Table 4.7; it shows that the present state is 00, and that on the next clock pulse the state must change to 01. Thus $Y$ does not change, while $X$ must change from 0 to 1. The question to be answered is: what values are required for the D-type flip-flop inputs $D_X$ and $D_Y$ so that the state will change from 00 to 01 on the next clock pulse? The answer is to be found in Table 4.4, the state table for the D-type flip-flop. This table shows that the characteristic equation for the D-type flip-flop is:

$$Q_{t+1} = D$$

This equation shows that the next output, or state, of the flip-flop is just equal to the present value of the $D$ input. Thus the entries in Table 4.7 for the next state are just those required for the $D$ inputs, $D_X$ and $D_Y$. Scanning down the column labelled $Y'$ shows that there are only two '1' entries, corresponding to the present states $S_1$ ($\bar{Y}X$) and $S_2$ ($X\bar{Y}$), so that

$$D_Y = \bar{Y}.X + Y.\bar{X} = X \oplus Y$$

Similarly for the $X'$ column there are also two '1' entries corresponding to states $S_0$ and $S_2$, and so

$$D_X = \bar{Y}.\bar{X} + Y.\bar{X} = \bar{X}$$

Fig. 4.12 shows the two D-type flip-flops with the logic required to generate $D_X$ and $D_Y$. Finally the logic required to generate the output signals must be determined.

Returning to the state diagram, it will be seen that the following output signals are required:

1. Red in state $S_0$ or $S_1$, i.e. Red $= \bar{X}.\bar{Y} + X.\bar{Y} = \bar{Y}$
2. Yellow in states $S_1$ or $S_3$, i.e. Yellow $= X.\bar{Y} + X.Y = X$
3. Green in state $S_2$, i.e. Green $= \bar{X}.Y$

The combinatorial logic to give these outputs is also shown in Fig. 4.12.

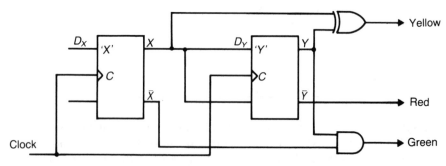

**Fig. 4.12**   D-type flip-flop implementation of traffic light controller.

## 4.5.2    Combination door lock

As in the previous example the state table of Table 4.2 is modified once the state variables for the states $S_0$–$S_3$ have been chosen. Again, there are four states, so two state variables are required, labelled $X$ and $Y$. However, the excitation table is considerably more complicated since there are three inputs to consider, $a$, $b$ and $c$. Thus the state table will have $4 \times 2^3 = 32$ rows, one row for each unique combination of the present state and the input values. Table 4.8 shows the state table for the combination lock.

Notice that many of the rows are identical. Examination of the $X'$ and $Y'$ columns for the '1' entries gives:

$$D_X = X' = \bar{Y}.\bar{X}.\bar{a}.b.\bar{c} + Y.\bar{X}.\bar{a}.\bar{b}.c + Y.X$$
$$D_Y = Y' = \bar{Y}.X.a.\bar{b}.\bar{c} + Y.\bar{X}.\bar{a}.\bar{b}.c + Y.X$$

Note that the last eight '1' entries in both columns correspond to state $S_3$ ($YX$) for all values of the $a$, $b$ and $c$, and so these eight terms can be combined to give $YX$. The K-map technique can be used to minimize the $D_X$ and $D_Y$ equations, but since there are five variables ($X$, $Y$, $a$, $b$ and $c$) 5-variable K-maps are required, which are beyond the scope of this book, so this is not attempted. The logic required to generate the output signal, open, is very straightforward, since open = 1 only in state $S_3$. Thus open = $XY$ and is generated by ANDing the state variables $X$ and $Y$.

## 4.6    Implementing sequential logic circuits with read-only memories

The previous example, although not difficult, does show that the combinatorial logic of sequential logic designs that have more than a few inputs and/or outputs can quickly become very cumbersome, and result in implementations requiring many gates. An alternative approach is to use a read-only memory (ROM) for the combinatorial logic.

Figure 4.13 shows a block diagram of the general sequential digital machine (or finite state machine) in which all the combinatorial logic is implemented with a ROM. Note that this diagram is essentially identical to that of Fig. 2.2. The flip-flops hold the present values of the state variables. The outputs of these flip-flops are taken, together with the input digial lines, to the ROM address lines. Thus the ROM word that is currently being addressed is determined by the present state and the current values of the inputs. The ROM outputs must contain the next state information, i.e. the next state values, and the present state outputs.

In the combination door lock problem discussed in the previous section

**Table 4.8**   Combination door lock excitation table

|  | Present state | | Inputs | | | Next state | |
|  | $Y$ | $X$ | $a$ | $b$ | $c$ | $Y'$ | $X'$ |
|---|---|---|---|---|---|---|---|
| | 0 | 0 | 0 | 0 | 0 | 0 | 0 |
| | 0 | 0 | 0 | 0 | 1 | 0 | 0 |
| | 0 | 0 | 0 | 1 | 0 | 0 | 1 |
| $S_0$ | 0 | 0 | 0 | 1 | 1 | 0 | 0 |
| | 0 | 0 | 1 | 0 | 0 | 0 | 0 |
| | 0 | 0 | 1 | 0 | 1 | 0 | 0 |
| | 0 | 0 | 1 | 1 | 0 | 0 | 0 |
| | 0 | 0 | 1 | 1 | 1 | 0 | 0 |
| | 0 | 1 | 0 | 0 | 0 | 0 | 0 |
| | 0 | 1 | 0 | 0 | 1 | 0 | 0 |
| | 0 | 1 | 0 | 1 | 0 | 0 | 0 |
| $S_1$ | 0 | 1 | 0 | 1 | 1 | 0 | 0 |
| | 0 | 1 | 1 | 0 | 0 | 1 | 0 |
| | 0 | 1 | 1 | 0 | 1 | 0 | 0 |
| | 0 | 1 | 1 | 1 | 0 | 0 | 0 |
| | 0 | 1 | 1 | 1 | 1 | 0 | 0 |
| | 1 | 0 | 0 | 0 | 0 | 0 | 0 |
| | 1 | 0 | 0 | 0 | 1 | 1 | 1 |
| | 1 | 0 | 0 | 1 | 0 | 0 | 0 |
| $S_2$ | 1 | 0 | 0 | 1 | 1 | 0 | 0 |
| | 1 | 0 | 1 | 0 | 0 | 0 | 0 |
| | 1 | 0 | 1 | 0 | 1 | 0 | 0 |
| | 1 | 0 | 1 | 1 | 0 | 0 | 0 |
| | 1 | 0 | 1 | 1 | 1 | 0 | 0 |
| | 1 | 1 | 0 | 0 | 0 | 1 | 1 |
| | 1 | 1 | 0 | 0 | 1 | 1 | 1 |
| | 1 | 1 | 0 | 1 | 0 | 1 | 1 |
| $S_3$ | 1 | 1 | 0 | 1 | 1 | 1 | 1 |
| | 1 | 1 | 1 | 0 | 0 | 1 | 1 |
| | 1 | 1 | 1 | 0 | 1 | 1 | 1 |
| | 1 | 1 | 1 | 1 | 0 | 1 | 1 |
| | 1 | 1 | 1 | 1 | 1 | 1 | 1 |

there are two state variables, three inputs and one output. To implement the door lock a ROM with five address inputs and a minimum word length of three bits is required. Five address lines gives an address range of $2^5 = 32$, so the minimum size ROM required is $32 \times 3$, as shown in Fig. 4.14. In practice a $32 \times 4$ ROM would be used, since ROMs with 3-bit words are generally not

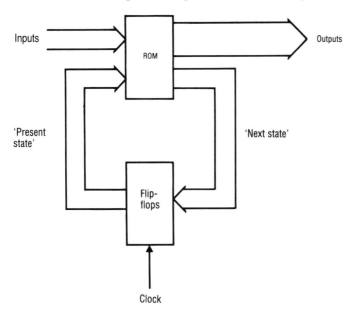

**Fig. 4.13**   Implementing the combinatorial logic of a sequential machine with a ROM.

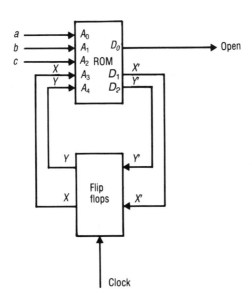

**Fig. 4.14**   Implementation of combination door lock, with a ROM to generate the combinatorial logic.

available. The programming information for the ROM is effectively already available in the state table, Table 4.8, with the exception of the output information. This state table has been rewritten in Table 4.9 in a form that is more suitable for the programming of the ROM. The inputs $a$, $b$ and $c$ are connected to the address lines $A_0$, $A_1$ and $A_2$, while the state variable outputs from the flip-flops, $X$ and $Y$, are connected to $A_3$ and $A_4$. The ROM output data line $D_0$ is used as the open output, while data lines $D_1$ and $D_2$ hold the next state information and are connected as inputs to the state variable flip-flops. Data line $D_3$ is not used, and when programming the ROM it does not matter whether its value is 0 or 1.

Consider the operation of the circuit shown in Fig. 4.14. Assume that it is initially in the idle or reset state. The address lines are all 0, so word 0 in the ROM is being addressed. This word contains all 0s (Table 4.9), so that open $= 0$ and the next state is 00. Now suppose button $b$ is pushed. This changes address line $A_1$ from 0 to 1, so that word 2 is addressed. This word contains the binary pattern 010, so that the next state is 01, while open remains 0. The next clock pulse, generated by pushing button $b$, now occurs and the next state information is clocked into the state flip-flops, to become the new present state, 01. Address line $A_3$ is now changed from 0 to 1. Thus word 8 is now being addressed. The operation of the circuit continues in this way, being entirely determined by the state table and the sequence in which the buttons are pushed.

In this particular example, many of the entries in the ROM table are identical, because many of the terms in the state table are identical. When this is the case the ROM implementation is inefficient, although this will often not matter since a ROM is a standard component available at low cost. In cases where efficiency is important, and where the state table is sparsely populated with 1s, a programmable logic array (PLA or FPLA) may be used instead of a ROM. For example, Table 4.9 shows that in the combination door lock, the next state variables $X'$ and $Y'$ both contain only three different product terms:

$$X' = \bar{X}.\bar{Y}.\bar{a}.b.\bar{c} + \bar{X}.Y.a.\bar{b}.c + X.Y$$
$$\bar{Y} = X.\bar{Y}.a.\bar{b}.\bar{c} + \bar{X}.Y.\bar{a}.\bar{b}.c + X.Y$$

i.e. there are only four different terms. Similarly the output is a single term:

$$\text{open} = X.Y$$

A PLA implementation of the combinatorial part of the door lock is shown in Fig. 4.15.

**Table 4.9**  Excitation table for the combination door lock rewritten in a form suitable for implementation with a ROM

| $A_4$ | $A_3$ | $A_2$ | $A_1$ | $A_0$ | $D_3$ | $D_2$ | $D_1$ | $D_0$ |
|---|---|---|---|---|---|---|---|---|
| Present state | | | Inputs | | Not | Next state | | Output |
| Y | X | a | b | c | used | Y' | X' | |
| 0 | 0 | 0 | 0 | 0 | | 0 | 0 | 0 |
| 0 | 0 | 0 | 0 | 1 | | 0 | 0 | 0 |
| 0 | 0 | 0 | 1 | 0 | | 0 | 1 | 0 |
| 0 | 0 | 0 | 1 | 1 | | 0 | 0 | 0 |
| 0 | 0 | 1 | 0 | 0 | | 0 | 0 | 0 |
| 0 | 0 | 1 | 0 | 1 | | 0 | 0 | 0 |
| 0 | 0 | 1 | 1 | 0 | | 0 | 0 | 0 |
| 0 | 0 | 1 | 1 | 1 | | 0 | 0 | 0 |
| 0 | 1 | 0 | 0 | 0 | | 0 | 0 | 0 |
| 0 | 1 | 0 | 0 | 1 | | 0 | 0 | 0 |
| 0 | 1 | 0 | 1 | 0 | | 0 | 0 | 0 |
| 0 | 1 | 0 | 1 | 1 | | 0 | 0 | 0 |
| 0 | 1 | 1 | 0 | 0 | | 1 | 0 | 0 |
| 0 | 1 | 1 | 0 | 1 | | 0 | 0 | 0 |
| 0 | 1 | 1 | 1 | 0 | | 0 | 0 | 0 |
| 0 | 1 | 1 | 1 | 1 | | 0 | 0 | 0 |
| 1 | 0 | 0 | 0 | 0 | | 0 | 0 | 0 |
| 1 | 0 | 0 | 0 | 1 | | 1 | 1 | 0 |
| 1 | 0 | 0 | 1 | 0 | | 0 | 0 | 0 |
| 1 | 0 | 0 | 1 | 1 | | 0 | 0 | 0 |
| 1 | 0 | 1 | 0 | 0 | | 0 | 0 | 0 |
| 1 | 0 | 1 | 0 | 1 | | 0 | 0 | 0 |
| 1 | 0 | 1 | 1 | 0 | | 0 | 0 | 0 |
| 1 | 0 | 1 | 1 | 1 | | 0 | 0 | 0 |
| 1 | 1 | 0 | 0 | 0 | | 1 | 1 | 1 |
| 1 | 1 | 0 | 0 | 1 | | 1 | 1 | 1 |
| 1 | 1 | 0 | 1 | 0 | | 1 | 1 | 1 |
| 1 | 1 | 0 | 1 | 1 | | 1 | 1 | 1 |
| 1 | 1 | 1 | 0 | 0 | | 1 | 1 | 1 |
| 1 | 1 | 1 | 0 | 1 | | 1 | 1 | 1 |
| 1 | 1 | 1 | 1 | 0 | | 1 | 1 | 1 |
| 1 | 1 | 1 | 1 | 1 | | 1 | 1 | 1 |

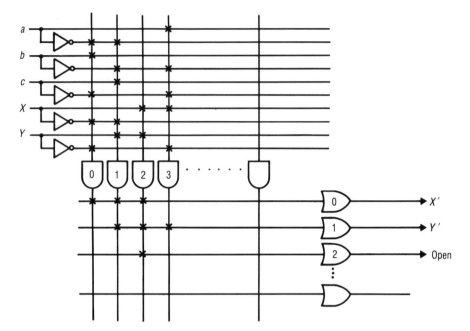

**Fig. 4.15**   PLA implementation of the combinatorial logic required in the combination door lock.

## 4.7   Counter design

Counters are a special class of finite state machines. A counter follows a preset sequence and repeatedly outputs the same pattern. The simplest counter is the binary-up counter in which the counter is incremented by one each time a clock pulse occurs, until the maximum count is reached. Figure 4.16 shows the state diagram for a modulo-8 counter. By convention the count begins at 0 and is then incremented by 1 on the next clock pulse until the maximum of 7 occurs. When the next clock pulse occurs the counter is reset to zero, and the sequence starts again. Note that there are no inputs, apart from the clock. Eight states require three state variables, $X$, $Y$ and $Z$. The circuit outputs are just the state variables, $X$, $Y$ and $Z$. The design of a synchronous counter proceeds in exactly the same way as discussed above for any synchronous sequential circuit.

Consider the design of a modulo-3 up/down synchronous counter. This counter has a single input labelled up/down, in addition to the normal clock. If up/down = 1 the counter is to count up in the normal way, following the sequence 0, 1, 2, 0 ..., while if up/down = 0 it is required to count down following the sequence 0, 2, 1, 0 ... There are three states, so two state

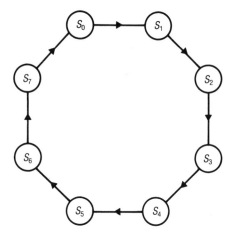

**Fig. 4.16**  State diagrams for a modulo-8 up-counter.

variables are required, $X$ and $Y$. In normal operation the fourth state, state 4, is never entered and so could be regarded as a 'don't care' state. However, if state 4 is ever entered, for example, as the random state entered at initial switch on, then the next state should be one of the three states, state 0 say, so that the count sequence is properly resumed. The state table is shown in Table 4.10(a). In this example it will be assumed that each of the state variables, $X$ and $Y$, is stored in a JK flip-flop, as shown in Fig. 4.17. As before, the problem comes down to designing the combinatorial logic required for the connections to the J and K inputs of the two flip-flops, and the logic to generate the output signals. The logic is determined by expanding the state table into a new modified table, called an **excitation** table (Table 4.10b). Again the normal binary pattern has been assumed for the state variables. The column labelled JK flip-flop controls is filled in with the aid of the JK flip-flop state change table, Table 4.6. For example, in the first row the transition from state 00 to state 10, the state variable $Y$ changes from 0 to 1. This requires that $J_Y = 1$ and $K_Y = $ x (don't care). The state variable $X$ does not change $(0 \rightarrow 0)$ and so $J_X = 0$ and $K_X = $ x. Boolean equations for the J and K values may then be written down directly by scanning each column for the '1' entries, as before, giving:

$$J_Y = \bar{Y}.\bar{X}.\bar{U} + \bar{Y}.X.U$$
$$K_Y = 1$$
$$J_X = \bar{Y}.\bar{X}.U + Y.\bar{X}.\bar{U}$$
$$K_X = 1$$

These equations can be minimized using K-maps, as shown in Fig. 4.17. The resulting implementation is given in Fig. 4.17.

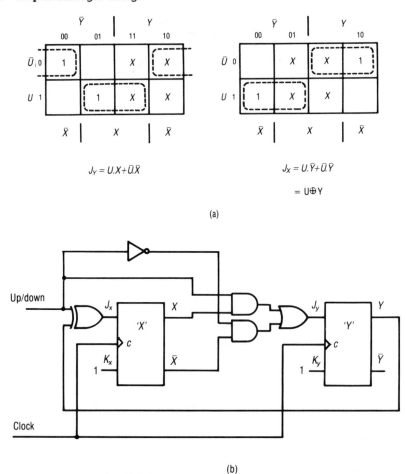

Fig. 4.17 Up/down counter: (a) K-maps for $J_X$ and $J_Y$ flip-flop control signals; (b) implementation.

The decision on whether to use D-type or JK flip-flops is really a matter of choice. A JK flip-flop implementation is slightly more difficult to design, but will often result in less hardware being required for the combinatorial logic, than an equivalent design using D-type flip-flops.

Another type of counter that is frequently used is the asynchronous or ripple counter. These counters use JK flip-flops connected in the toggle mode, with $J = K = 1$. Figure 4.18a shows a modulo-16 ripple counter. The pulses to be counted are applied to the clock input of the first JK flip-flop. The output of this flip-flop, $Q_A$, is applied to the clock input of the second flip-flop. Its output is applied in turn to the clock input of the third flip-flop, and so on.

**Table 4.10** Modulo-3 up/down counter: (a) state table; (b) excitation table

| Present State Y | X | Up/down U | Next state Y' | X' |
|---|---|---|---|---|
| 0 | 0 | 0 | 1 | 0 |
| 0 | 0 | 1 | 0 | 1 |
| 0 | 1 | 0 | 0 | 0 |
| 0 | 1 | 1 | 1 | 0 |
| 1 | 0 | 0 | 0 | 1 |
| 1 | 0 | 1 | 0 | 0 |
| 1 | 1 | x | 0 | 0 |

(a)

| Present state Y | X | Up/down U | Next state Y' | X' | $J_Y$ | Flip-flop controls $K_Y$ | $J_X$ | $K_X$ |
|---|---|---|---|---|---|---|---|---|
| 0 | 0 | 0 | 1 | 0 | 1 | x | 0 | x |
| 0 | 0 | 1 | 0 | 1 | 0 | x | 1 | x |
| 0 | 1 | 0 | 0 | 0 | 0 | x | x | 1 |
| 0 | 1 | 1 | 1 | 0 | 1 | x | x | 1 |
| 1 | 0 | 0 | 0 | 1 | x | 1 | 1 | x |
| 1 | 0 | 1 | 0 | 0 | x | 1 | 0 | x |
| 1 | 1 | x | 0 | 0 | x | 1 | x | 1 |

(b)

Figure 4.18b shows the input and output signals that are observed in this counter. The first flip-flop toggles, i.e. changes state, on the rising edge of each of the pulses to be counted. It effectively divides the pulse frequency by 2. The second flip-flop toggles on every rising edge of $Q_A$, so effectively dividing the input pulse frequency by 4. The outputs of the flip-flops are thus a binary count of the input pulses, with $Q_A$ being the least significant digit, and $Q_D$ the most significant digit. Clearly the design can be extended to any number of stages to produce a modulo-$N$ counter, but with the limitation that $N$ is a power of two. It is also possible to design ripple counters where $N$ is not a power of two, but their design is not considered here. Note also that a modulo-$N$ counter may also be used as a divide-by-$N$ frequency divider, dividing the input frequency by $N$, $N^2$, $N^4$, etc. The name 'ripple counter' comes from the fact that changes in the state of the counter ripple through the chain of flip-flops, with the result that there is a propagation delay between the outputs of the flip-flops changing. If this is important then a synchronous counter must be used where all the changes occur instantaneously coincident with the clock pulse.

A variety of counters are available as MSI packages.

## 4.8 Design of a register bank

The basic ideas, including the design of combinatorial and sequential logic circuits, required for the understanding of how a computer works have now been discussed. As an introduction to the following chapters that consider the concept of a computer as a finite state machine, the evolution of a memory from a single D-type flip-flop to a register bank will now be discussed.

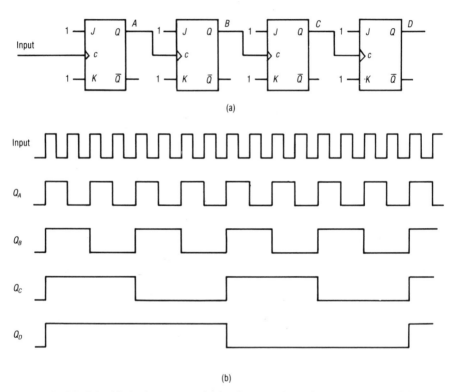

**Fig. 4.18** Modulo-16 ripple counter: (a) implementation using JK flip-flops; (b) input and output signals.

A register is a device in which a number of **binary digits** (bits) can be stored and retrieved, or read back. The use of a D-type flip-flop to store a single bit of information has been considered in section 4.4.2 above. The data bit to be

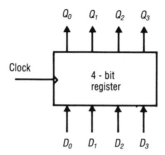

**Fig. 4.19**  Register formed from a set of four D-type flip-flops.

stored in, or written to, the memory (0 or 1) is placed on the D input (see Figs 4.8 and 4.9) and a clock pulse is then applied to the clock input, $C$. This results in the data bit being stored in the flip-flop. Its value can be ascertained at any time from the memory by reading the value of the $Q$ output. A set $n$ of these D-type flip-flops, fabricated as a single unit, can be used to store $n$ bits of information, and is known as a register. Frequently, $n$ is a power of 2, usually 4, 8 or 16 (although there are exceptions). Figure 4.19 is a schematic diagram of a single 4-bit register. The inputs are labelled $D_0$ to $D_3$, and the outputs $Q_0$ to $Q_3$. The pattern of bits stored in the register will be referred to as a (4-bit) word. The four clock inputs to the individual flip-flops within the register are connected to a common clock line. When a pulse is applied to this line the data on the input lines are written into the memory, over-writing the previous word stored.

Clearly a set of registers is required to store a set of words; Fig. 4.20 shows two 4-bit registers, $R_0$ and $R_1$. In a computer system data are transferred between the various units that make up the computer on a common data bus, which in practice is just a set of wires, or tracks on a printed circuit board, or

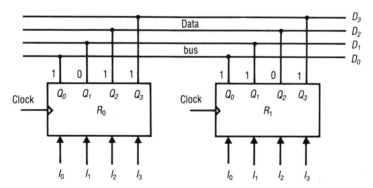

**Fig. 4.20**  Two 4-bit registers connected to a data bus.

interconnections in an integrated circuit. In Fig. 4.20 the outputs of the two registers are shown connected to the data bus. This bus is a 4-bit wide bus, since four bits of information are passed between the registers and computer (or other devices using the registers) at once. Note that the inputs to the registers have been relabelled $I_0$ to $I_3$, to avoid confusion with the data bus which is labelled according to the accepted convention $D_0$ to $D_3$.

Figure 4.20 shows that each output of register $R_0$ is connected to the corresponding output of register $R_1$ via the data bus, and so breaks one of the cardinal rules of constructing logic systems. This rule states that the outputs of ordinary gates or components such as flip-flops must not be connected together. To see why, suppose the two words stored in $R_0$ and $R_1$ are 1101 and 1011, respectively, and consider what will be the logic states of the data bus lines. $D_0$ and $D_3$ will both be 1 since $Q_0$ and $Q_3$ are 1 for both registers. However, it is not at all clear what the states of $D_1$ and $D_2$ will be. In the case of $D_1$ register $R_0$ is trying to output a 0, while register $R_1$ is trying to output a 1 (and conversely for $D_2$). At best, $D_1$ and $D_2$ will be indeterminate, while at worst both registers will be destroyed. This is because $Q_1$ of $R_0$ is effectively connected to the 0 volt supply line, and $Q_1$ of $R_1$ to the $V_{cc}$ supply line. The result is a short circuit path between $V_{cc}$ and 0 volts leading to the probable destruction of both circuits. Moreover, logically, the device at the other end of the data bus is attempting to read from both registers at once, which is clearly not sensible.

**Table 4.11**   Truth table of tristate buffer

| $D$ | $E$ | $Y$ |
|---|---|---|
| 0 | 1 | 0 |
| 1 | 1 | 1 |
| 0 | 0 | high-Z |
| 1 | 0 | high-Z |

One solution is to connect only the output lines of one register at a time to the data bus. This is achieved by inserting a special type of buffer circuit, known as a 3-state or tristate buffer, into each output line of the registers. Figure 4.21 shows the circuit symbol and schematic circuit diagram of a tristate buffer. Its truth table is given in Table 4.11. If the enable line is high then the tristate buffer behaves like an ordinary buffer: the 'switch' is closed and the output logic state is the same as the input. However, if the enable line is low the 'switch' is open, effectively disconnecting the output from the input. The design of a tristate buffer is such that there is a very high impedance between the input and output, shown in the truth table by the 'high-Z' entries. Tristate buffers are also available with an inverting action ($Y = \bar{D}$),

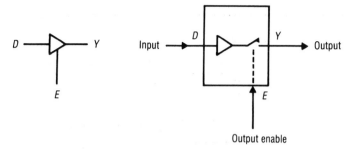

**Fig. 4.21**    Tristate buffer.

and with active low enable. Thus each output line in each register has a tristate buffer controlled by the 'output enable' control line. Clearly only one register 'output enable' must be true at any one time, or else the same problem of two registers trying to drive the data bus at the same time occurs.

The next problem is how to write data into a register. Again, the data bus is used, but this time data are placed on the bus by a device such as a computer, and the task is to route the data from the data bus to the desired register. Connections can be made directly from the data bus to the register inputs ($I_0$ to $I_3$), since the data will only be written into the register when a clock pulse is applied. Figure 4.22 shows the connections between a data bus line and a single flip-flop of a register. The read, write and select control lines are common to all the cells within a register. The select line is used to select, or address, a particular register within a system. This selection is usually done with the aid of a decoder, and will be discussed in detail in Chapter 9. Read and write are control lines used to control the reading from, and writing to, the registers. These operations are as follows.

1.  Read from memory cell: select and read = 1; write = 0. The output of the tristate buffer is enabled, so the data bit stored in the cell is routed to the data bus line $D$.
2.  Write to memory cell: select and write = 1; read = 0. The input **AND** gate $A$ is enabled so the data bit present on the data bus line is routed to the input of the memory flip-flop. A clock pulse is then applied, and since **AND** gate $B$ is enabled, the flip-flop is clocked, so copying the data bit into the flip-flop. The output tristate buffer is in its high-impedance state, so there is no connection between the output of the flip-flop and the data bus.

## 4.9  Summary

The design and implementation of synchronous sequential logic circuits has been discussed in this chapter. A sequential logic design is commenced by

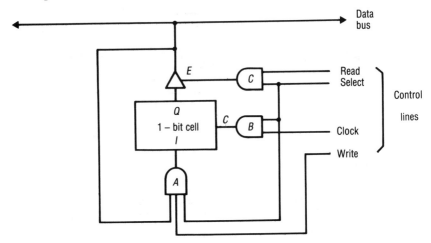

**Fig. 4.22** 1-bit memory cell.

drawing a state diagram, the normal starting point of the design process. Once this diagram is complete, and checked against the specification for the system required, the implementation process is then essentially a mechanical exercise, following a given 'recipe'. The implementation discussed in this text uses JK flip-flops as memory elements for the state variables, and a simple procedure is given which allows the combinatorial logic for each of the $J$ and $K$ flip-flop inputs to be determined easily. If implementing the combinatorial logic using discrete gates becomes too extensive then an alternative approach is to use either a read-only memory (ROM) or a programmable logic array (PLA) or an EPLD. The implementation of simple counters, both synchronous and asynchronous (ripple), has also been introduced.

## Exercises

4.1 Design a synchronous circuit using D-type flip-flops to detect the sequence 0101. The circuit has a single input, $x$, and a single output $z$. The output is logic-1 whenever the input sequence 0101 is detected, logic-0 otherwise. Note that overlapping sequences are allowed.

4.2 Design a synchronous circuit that has a single binary input, $x$, and a single binary output, $z$. The output is to be logic-1 whenever the previous three inputs contain an even number of logic-1s. For example, the input sequence

   0 1 1 0 1 0 1 1 ...

should give rise to the output sequence

   0 0 1 1 1 0 1 1 ...

4.3 A synchronous circuit is to be designed to perform the serial addition of two binary numbers. These numbers are fed a bit at a time, starting with the least significant bits, to the two inputs of the circuit, $x_1$ and $x_2$. The circuit has a single output, $z$, which is to produce the sum of the two inputs, in serial form.

4.4 Design a synchronous modulo-3 counter (that is, one that continually counts in the sequence 0, 1, 2, 0, 1, 2, ...) using (a) D-type and (b) JK flip-flops.

4.5 Design a modulo-6 up/down counter using a ROM and a set of D-type flip-flops. You should specify the size and the contents of the ROM.

# 5

# The structure of a computer

A computer, strictly a stored program computer, consists of a set of sequential and combinatorial logic components which act in a similar way to the sequential logic described in the previous chapter.

The basic difference between a computer and a sequential logic machine is that whereas in a sequential logic machine the combinatorial and sequential logic defines the function performed, in a computer it is the stored instructions, the program, which determine its action. Because the program may be changed easily, the computer is much more flexible than a hardwired design.

A computer can be represented in block-diagram form as shown in Fig. 5.1. It consists of five functional blocks: memory, input, output, control and the arithmetic and logic unit. The memory is used to store instructions and data which are processed by the arithmetic and logic unit. The input and output devices, often called peripherals, are used to input and output instructions and data. The control unit coordinates the operation of the computer and most of the control resides in a central unit which, since it normally also contains the arithmetic and logic unit, is known as the central processing unit (CPU). In a simple microcomputer system, integrated circuits often correspond to this functional division of a computer system. An example of simple Intel 8085- and Motorola 68000-based microcomputer systems is given in Chapter 9.

## 5.1   The operation of a computer

The operation cycle of a computer consists of four basic steps:

1. Fetch the next instruction from memory to the control unit $\left.\right\}$ *Fetch cycle*
2. Decode this instruction

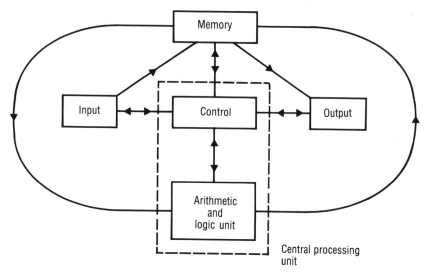

Fig. 5.1  Block diagram of a computer.

3. Obey the instruction  *Execution cycle*
4. Go to 1

Memory consists of a large number of locations, each comprising the same number of bits and called a word. Some of these locations contain instructions and some contain data. This information is stored encoded into groups of bits. Each separate memory location is identified by a unique address. To write information to memory the address of the location where the information is to reside has to be presented, together with the data. To read information already present in memory only the address of the location is required.

The bit pattern representing an instruction can be considered as split into a number of fields. One of the fields specifies the operation to be carried out; other fields may specify the address in memory of operands of the instruction and the address where the results, if any, are to be put. The number and type of operand fields will depend on the operation to be performed and on the computer architecture. For example, the **HALT** instruction, which will halt operation of the computer, needs no operands. An **ADD** instruction, however, needs to know the addresses of two operands and the address in memory to place the result. A full discussion of instruction sets and memory addressing modes is given in Chapter 11.

While the fetch cycle is identical for all instructions within the computer, the execution cycle depends on the particular instruction being executed.

Hence there will be as many different execution cycles as there are instructions defined for that particular computer.

Instructions typically fall into several groups. One group, the arithmetic and logic group, includes instructions such as add, subtract, multiply and divide in the arithmetic group and **ADD**, **OR** and **XOR** in the logic group. A second group consists of move or copy operations which provide a means of transferring information from memory location to memory location and between memory and input and output devices. A third group involves transfer of control. These instructions modify the instruction flow through the program, often conditionally on the result of the previous operation by forcing the next instruction to be obtained not from the next memory location but from somewhere else in memory. In addition to these groups of instructions there are usually instructions to perform specialized operations, such as halting the computer. More details of these groups of instructions for the Intel 8085 and Motorola 68000 microprocessors are given in Chapter 11.

## 5.2 The bus

The main method of communication between the various component parts of a computer is by the use of one or more buses. A bus consists of a group of signal lines used to carry information. Usually the components tap on to the bus to send and receive information as shown in Fig. 5.2.

In order to work correctly, only one sender must be active on the bus at any one time. In a simple computer this is achieved by having a single master, the central processing unit, which controls the whole system. The other devices on the bus, called slaves, respond to commands from the central processing unit which controls what information is on the bus at any one time. Any device connected to the bus may read information on it; logic has to be provided so that only the addressd device responds. Buses carry three different types of information, address, data and control, and a bus is often subdivided into these three types.

In a computer system there will be a number of groups of buses. In this text only the two lowest level buses will be considered; those between components of the CPU and those between the CPU, memory and input−output interfaces on a single printed circuit board.

As mentioned previously in this chapter, a typical microcomputer system is made up from a number of integrated circuits providing the functions described in Fig. 5.1. The CPU is normally provided as a single integrated circuit which is connected via buses to the appropriate number of memory and input−output interfaces to produce the required computer system. This division is followed in this book, with this chapter concentrating on the internal structure of the CPU.

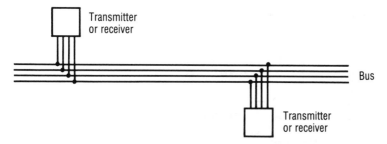

**Fig. 5.2**   The bus.

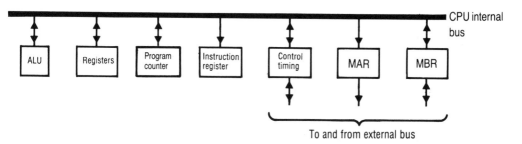

**Fig. 5.3**   The CPU bus structure.

## 5.3   The central processing unit

The central processing unit (CPU) consists of a control unit and an arithmetic and logic unit. In this section these two subunits are described in detail.

The CPU is organized around a bus structure and although individual computers differ as to the exact organization, Fig. 5.3 is typical.

Not all registers have to be the same size because they hold different types of information. Those registers which hold data or instructions have to be the same size as a memory location. Registers which hold the address of a memory location, the program counter and the memory address register of Fig. 5.3, need to be large enough to contain the highest memory address. In a typical 8-bit microcomputer the registers which hold data are 8 bits wide, whereas those which hold memory addresses are 16 bits wide to allow for a maximum memory size of $2^{16}$ (65 536) locations. A 16-bit microcomputer normally has a wider address range, typically in the megabyte range. For example, the Motorola 68000 has 24 address lines giving a maximum memory size of $2^{24}$ (16 777 216) locations.

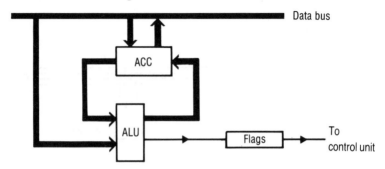

**Fig. 5.4**   A single accumulator ALU structure.

## 5.4   The arithmetic and logic unit

The arithmetic and logic unit (ALU) is involved in the execution of arithmetic and logical operations. The operands of an arithmetic or logical operation are to be found in memory, but to speed up the operation many computers have several, typically 8 or 16, faster memory locations, called registers, within the CPU. Many computers have a single special register, called the accumulator, which is the source of one of the operands and the destination of an arithmetic or logical operation. If this is the case, the structure of the processor can be represented as in Fig. 5.4, which also shows a flag register. This register contains a number of individual bits to store information about the result of the last ALU operation, for example, whether it resulted in a zero result, negative result, or produced a carry or an overflow. This information may be used by later instructions.

### 5.4.1   The structure of an arithmetic logic unit

A simple block diagram of an ALU is shown in Fig. 5.5. The inputs and the output will typically be 8 or 16 bits wide, depending on the size of the ALU. The number of control signals will depend upon the number of functions which the ALU is capable of performing; $n$ control signals are required for $2^n$ opreations.

### 5.4.2   The subunits of the arithmetic logic unit

An ALU can perform a range of arithmetic and logic operations and this section describes a few of the circuits required to perform these operations. The circuits described would not necessarily be found in this form in a modern CPU; usually they are implemented by more regular structures such as PLAs.

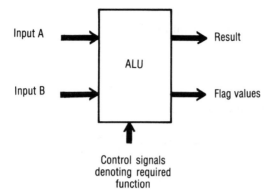

**Fig. 5.5**  ALU structure.

## (a)  An adder

A computer works on a pattern of bits and so the lowest level of adder is a
1-bit adder. This adder has to implement the truth table:

| A | B | Carry | Sum |
|---|---|---|---|
| 0 | 0 | 0 | 0 |
| 0 | 1 | 0 | 1 |
| 1 | 0 | 0 | 1 |
| 1 | 1 | 1 | 0 |

The circuit that implements this truth table is called a half adder, since for
addition of multiple bits an additional circuit is needed which has as an extra
input, the carry from the previous bit addition. This is called a full adder and
its truth table is:

| A | B | Carry in | Carry out | Sum |
|---|---|---|---|---|
| 0 | 0 | 0 | 0 | 0 |
| 0 | 0 | 1 | 0 | 1 |
| 0 | 1 | 0 | 0 | 1 |
| 0 | 1 | 1 | 1 | 0 |
| 1 | 0 | 0 | 0 | 1 |
| 1 | 0 | 1 | 1 | 0 |
| 1 | 1 | 0 | 1 | 0 |
| 1 | 1 | 1 | 1 | 1 |

For the half adder, the circuit is simple and can be produced by inspection of the truth table, as was shown in Chapter 1, i.e.:

$$S = A \oplus B$$
$$C = A \cdot B$$

giving the circuit shown in Fig. 5.6.

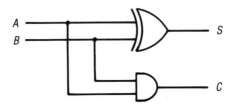

**Fig. 5.6** Half adder structure.

The full adder circuit is more complex. Using the combinatorial logic design techniques described in Chapter 3 the required logic is:

$$
\begin{aligned}
C_{out} &= \bar{A}.B.C_{in} + A.\bar{B}.C_{in} + A.B.\bar{C}_{in} + A.B.C_{in} \\
&= C_{in}\,(A \oplus B) + A.B \\
S &= \bar{A}.\bar{B}.C_{in} + \bar{A}.B.\bar{C}_{in} + A.\bar{B}.\bar{C}_{in} + A.B.C_{in} \\
&= \bar{C}_{in}\,.\,(A \oplus B) + C_{in}\,(\overline{A \oplus B}) \\
&= C_{in} \oplus (A \oplus B)
\end{aligned}
$$

which gives the circuit shown in Fig. 5.7.

Full adders may be cascaded together to produce multiple bit adders as shown in Fig. 5.8. A point to notice here is that if one of the input values is 0, for example $B_0$–$B_3$, then, if the initial carry $C_0$ is set to 1, the result will be $A + 1$. This is a quick method of incrementing a value by 1.

An adder may also be used as a subtractor, using the rules of 'two's complement' arithmetic, the arithmetic normally performed by a computer. In this number system (see Chapter 10 on computer arithmetic), subtraction may be performed by one's complementing (inverting all the bits of) the value

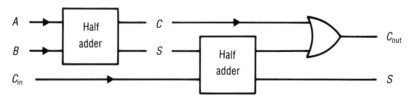

**Fig. 5.7** Full adder circuit.

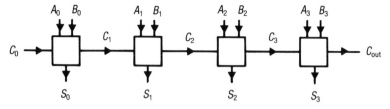

**Fig. 5.8**   Multiple bit full adder.

to be subtracted, incrementing the one's complement to form the two's complement and then adding this complemented value to the other operand. Hence for subtraction the circuit required is a set of inverters on one of the input paths to the ALU and the adder circuitry described above. The carry input to the least significant bit of the adder provides a simple incrementing mechanism.

### (b)   Logical tests

An ALU normally contains logic to perform a number of different logical tests, such as a test to see if the result of an operation is zero. Some of these logical tests affect the flag register used to store information regarding the result of the last operation; other logical tests produce a result used as data in further processing.

### (c)   Logical test for zero

All that is needed for a test for zero on a word is an **OR** gate with the requisite number of inputs as shown in Fig. 5.9. This circuit may be used to set the zero flag on the result of an operation.

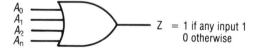

**Fig. 5.9**   Logical test for zero.

### (d)   Bitwise **AND** of two operands

As this operation suggests, what is required is a set of **AND** gates which have as inputs the corresponding bits of the two operands. The outputs are the resultant **AND** of the bit pairs as shown by the circuit in Fig. 5.10.

The other bit operations, for example bitwise **OR**, may be implemented by similar schemes using different gates.

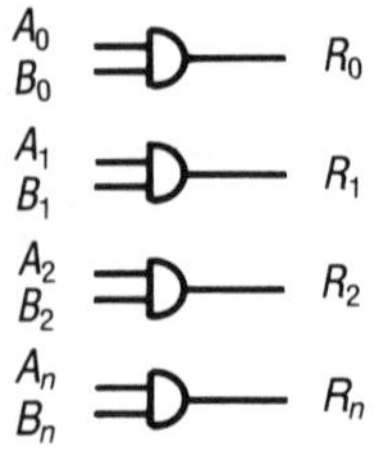

$A_0$ =D— $R_0$
$B_0$

$A_1$ =D— $R_1$
$B_1$

$A_2$ =D— $R_2$
$B_2$

$A_n$ =D— $R_n$
$B_n$

**Fig. 5.10** Bitwise **AND** of two words.

### (e) Shifting

Most computers include some form of shift or rotate instructions in their instruction set. These instructions move bits right or left within a word. The various shift and rotate operations differ in what is placed in the bit position left vacant by the moving of the bit pattern and by what happens to the bit which is moved out of the word by the shifting operation.

A shift register may be implemented by a series of edge-triggered flip-flops as shown in Fig. 5.11. On the occurrence of a clock pulse, the external input is clocked into the first flip-flop, the output from the first flip-flop is clocked into the second one, and so on. Thus all the bits are shifted one place to the right. The output and input will be connected in the particular way required for the shift operation and initial loading of all the bits of the shift register in parallel is normally allowed.

### (f) Comparator

Most computers include a number of comparison operations such as test for equality, greater than and less than. All these comparisons can be performed by subtraction, as described previously with the setting of the appropriate status flags, without the storing of the subtraction result.

### (g) Multiplication and division

In most small computers, multiplication and division are not implemented in hardware but have to be implemented by the programmer in software. In larger computers special hardware is provided, but it will not be discussed here.

## 5.4.3 Control

As shown earlier, control signals are required to connect registers to the bus, to control the function of the ALU and to provide timing signals to the rest of

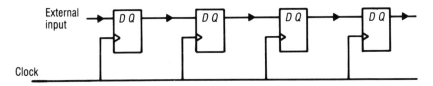

Clock

**Fig. 5.11**   A shift register.

the computer system. Most of the these control signals originate in the control section of the central processing unit.

All the actions of the control unit are connected with the decoding and execution of instructions, the fetch and execute cycles.

### (a)   The fetch cycle

The instruction cycle, as described in the beginning of this chapter, involves reading the next instruction to be obeyed from memory into an internal register in the CPU, the instruction register (IR), and then decoding and obeying the instruction.

In order to explain these actions in more detail a simple computer system will be used for illustrative purposes as shown in Fig. 5.12.

For an instruction to be fetched from memory the following sequence of operations has to be performed:

1. load the contents of the program counter into the memory address register (MAR) which is then put on the bus;
2. instruct the memory to perform a read operation which will result in data being placed on the data bus;

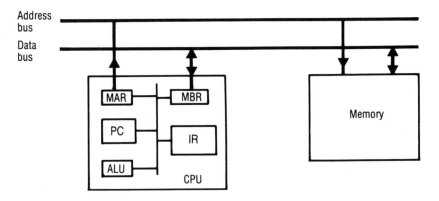

**Fig. 5.12**   Illustrative system.

3. store the value on the data bus in the memory buffer register (MBR) in the CPU;
4. transfer the value in the MBR into the instruction register (IR);
5. increment the contents of the program counter to point to the next location in memory.

In order to carry out these operations, a number of different control signals have to be sent to the various registers within the CPU and to the memory subsystem. For example, for the first operation the control system has to disable all the register outputs to the bus, to enable the output of the program counter on to the bus and to load the bus contents into the memory address register. The control signals required to perform these operations have to occur in the correct order and at the correct time relative to each other.

*(b)   The execute cycle*

The set of operations described above are performed as the fetch cycle of every instruction, but the execute cycle differs from instruction to instruction and from computer to computer as the architecture of the computer will greatly influence how an operation is performed.

As an example of an execution sequence, consider the architecture of Fig. 5.12 where an **ADD** instruction is defined as adding the contents of a named register to the accumulator and leaving the result in the accumulator. Since the registers reside in the CPU the execution sequence would be:

1. transfer the accumulator contents to the ALU via the internal bus;
2. transfer the addressed register contents to the other ALU input via the internal bus;
3. signal the ALU to add;
4. store the result in the accumulator.

A much fuller discussion of control is given in Chapter 8 on micro-programming.

## 5.5   Examples of processors – the Intel 8085 and the Motorola 68000

In this section two examples of real microprocessors will be outlined, namely the Intel 8085, an 8-bit processor, and the Motorola 68000, a 16-bit processor.

### 5.5.1   The Intel 8085 processor

A slightly simplified diagram of the Intel 8085 8-bit processor is shown in Fig. 5.13. It consists of an internal 8-bit bus, to which a bank of registers and an

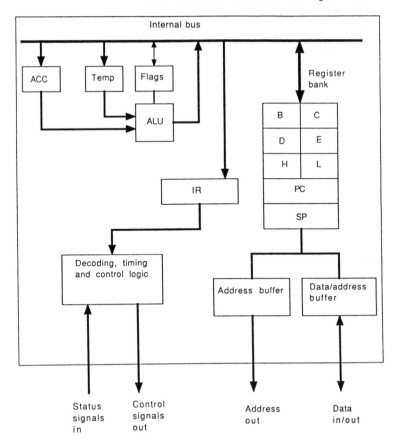

**Fig. 5.13**   Intel 8085 CPU.

ALU are connected. The register bank is made up of six 8-bit registers (B, C, D, E, H and L) and two 16-bit registers, the program counter (PC) and the stack pointer (SP). For some instructions the 8-bit registers are used as register-pairs (BC, DE and HL) to hold 16-bit values. One of the inputs to the ALU comes from a special register, called the accumulator (ACC), while the second input is from a temporary register. The output from the ALU is routed back to either the accumulator or to one of the registers via the internal bus. The flag register containing the status bits is also connected to the internal bus. Similarly, the instruction register (IR) is connected to the same internal bus and also to the timing and control unit via the instruction decoder. The control unit generates all the appropriate control signals both for the internal registers, and for external memory and input–output device synchronization.

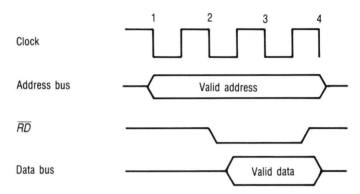

**Fig. 5.14**   Timing diagram for the Intel 8085 processor.

The 8085 processor is a synchronous machine, controlled by a single clock, with every action occurring on a transition of the clock. Fig. 5.14 shows the basic timing operation for the processor to perform a *read* operation, that is, to read an 8-bit value from memory. In the first cycle, $T_1$, the address of the location that is to be read is placed on the address and data buses, and the ALE (address latch enable) control signal is activated to indicate to the external latch that the data bus contains the least significant byte of the address. During the second cycle, $T_2$, the read control line, $\overline{RD}$, is activated, indicating to the external memory that the value in the location addressed should be placed on the data bus. The processor then normally assumes that the external memory responds quickly enough so that the data are available to the processor during the third cycle, $T_3$. These data are then latched into the appropriate processor register at the end of $T_3$. This completes the normal read operation. The write operation proceeds in a similar way, except that the write control signal $\overline{WR}$ is used instead of $\overline{RD}$.

## 5.5.2   The Motorola 68000 processor

The Motorola 68000 processor is actually one member of a family of compatible processors, ranging from the 8-bit 68008 to the newest 32-bit 68030. All the processors are object-code compatible, which means that they all execute the same base-level instructions. The 68000 is a very much more complicated and sophisticated processor than the Intel 8085, and is a good example of a CISC, a complex instruction set computer. It is available in a number of different packages; Fig. 5.15 shows the logical layout of the pins. The data bus is 16-bits wide, and the address bus is effectively 24-bits wide, so that $2^{24}$ or 16 Mbytes of memory can be addressed. The remainder of the pins are for power and control signals, some of which will be discussed below. The

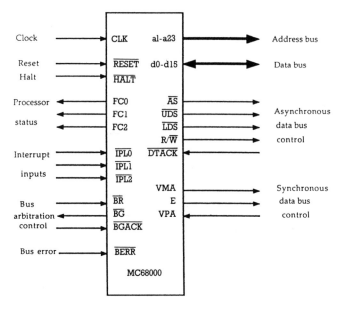

| | | |
|---|---|---|
| Clock | CLK | a1-a23 | Address bus |
| Reset | $\overline{\text{RESET}}$ | d0-d15 | Data bus |
| Halt | $\overline{\text{HALT}}$ | | |
| Processor | FC0 | $\overline{\text{AS}}$ | |
| | FC1 | $\overline{\text{UDS}}$ | Asynchronous |
| status | FC2 | $\overline{\text{LDS}}$ | data bus |
| | | R/$\overline{\text{W}}$ | control |
| Interrupt | $\overline{\text{IPL0}}$ | $\overline{\text{DTACK}}$ | |
| | $\overline{\text{IPL1}}$ | | |
| inputs | $\overline{\text{IPL2}}$ | | |
| | | VMA | Synchronous |
| Bus | $\overline{\text{BR}}$ | E | data bus |
| arbitration | $\overline{\text{BG}}$ | VPA | control |
| control | $\overline{\text{BGACK}}$ | | |
| Bus error | $\overline{\text{BERR}}$ | | |
| | MC68000 | | |

**Fig. 5.15**  Motorola 68000 processor.

processor contains seventeen registers: 8 data registers, 7 address registers, 2 stack pointers and a status register. With the exception of the status register, all the other registers are 32-bits wide, so that 32-bit values can be stored and operated upon. The 68000 allows operations on bytes (8-bits), words (16-bits), and long words (32-bits). The registers are connected via internal buses which are 32-bits wide. The main difference between the members of the 68000 family of processors is the number of read–write operations to fetch–store a value from–to memory. For example, the 68008 requires four read operations to fetch a 32-bit value from memory, the 68030 just one operation.

The 68000 has a full 32-bit ALU. As well as the normal logical and arithmetic operations, it also supports hardware multiplication and division of integer values. For the arithmetic operations one of the operands must be in a register (usually a data register), while the second operand can be in another register or in memory. A description of some of the 68000's addressing modes and instructions is given in Chapter 11.

Consider now a read operation from memory to a 68000 internal register. Fig. 5.16 shows a slightly simplified timing diagram. The read operation takes a minimum of four clock cycles, or eight states which are labelled S0–S7. Note that two states make up one clock cycle. The read operation starts in state S0. Unlike the Intel 8085 the 68000 has a single signal R/$\overline{\text{W}}$ to tell the memory whether it is doing a read operation (R/$\overline{\text{W}}$ = 1), or a write operation (R/$\overline{\text{W}}$ = 0). During S0 R/$\overline{\text{W}}$ is set high (logic level 1) to indicate a read

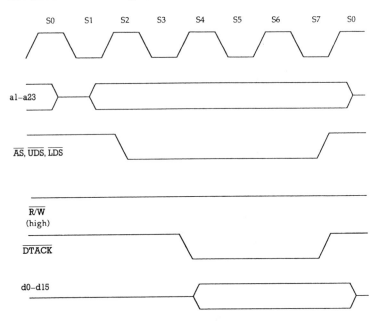

**Fig. 5.16**    Read timing diagram for the 68000 processor.

operation. In state S1 the address of the memory location to be read is output onto the address bus, while in state S2 the address strobe signal $\overline{AS}$ is activated, that is, goes low to logic level 0. This signal is used by the memory to detect that there is a valid address on the address bus. It has already been noted that the 68000 has a 16-bits wide data bus, so that it can transfer 16-bit values (words) at a time. If this is required then the two control lines labelled $\overline{UDS}$ and $\overline{LDS}$, upper and lower data strobes respectively, are activated (go low). However, if the processor is to read a single byte then only one of the two strobes is activated depending on whether the processor is to read a byte from the upper or lower half of the data bus. All control signals are now set for the read to proceed. The processor now waits for the external memory to place the value stored in the location addressed onto the data bus, and then to *signal back to the processor* that it has done so, and that there are valid data on the data bus. This is achieved via the data acknowledge signal $\overline{DTACK}$. If $\overline{DTACK}$ is activated (goes low) before the end of state S4 then the read operation is completed by the end of state S7. During S7 the address and data strobes ($\overline{AS}$, $\overline{UDS}$ and $\overline{LDS}$) are negated, and the data are latched internally into the appropriate 68000 register. If $\overline{DTACK}$ does not go low by the end of S4 then wait states are automatically inserted between S4 and S5, until the external memory does respond. A write operation occurs in a very similar way, with the processor again waiting until $\overline{DTACK}$ is asserted.

This data transfer scheme between processor and memory is fundamentally different from that of the Intel 8085. The 68000 data transfer is asynchronous, because the processor always waits for the memory to inform it that the data transfer has taken place. A full 'hand-shake' protocol is used, with the signals $\overline{AS}$, R/$\overline{W}$, $\overline{UDS}$, $\overline{LDS}$ and $\overline{DTACK}$ forming the asynchronous bus control.

Examination of Fig. 5.15 shows that there are a number of other groups of control signals. The synchronous bus control signals ($\overline{VPA}$, valid peripheral address, $\overline{VMA}$, valid memory address, and E, enable) allows older 8-bit peripheral input–output devices, originally developed for the Motorola 68000 processor, to be used by the 68000. This will be discussed further in Chapter 9. The interrupt control signals and the bus arbitration control signals are generally used by peripheral devices to transfer data quickly between the 'real world' and the processor; they will be discussed in Chapter 7. Finally, the three processor status lines are used to output a code to indicate the processing state of the 68000 processor. Full details of all the signals and the timing relationships can be found in the Motorola 16-bit Microprocessor Data Manual.

## 5.6   Input and output

Clearly a computer is useless unless information can be input from the 'real world', and the results of information processing passed back to the 'real world'. The subject of input/output is so important that a separate chapter (Chapter 7) is devoted to it. At this point it is only necessary to realize that a wide range of devices exist for input and output for most computer systems. These devices usually contain registers, which then appear as normal memory to the computer, and can be manipulated in the same way as memory. Thus an input device assembles information from the real world and places it in a register; the computer can then read this information from the register. The converse is true for output. The computer places information to be output in a register in the selected output device; the device then presents this information to the outside world.

## 5.7   Summary

The hardware of a computer consists of combinatorial and sequential logic. This logic is organized around a central bus structure which provides the communication between the memory, processor and input/output devices. The processor consists of a control and timing section, together with a set of registers and the arithmetic and logic unit (ALU). The ALU consists of a set of circuits which implements the arithmetic and logical operations provided by the instruction set of the computer.

## Exercises

5.1   A 4-bit arithmetic and logic unit (ALU) is to be designed for a 4-bit microprocessor. The ALU has two 4-bit wide inputs, labelled $i_1$ and $i_2$ and a 4-bit output labelled *out*. In addition there is a carry-out bit. Design the ALU so that it implements the following functions:

        add:           *out* $= i_1 + i_2$
        subtract:    *out* $= i_1 - i_2$
        shift-left:  *out* $= i_1$ shifted-left by 1-bit
        shift-right: *out* $= i_1$ shifted-right by 1-bit
        transfer:   *out* $= i_1$

5.2   A 4-bit microprocessor is to be designed. The processor is to use the ALU designed in Exercise 5.1, and in addition should have four general-purpose registers, a program counter (PC), an instruction register (IR), a memory address register (MAR) and a memory buffer register (MBR). Investigate a possible architecture for the organization of these registers and the ALU, and consider how the registers are to be connected to the various internal buses of the processor. Finally consider how the data flow between the registers, the ALU and external memory should be controlled, and in particular consider what control signals are necessary. (Although the control unit for a processor will be discussed in detail in Chapter 8, it is interesting at this stage to consider what it has to do, and what control signals are necessary.)

# 6

# Memory systems

In the previous chapter the structure of processors was considered, together with two examples of microprocessors, namely the 8-bit Intel 8085 and the 16-bit Motorola 68000. To make a useable computer system the processor requires a memory system to store programs and data, and input–output interfaces to connect it to the 'real world'. Memory systems will be considered in detail in this chapter, and input–output interfaces in Chapter 7.

## 6.1 Memory

Chapter 4 showed some simple memory circuits such as flip-flops and registers. The central processing unit contains a number of registers used for special purposes, such as the program counter and the accumulator, but the main directly accessible storage of the computer is concentrated in a separate unit, the memory subsystem. The memory can be thought of as a set of registers, each the same length, the word length of the computer. Each memory location has a unique address which is used by other devices within the computer to access that location.

Two memory parameters of interest are the size of each memory location (normally the word length of the computer) and the number of memory locations. The number of memory cells is usually a power of two, since an $n$-bit pattern, used to store an address of a memory cell, may contain $2^n$ separate values. The size of a memory is normally quoted in multiples of 1024 (i.e. $2^{10}$) called K; hence a 64K byte memory contains $64 \times 1024 = 65\,536$ bytes.

### 6.1.1 The basic memory structure

The basic operations on a memory location are read and write. Since basic memory operations are concerned with one word, the address of this word

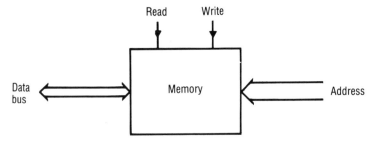

**Fig. 6.1** Basic memory structure.

must be presented to the memory with the read/write control signal(s). The operations read and write operate on one word of data and hence a data route one word wide must be provided to the memory. This gives the basic memory structure as shown in Fig. 6.1.

There is typically a delay of several hundred nanoseconds between the start and finish of an operation in memory. In Chapter 3 the operation of a decoder was shown and this can be used to decode the address of a register in a register bank. In a similar manner a decoder is used in the memory subsystem to convert from an *n*-bit address stored in the address register to a control line to a single memory location. This will be shown in more detail later in this chapter.

### 6.1.2 The operation of memory

Consider the state of memory as shown in Fig. 6.2. In this example it has been assumed that the word length is four bits and the memory size 256 words. If the memory size is 256 words then the address register needs to be eight bits

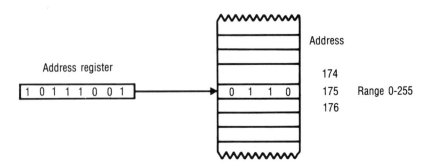

**Fig. 6.2** Memory addressing.

wide (since $2^8 = 256$). To read the contents of word 175 from the memory it is necessary to perform the following operations:

1. load the address register with 175;
2. set the read control signal.

At some time later, determined by the propagation time of the memory, the contents of word 175, 6 in the example, will be available at the data outputs of the memory.

To perform a write operation the following sequence is required:

1. load the address register with 175;
2. load the data buffer register with the required new contents of word 175;
3. set the write control signal.

At some time later, again depending on the characteristics of the memory, the contents of word 175 will reflect the new value.

### 6.1.3    Properties of memories

Having described the basic operation of memory, the properties of different types of memories are considered.

### (a)    Random access

The type of memory described above is known as random access (RAM) since it takes the same time, the access time, to access any memory location. In most computer systems there are several forms of memory and not all of them have this random-access property. For example, it is usual to store programs on some form of magnetic media such as tapes or disks, and access to these memories is not random. In the case of magnetic tape the access is sequential since each item is read in sequence from the tape, starting at the beginning. A magnetic disk, on the other hand, provides a quicker access mechanism, somewhere between random and sequential access, depending on the type of disk and organization of the information.

Random-access memory is often used as a synonym for read–write memory (RWM) as opposed to read-only memory (ROM). Strictly, both RWM and ROM are random-access memories since access to any memory location takes the same time.

### (b)    Cycle time

This is the minimum time required between two successive read or write operations to memory. It is a basic physical property of the memory, as is the access time, defined above.

## (c)  Volatility

A memory that loses its information when power is removed is said to be volatile. Semiconductor read–write memories are volatile because they rely on external power to maintain the information stored. Magnetic disks and tapes, however, are non-volatile and can keep their information almost indefinitely. It is because of the volatility of semiconductor memory (RAM) that most processors have power-fail circuitry. If power is lost, there is a small amount of time for the processor to store away vital information in non-volatile memory. One method of saving information in volatile memory is to provide battery back-up so that battery power take over if mains power fails.

## (d)  Static and dynamic memory

The memory described above is known as a static memory. Once a value has been stored in the memory, no action is required to maintain it other than to maintain the power supply. In contrast to this, there is a type of memory known as dynamic memory where the information is stored as charge on a capacitor. Since a capacitor will gradually discharge itself over a period of time this type of memory has to be continually recharged (refreshed) in order to avoid loss of information. The read operation in dynamic memory is destructive so the cell includes circuitry to rewrite the contents after a read operation. Thus a read operation may be used to refresh the memory. Dynamic memory systems normally include some means to refresh memory by periodic read operations. The refresh may be performed by software but, since memory has to be refreshed every 1 or 2 milliseconds, this imposes a high burden on the processor. A more satisfactory solution is to use some of the period when the processor is not accessing memory to perform the refresh, or to use an independent refresh controller.

Because of the need for this extra circuitry, the use of dynamic memory may seem undesirable, but a dynamic memory uses about one-quarter of the silicon area of the equivalent static memory and hence the extra density on an integrated circuit makes its use attractive. For the same area a dynamic memory will contain about four times as many memory cells as the corresponding static memory chip. Since system costs are directly related to the number of integrated circuits used in their production, the reduction in chip count using dynamic memories outweighs the complication of adding refresh circuitry in large memory system. Also, with the ever-increasing amount of logic which can be put on a chip, dynamic memories with internal refresh become feasible.

## (e)  Read-only memory

Some types of memory may be both read from and written to, read–write memory (RWM), whilst others may only be read, read-only memory (ROM).

This latter type appears to be less useful but has the additional property that it is non-volatile, that is that the contents of the memory are not lost when power is removed from the circuit. This means that by using ROMs to contain programs, equipment can be produced which will function immediately it is switched on without having to be loaded with programs from media such as floppy disks. For embedded systems, such as microcomputers in washing machines, cars or general laboratory instruments, this is essential. There are several types of ROMs available, the differences being in the method initially used to write the information into memory. In mask programmed ROMs the program is inserted during the manufacturing process and cannot be changed. This type of memory is used for standard programs which are produced in large quantities. Erasable programmable ROMs (EPROMS) can be programmed by the user using special programming equipment and may be erased for reuse by exposure to ultraviolet light.

### 6.1.4   An integrated circuit random-access memory

The basic binary storage cell which is the building block for static memory is shown in Fig. 6.3. The select signal is generated by the address decoder and applies to all the bits of the selected word. The read and write inputs determine the cell operation and the 1-bit input and output are the data interfaces to the rest of the computer system. A slightly different form of the basic cell, incorporating a tristate buffer, is shown in Fig. 4.22.

A clock signal is shown in the cell in Fig.6.3. This is not strictly necessary as one of the other control signals, such as read or write, could be used to gate the input and output to and from a non-clocked flip-flop. However, many memories operate with a clock signal to synchronize their operation with the rest of the computer.

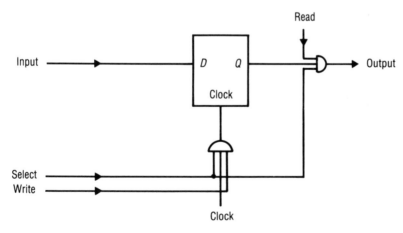

**Fig. 6.3**   Memory storage cell.

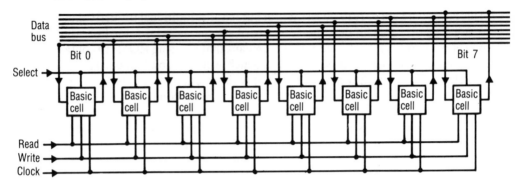

**Fig. 6.4**   Organization of a byte of memory.

The circuit in Fig. 6.3 contains storage for one bit. Memories are normally organized as a number of bytes or words. Since the basic memory operations work on these larger quantities, usually bytes, the organization of a byte of memory is shown in Fig. 6.4.

All the basic cells in the byte are accessed in parallel and operate on different bits. The select signal is produced from the address decoder and only one select signal will be active at any one time, limiting access to one byte.

The data bus is attached to all the bytes of memory, for example, bit 0 of all the bytes of memory will be attached to bit 0 of the data bus. The memory can be thought of as an array of basic cells $n$ bits wide, where $n$ is the word length, and $m$ bits long, where $m$ is the number of words in memory. Each bit in the row of this matrix is connected by the select line, and equivalent bits in different words are connected by the data lines for input and output. All the cells are connected to the same read, write and clock lines. This structure is shown in outline in Fig. 6.5.

### 6.1.5   The structure of a typical integrated circuit memory

In this section some typical memory chips are considered and their mode of action explained.

#### (a)   Static memory

The Hitatchi HM6116 RAM chip shown in Fig. 6.6 corresponds closely to the logical structure described before. Since there are 2048 ($2^{11}$) words of memory, eleven address lines ($A_0$–$A_{10}$) are required. Each word is 8 bits wide and hence eight lines ($I/O_1$–$I/O_8$) are required for data input/output. Instead of two separate controls for read and write they are multiplexed onto a single

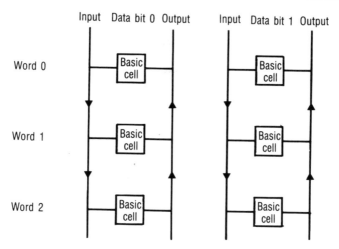

**Fig. 6.5** The memory matrix.

pin, write enable which is active low, since they are mutually exclusive. This signal is usually referred to as read/write ($R/\overline{W}$). The chip requires the standard power supply of 5 V. Since this chip will be one of many which has to be interfaced to the data bus of the computer, it must only be active when it is being addressed; the chip select signal is used for this purpose. Some external decoding circuitry is necessary to generate chip select from bits $A_{11} \ldots A_n$ of the address bus which is used to control the tristate buffers on to the data bus.

The example shown here is eight bits wide. At any point in time, technology limits the total number of bits in a memory chip. This leads to the availability

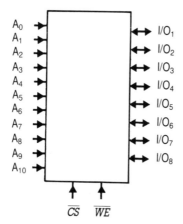

**Fig. 6.6** The Hitachi HM6116 $2048 \times 8$ static RAM.

of memory chips with differing widths and differing numbers of words, but with approximately the same number of bits. Newer and larger 8-bit wide memories, typically 2048 × 8 and 8192 × 8, provide a simple, convenient means of implementing a small memory for an 8-bit computer. The advantage of static memory over its dynamic counterpart is its ease of interfacing to the rest of the system.

### (b)  Dynamic memory

In order to address 16384 locations, 14 address bits are required. The chip shown in Fig. 6.7 only has seven address lines, owing to technological limitations on the number of pins on the integrated circuit. The 14 bits required are multiplexed on these seven pins. The memory is organized as two 128 × 128 cell arrays and these are accessed by row and column addresses, each of seven bits. The control signals $\overline{RAS}$, row address strobe, and $\overline{CAS}$, column address strobe, replacing the single address select of the static RAM chip, are used to latch the appropriate address into an internal register. These control signals indicate which seven address bits are currently being accessed via the address lines. The internal register is needed in this case to assemble the 14-bit address from the two 7-bit values presented. The read and write signals are multiplexed, as in the static RAM, onto a single pin, $\overline{WE}$. In this chip there are two separate data buffers, one for input and one for output; hence the need for separate pins for data input and output.

Since dynamic memory gradually loses its information with time, refreshing of this information is periodically necessary, in this chip every 2 ms. It may be performed by cycling through all the rows of memory with RAS low and CAS high. This refreshes the memory a row (128 bits) at a time. Alternatively, normal read operations or hidden refresh cycles can be used. This latter

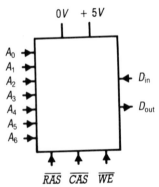

**Fig. 6.7**   The Intel 2118  16384 × 1 dynamic RAM.

technique allows data to be read from the memory as well as performing a refresh operation.

### (c)   Read-only memory

A read-only memory circuit looks very similar to the equivalent static RAM circuit; the differences being the output only data lines and the presence of output enable and a $V_{pp}$ signal. The $V_{pp}$ signal is needed to program the memory. In program mode the $V_{pp}$ pin has to be kept at +25 V, the address and data lines set to the required values and a 50 ms pulse applied to the $\overline{CE}/PGM$ (program) pin. This operation has to be carried out for every memory address which has to be written to. The complete memory may be erased by exposure to ultraviolet radiation of the correct wavelength. The output enable signal is provided for the same purpose as chip select on a static RAM, that is, to turn the tristate drivers on the data lines on and off. Chip select is provided because the ROM can operate in standby mode when not in use, consuming less power than normal, and the chip select signal is used to determine whether the chip is in use or in standby mode. The appropriate combination of chip select and output enable should be used to obtain maximum benefit from the device.

## 6.2   Architectural considerations and memory

In the system described in the last chapter there was a single composite bus, carrying address, data and control between processor and memory. This is the

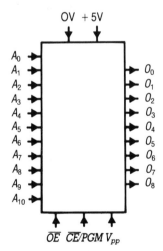

OV  + 5V

$A_0$   $O_0$
$A_1$   $O_1$
$A_2$   $O_2$
$A_3$   $O_3$
$A_4$   $O_4$
$A_5$   $O_5$
$A_6$   $O_6$
$A_7$   $O_7$
$A_8$   $O_8$
$A_9$
$A_{10}$

$\overline{OE}$  $\overline{CE}/PGM$ $V_{pp}$

**Fig. 6.8**   The Intel 2716  2048 × 8 UV erasable PROM.

most common architecture in small computer systems. In this section, options for increasing performance and producing cost-effective memory subsystems are investigated.

### 6.2.1 The memory hierarchy

One of the objectives of the computer architect is to produce a computer that is fast, bearing in mind the technology used. Since much of a processor's time is spent reading and writing to memory, one critical area of attention for the architect is the processor–memory interface. It would appear, at first sight, that the ideal solution would be to have the maximum amount of fast, directly accessible memory placed as close to the processor as possible. This is not feasible, both on space and economic grounds, but, perhaps surprisingly, memory systems can be built with almost the same performance. This is possible because programs typically exhibit a property called locality. This phenomenon concerns the way in which references to instructions and data are grouped in a program. Analysis of programs has shown that references to the address space of a program, instructions and data, tend to become confined to a few localized areas over a period of time. The crucial fact is that membership of these small, localized areas only changes slowly with time, owing to the way in which humans structure their programs. This means that if the members of these areas are kept in fast memory, the program will execute quickly even if the rest of the instructions and data are stored in slower memory. Using this scheme there has to be some method of transferring instructions and data between memories when this becomes necessary.

There are several levels in the memory hierarchy. The first level, the fastest, is a set of registers, typically 8 or 16, which resides within the CPU. This level of the hierarchy is found in virtually all computer systems. The next level is cache memory, typically 2K words, which is not as fast as the internal

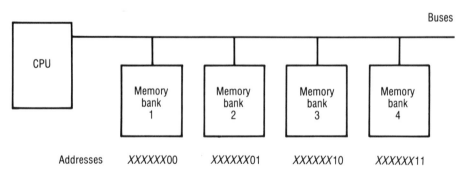

**Fig. 6.9** Interleaved memory.

registers but faster than main memory, the third level. The fourth level is backing storage such as disks and tapes, and this has the property of not being directly accessible. In order for the processor to process information from backing store, the information must first be read into directly accessible memory, modified and then written back. In order to relieve the programmer of this chore, some systems implement a virtual memory, where the programmer is given access to a large address space, only part of which resides in directly accessible memory at any one time. Transfer to and from the directly accessible memory is transparent to the programmer who can assume that any information he requires is directly accessible. From the programmer's point of view, virtual memory systems are very convenient to use, hence the current trend for an increase in their use. Not all computer systems have all the levels of the memory hierarchy; those levels present will be determined by the cost and the use of the computer.

In the following sections some of the techniques used to speed access to memory, while being transparent to the programmer, are discussed.

## 6.2.2   Interleaving

In a normal memory subsystem there is a time lapse, called the access time, between the time when the address is presented to memory and the time when the operation, read or write, is complete. One way of using this 'dead time' on the bus is to split the memory into a number of memory banks, each containing a subset of the memory space. Assuming that each of these memories has its own address and data buffers, then operations to access memory may be overlapped.

There are, however, a number of problems with this technique. For example, for maximum efficiency, memory references have to be distributed so that consecutive accesses are to different memory banks. Since instruction flow through a program is normally sequential, memory banks are usually divided using the lower address bits as the bank number. This means that sequential access will cycle through all the memory banks in order. Interleaving also assumes a more complicated processor which can control several concurrent memory activities.

## 6.2.3   Cache memory

Normally, fast devices are more expensive than slow ones and this is true for memory; the faster the memory, the more expensive. Thus the use of large amounts of fast memory is precluded on economic grounds for even the most expensive computer system. Fortunately, using the property of program locality, only a small proportion of the program address space need be kept in fast memory and yet the program will run as quickly as if it were all in fast memory. This is the basis of the use of cache memory; small, fast memory placed between the CPU and main memory.

The basic operation of the cache is as follows. An access to memory is made to the cache. If the required address (or data) resides there then it is used, but if it is absent then a block of memory is transferred from main memory to the cache, typically consisting of 1–16 words containing the addressed word. This block of words will displace some other information in the cache if it is already full.

The performance of the cache is measured by the hit ratio which is the ratio of the number of successful accesses to the cache compared with the total number of accesses to memory. The hit ratio measures the locality of reference of the program being executed and so should be measured experimentally. The hit ratio obviously depends upon the size of the cache as well as the degree of locality in the program. Typical cache memories are of the order of 2K words and studies of their use have shown a number of programs to exhibit hit ratios between 0.9 and 1.0, that is, almost all references to the cache were successful.

There are two ways in which memory can respond to a write request to memory. The first method is the write through method where the main memory is updated on every write, and also the cache if the information is stored there. This method ensures that main memory always contains up-to-date information. The second method, called write back, only updates the cache copy of the information on a write. A flag, associated with each word of cache, is set so that when the information is removed from the cache it is written back to main memory. The fact that main memory is not always up-to-date does not matter, since access will always be to the cache until the information is updated in main memory.

Each word of cache has a bit associated with it called the valid bit. On initialization, all the valid bits are set to zero, indicating that the associated words do not contain valid data. The valid bit of a word is set to 1 the first time valid data are copied into the word.

## 6.2.4 Cache organization

Important features of a cache include the internal organization and that part involved with the transfer of information to and from main memory (Fig. 6.10).

One form of cache organization uses an associative memory which stores both the memory address and the contents (Fig. 6.11). Access to information in the cache requires a search for the required address among all the stored addresses. In an associative memory, the comparisons between the required address and the table of stored addresses can be performed in parallel, thus making them fast. If a match is found, the data associated with the required

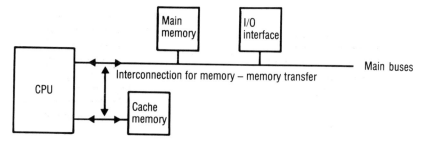

**Fig. 6.10**   Typical cache memory structure.

address may be read or written to. If no match is found then access to main memory is initiated. If there is no free space in the cache then a block of address/data pairs from main memory has to overwrite pairs already in the cache. Typically this will be done in a round robin fashion, i.e. first-in-first-out (FIFO).

Another form of cache organization is direct mapping (Fig. 6.12) which may be used where associative memory is considered too costly. In this case, normal random-access memory (RAM) may be used for the cache. Concurrently with main memory access, the cache is addressed using the $n$ least significant bits of the memory address. In the cache are stored the remaining memory address bits, called the tag bits, and the data. Since the cache is addressed using only some of the memory address bits, several main memory addresses map onto the same cache address. The tag bits in cache will only match one of the possible mapped addresses – the one presently stored in the cache. This can lead to inefficiencies, since only one of the mapped main memory addresses can reside in the cache at any one time. To overcome this,

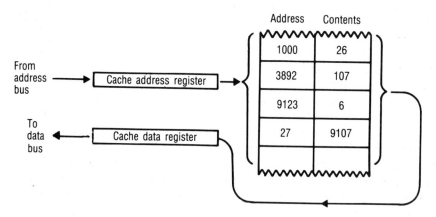

**Fig. 6.11**   Associative cache memory.

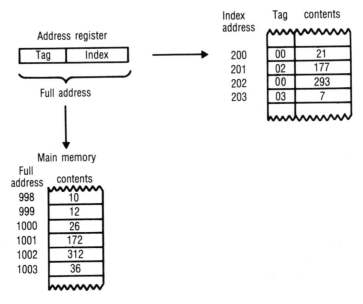

**Fig. 6.12** Direct mapping cache.

a method called set associative mapping has been developed which allows each word of cache to store multiple values, thus allowing several main memory locations mapping onto the same cache address to be stored concurrently.

## 6.2.5 Virtual memory systems

The instruction set of a computer allows the user to access a range of addresses, the address space. In many computers the address space is identical to the main memory address space. In a virtual memory system, however, the address space is very much larger than the main memory address space and the virtual memory subsystem, software and hardware, are responsible for mapping virtual memory references to main memory addresses. Thus main memory, at any one time, only contains a subset of the total memory contents as shown in Fig. 6.13. In order to make the transfers between main memory and backing store relatively simple, transfers are normally restricted to fixed size blocks. These blocks, typically 1K words, are known as blocks of main memory or pages of virtual address space. This gives rise to the term 'paging' because a page is the unit of transfer between main memory and backing store. For example, if the size of backing store used for paging was 512K words, it could hold 512 pages of 1024 words, and a main memory of 32K words could hold 32 pages and would be divided into 32 blocks. In this example, the main memory could hold one-sixteenth of the information on

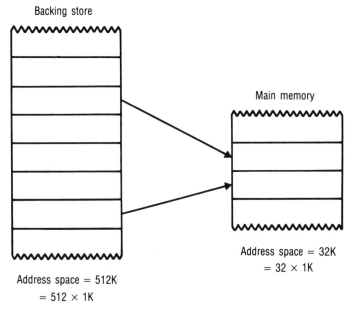

Fig. 6.13    Address space and memory space.

backing store. The reason for pages being of size $2^N$ is that any address in the page can be represented by $N$ bits. Thus a virtual memory address can be subdivided into two fields; the top $M$ bits representing the page number and the bottom $N$ bits the address within the page. To produce the real memory address from the virtual address, the translation mechanism has to replace the page number by the appropriate memory block address. This is the task of the virtual memory architecture. Since the addressing mechanism is used frequently, address translation from virtual to real has to be performed by hardware. The moving of pages between main memory and backing store is not so critical because it happens less frequently and almost all virtual memory computers are multiprogrammed so that the time needed to move a page can usefully be used by another program. The moving of pages is controlled by software. A block diagram of the memory mapping hardware required is shown in Fig. 6.14 and an example showing the translation for a small address space is given in Fig. 6.15. The blank entries in the page table would cause a page fault. Because this address translation scheme is applied to every memory access it must be fast. The time-consuming operation is the page table look-up and in many computers associative memory is used to perform a parallel search of all the entries.

Because of the locality of programs, as mentioned previously, most accesses to the virtual address space will result in accesses to main memory, but a small

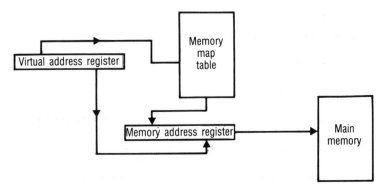

**Fig. 6.14**    Memory mapping hardware.

proportion will result in a page fault if the page requested is not in main memory. If this is the case, software is activated to initiate the transfer of the referenced page from backing store to main memory. The software has to decide which page to remove from main memory, assuming that it is full, and when to replace a page. The scheme outlined above is known as demand paging – a scheme in which a page is placed in main memory when demanded (referenced). There are several different types of replacement policy which are used; the most common being first-in-first-out (FIFO) and least recently used (LRU). The FIFO method is implemented by the system keeping a

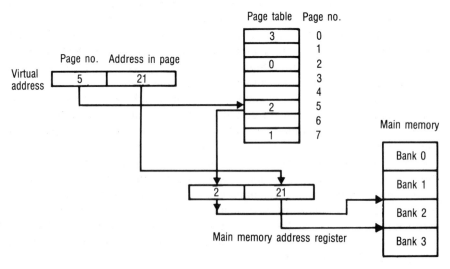

**Fig. 6.15**    Example of address translation scheme.

queue of the page numbers in the order in which they are placed in memory. If a page has to be replaced the one whose identification number is at the head of the queue is chosen. In the LRU method a counter is kept with each page in main memory and incremented at fixed time intervals. When a page is referenced, the counter is reset to zero. When a page has to be replaced, the page with the highest associated counter is selected to be overwritten.

There are other techniques similar to paging used in virtual memory systems. The most important one is segmentation where segments are equivalent to pages but are of variable length. This causes problems for the management system since both the mapping and page management policies become more complex. For this reason, segmentation is often used in conjunction with paging to get the best of both techniques; paging for hardware simplicity and segmentation for ease of use by the programmer.

The importance of segmentation is that access control can be applied to segments; one may be read-only for program code, another read-only for data and another read–write for data. An attempt to access a segment for the wrong usage leads to an immediate hardware-generated interrupt.

## 6.3  Summary

Memory is an integral part of a computer system; it is used to store programs and data. There is a hierarchy of memory types, ranging from the on-chip registers of a processor, through high-speed semiconductor memory (both ROM and RAM), to low-speed magnetic backing store, such as magnetic tape and floppy disks. The cost of memory depends on its speed – fast memory is more expensive than slow memory – so that while the amount of semi-conductor memory that a computer system has is usually limited, the amount of backing-store available is unlimited, or at least very large (typically hundreds of megabytes compared to a megabyte or less of semiconductor memory). This fact has led to the development of memory management schemes which automatically transfer program fragments and data from backing store to main memory when they are required by an executing program, and out again when they are no longer needed if they have been changed. In addition, many processors contain a cache memory, which may be either a part of the processor chip itself, or a separate set of chips. This cache memory is used to store the instructions that are currently being executed. Cache memory is faster than the main semiconductor memory, and is severely limited in size (usually a few tens of words). The efficiency of a cache memory depends on a factor called the 'hit rate', which is the effective probability that the next instruction to be executed is in the cache memory. If it is not, then the cache has to be re-loaded from the main semiconductor memory.

## Exercises

6.1  (a) How many address lines are required to access 64K words of memory?
     (b) How many words of memory can be accessed using 20 address lines?

6.2  In the Intel 8085 microprocessor the lower half of the address bus ($A_0$–$A_7$) is multiplexed onto the data bus; i.e. when an address is being output by the processor the data bus contains the least significant byte of the address. Does this impose a time penalty? If so estimate the penalty for a processor operating with a 10 MHz clock frequency.

6.3  In a Motorola 68020 microprocessor (an enhanced version of the 68000) an instruction fetch takes a minimum of 3 clock cycles. However, with most semiconductor memories at least 2 extra cycles are required for the memory to respond. These extra cycles are called 'wait states'. No such wait states are necessary for instruction fetches from the cache memory. Given that the hit rate to the cache memory for a particular program is 0.9, calculate the percentage by which the program is speeded-up by the use of a cache memory over a similar processor with no cache memory.

# 7

# Input–output

In this chapter the interfacing between the 'real world' and the computer will be discussed.

## 7.1 Input–output interfaces

The standard method of transferring data inside a computer is along parallel $n$-bit buses, where $n$ is the word size. Input–output devices interface to this parallel bus on one side and to the 'real world' on the other. Inside the computer, information is coded in a particular manner, for example, the 7-bit ASCII code for characters, and its physical realization has particular properties, for example, logic 0 and 1 are represented by 0 and 5 V approximately. The large number of interface circuits which exist within a computer are there to make signals from the 'real world' compatible with the internal representation. 'Real world' signals can take a variety of different forms and to convert them to the internal representation required, some of the following functions may be needed:

1. serial to parallel conversion and vice versa;
2. analogue to digital conversion and vice versa;
3. encoding and decoding;
4. changing the current drive capability;
5. changing voltage levels.

There are integrated circuits available to perform many of these tasks, for example, a USART which performs serial–parallel conversion and vice versa, a function required to interface a standard computer terminal, a visual display unit (VDU), to a computer.

This book is concerned with basic architectural principles rather than detailed interfacing, so only simple interfaces are considered here. The interested reader is referred to the books by Stone and Artwick in the bibliography for more information on interfacing techniques.

### 7.1.1   The logical structure of an input–output interface

In order for the processor to communicate with the input–output device, the interface must provide registers both to buffer the data and to control and monitor the input–output device. Buffers are required since the 'real world' operates asynchronously with the processor clock. The logical structure of the input–output interface is shown in Fig. 7.1.

There may be several registers of each of the three types shown, depending on the complexity of the external device. For the interfaces considered in the following sections a single control and status register suffices, but for more complicated interfaces, for example to a disk, several control and status registers would be present.

There are two different methods of implementing addressing of the interface. The first method, called memory mapping, places the registers of the interface in the normal address space of the processor. This permits access by any memory reference instruction at the expense of address space for real memory. The alternative scheme, called I/O mapping, involves creating a separate address space specifically for input–output registers and a special instruction set to address this space. This involves creating instructions such as **IN** and **OUT** which transfer information between a known place in memory, usually a register, and the input–output device. This scheme implies less flexibility but a larger total address space, which is useful when the addressing range is limited, as it is in most 4- and 8-bit microcomputers. The Intel 8085 is an example of a processor which has separate input–output mapping, while

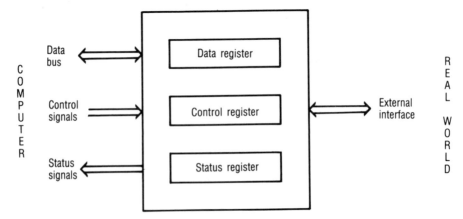

**Fig. 7.1**   Logical I/O port structure.

the Motorola 68000 is an example of a processor with memory-mapped input–output.

## 7.1.2  Parallel port

Even if a device with a bus-compatible parallel interface has to be linked to a computer, some interfacing circuitry is required, if only to provide buffering and control of the gating of input signals or output signals to and from the bus at the correct time, that is, to synchronize the 'real world' to the computer. The structure of a parallel interface is shown in Fig. 7.2.

In order for the processor to read and write from the port it must be selected, and this selection is carried out by some external decoding logic connected to the 'select' input. Because the computer has no control over the actions of the external world, it is important that the direction of transfer of information between the port and the external world is determined at all times. In order to do this, each port has a data direction register associated with it which is programmable for input or output mode. Furthermore, since the outside world needs to be synchronized to the computer for the transfer of data, it is usual to associate some control signals, used for handshaking, with each port and also some data buffering.

### (a)  The Intel 8255 programmable peripheral interface (PPI) (Fig. 7.3)

The three ports of eight bits provided by this parallel interface can be configured as two groups of 12 bits and can operate in one of three modes. In the simplest mode, mode 0, each of the two groups may be programmed, in sets of four bits, to be either input or output. Mode 1 allows each group to have eight data bits and four control and status bits for handshaking. Mode 2 is

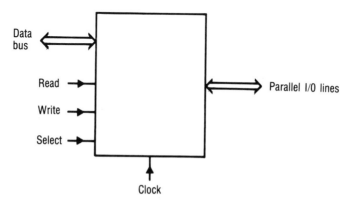

**Fig. 7.2**  Structure of a parallel port.

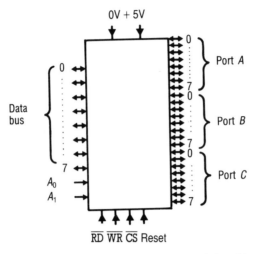

**Fig. 7.3** Intel 8255 programmable peripheral interface.

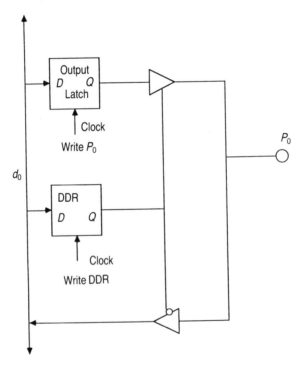

**Fig. 7.4** Schematic diagram showing 1 bit of the Intel 8255 programmable peripheral interface.

used to configure an 8-bit bidirectional bus with five control lines. The modes are set up under program control, typically at the beginning of the program.

The address lines $A_0$ and $A_1$, so called because they are normally controlled from the least significant bits of the address bus, are used in conjunction with $\overline{RD}$ and $\overline{WR}$ to select one of the 8-bit data registers associated with each port or the internal control register. The reset control signal clears the control register and sets all the ports to input mode.

The eight bits of the control word specify the mode of each group of 12 bits and whether the ports are in input or output mode. The details of the use of mode 1 and mode 2 are complex and are not dealt with here. To use all the ports in input mode, no programming is required on power up or reset, otherwise a control word has to be sent to the control register before any data transfer commences.

Figure 7.4 shows the schematic diagram of the logic for one bit of the PPI, $P_0$. Both the data direction register and the output register are D-type latches connected to $d_0$ of the internal data bus of the PPI (programmable peripheral interface). If the port has been set-up as an output, by writing a logic-1 into the data direction register, then the tristate buffer between the output latch and the $P_0$ pin is enabled, so that the output of the latch is connected to pin $P_0$. For the port to act as an input a logic-0 is written into the data direction register, so that the $P_0$ pin is isolated from the output latch. The input tristate buffer is then activated, enabling the logic level on $P_0$ to be read.

## (b)   A simple example of the use of a programmable peripheral interface

One simple use of a programmable peripheral interface (PPI) is to connect a keyboard to the computer system as shown in Fig. 7.5. Each key is connected to one input line and one output line as shown. When no key is depressed the pattern 1111 in binary will be read at the input port. If zeros are output from the output port then any key depression will result in one of the input lines going to zero. (The diodes are needed to stop multiple key depressions shorting the input port.) By changing the output pattern so that only one zero is output at any one time, both the row and column of the depressed key may be determined. This keyboard scanning algorithm has to be run in software on the host computer, and becomes quite complex when multiple key depressions and contact bounce have to be taken into account. Such a scheme might be used for a small special-purpose keypad. Because of this complexity and because control of a full keyboard is frequently required, special keyboard controller integrated circuits have been developed, such as the Intel 8279 keyboard/display controller, which provide a convenient way of connecting a keyboard and display to a microcomputer-based system.

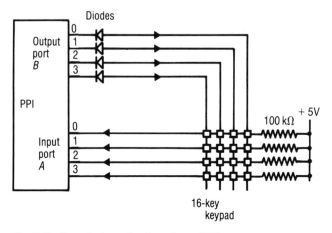

**Fig. 7.5**   Interfacing a keyboard to a PPI.

## 7.1.3   Serial port

With the simplicity of the parallel port it is not obvious why a large number of slow to medium speed peripherals do not use this method. Two of the reasons are cost and standardization.

1. Cost. A parallel interface requires $n$ wires, where $n$ is the word length, between interface and device, whereas a serial device, for the same purpose, uses only three, one for the signal in each direction and one for ground (reference). For long distances, the cost of the extra cable for a parallel interface is considerable.
2. Standardization. Because the original teletypes used over the telephone network worked serially, the telecommunications authority (CCITT) published a standard to allow networking across the world. The presence of a standard and the potentially large market in telecommunications motivated the industry to invest heavily in this method of communication.

The structure of a serial interface is shown Fig. 7.6. Internally the interface consists of a number of registers, one for transmitted data and one for received data, and one or more for control and status information.

An interesting difference between this logical structure and the parallel port is the need for two different clock signals. The clock signal shown is used for the same purpose as in the parallel port, namely to synchronize the interface to the processor. The clock signal, labelled $T_x/R_x$ clock (in reality two signals, one for data in and one for data out), is used to determine the speed of the serial transmission. Both transmitter and receiver have to agree on the transmission speed, usually between 300 and 9600 bits s$^{-1}$. Because the transmitter and receiver cannot be driven by the same clock, owing to the distances

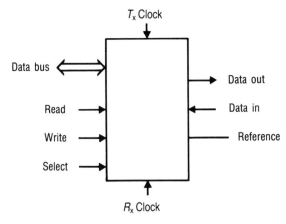

**Fig. 7.6**   Serial interface structure.

between the sending and receiving devices, the problem of keeping the transmitter and receiver in synchronization, *vis-à-vis* the characters that are transmitted, arises. There are two different solutions to this problem:

1. asynchronous, where each character contains its own synchronizing information, namely a start bit and one or more stop bits;
2. synchronous, where characters are always transmitted on the line even when there is no information to send. This keeps both ends permanently in synchronism.

Normally low-speed transmission uses the asynchronous method and higher speeds use the synchronous method.

### (a)   The standard

The standard for serial transmission is CCITT V24, also known by the American equivalent RS232C. This standard defines all the details of a serial connection including voltage levels, pin connections and plug types, as follows:

| | |
|---|---|
| Logic levels | logic 1 between −3 V and −25 V |
| | logic 0 between +3 V and +25 V |
| | (typically −12 and +12 V are used) |
| Plug type | 25-way D-type connector |
| Bit order | least significant bit first |
| Idle state | logic 1 |
| Pin connections | defined for data and control lines |

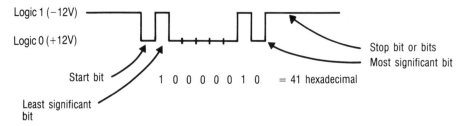

**Fig. 7.7** Transmission of the letter A.

Hence a typical character, such as the letter A (41 hexadecimal in the ASCII code), would be sent as shown in Fig. 7.7.

The penalty which has to be paid for serial transmission, apart from the slowness of transmission, is the translation from parallel to serial form and vice versa in the interface. Fortunately, this is relatively simple using a shift register.

Using serial interfaces is not always as simple as presented here, since the V24 standard defines a large number of control signals associated with a serial connection. The reason for this is that the CCITT standard was defined for use over telephone lines where a pair of modems (modulator–demodulators) is required between the transmitter and receiver. Many of the control signals are provided for signalling between the modem and transmitter or receiver. Where direct connection between transmitter and receiver is possible these additional control signals are not required, but there is no standard for this so the V24 standard is still used. In this case only the three signal lines defined above are required and the use of most of the control signals are undefined. This leads to confusion as some systems use the extra control signals whilst others do not. The reader is referred to the interfacing books in the bibliography for more details.

### (b)   The Intel 8251 USART

It is possible to get all the logic required for serial–parallel conversion on a single integrated circuit, normally called a UART or USART, universal synchronous asynchronous receiver transmitter, which microcomputer manufacturers produce. The Intel version is the 8251A USART shown in Fig. 7.8.

The transmitter and receiver have separate clocks, $T_xC$ and $R_xC$, and data lines, $T_x$ and $R_x$, to allow full duplex operation, at different speeds if required. The $T_xRDY$ and $R_xRDY$ signals are status lines indicating that the transmitter is ready to accept the next character to be output from the processor, and that the receiver has a character for the processor, respectively. In addition the

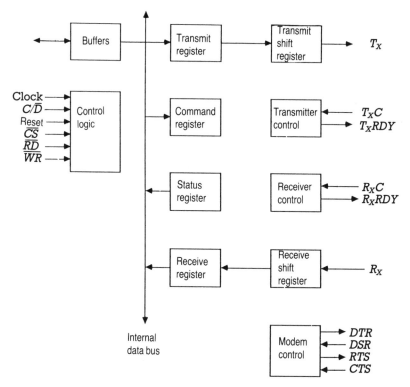

**Fig. 7.8**   Schematic diagram of Intel 8251 A USART.

status register has two bits which correspond to these conditions. The command register, which must be set-up before the USART is used, informs the USART the number of bits that are to be transmitted/received for each character, the number of stop-bits required, and whether a parity bit is to be added to a transmitted character, and checked for in an incoming character. The four registers (transmit, receive, command and status) are selected by the use of the three control signals, C/$\overline{\text{D}}$ (control/**NOT** data), $\overline{\text{RD}}$ and $\overline{\text{WR}}$ together with the chip select signal $\overline{\text{CS}}$.

The clock signals for the transmitter and receiver are normally generated by the use of a timer chip which is programmed to give a clock signal of the required frequency.

The extra control and status signals indicated in the diagram are needed when the device is used over a telephone line with a modem. The control signals are for controlling and sensing the state of the modem. For direct connection to another serial interface these control signals are not required but have to be tied to the correct voltage levels.

## 7.2 Controlling input–output devices

Input–output devices transfer data between the 'real world' and the processor. However because they are interacting with the real world they must operate a speed at which the real world can present and accept information to and from the computer. This speed is almost always different, and usually slower, than the speed at which the processor can transfer data to an I/O device, so it is necessary to synchronize the computer to the 'real world'. There are three main ways in which this can be achieved, namely polling, interrupts and direct memory access; these will now be discussed in turn.

### 7.2.1 Polling

Consider the transmission of a character string using the USART discussed in Section 7.1.3. If the transmitter baud rate is set at 9600 bits per second, then

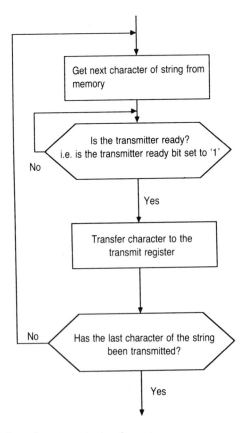

**Fig. 7.9**   Program flow-chart to output a character.

960 characters can be transmitted per second, assuming that there are 10 bits per character (1 start bit, 8 data bits and 1 stop bit). Thus it takes 1/960 s, or approximately 1 ms, to transmit each character. This is slow compared with the time that the processor will take to fetch the next character of the string from memory and transfer it to the USART (typically 10 $\mu$s). Thus, it is necessary to synchronize the transfer of characters to the USART to the speed at which the USART communicates with the real world. One way to do this is for the processor to continually check, or **poll**, the transmitter ready bit in the USART's status register. When this bit is set to 1 the transmitter register is empty, and so the next character can be transferred by the processor to the transmitter register. This automatically clears the transmitter ready bit in the status register, so that the next time it is polled it will indicate that the transmit register is not yet ready to be loaded with the next character. Fig. 7.9 shows the flow-chart of the program fragment for outputting a character. This technique is known as **polling** since the transmitter ready bit is continually sampled, or polled, until it is set to indicate that the transmitter register is empty. The processor spends the majority of its time polling since, as was said above, it will take only about 10 $\mu$s to execute the transfer of a character to the USART, while output to the USART's transmit register can occur only about every 1 ms.

The receiver operation is very similar. When a character is received by the USART into its receiving register the receiver ready bit in the status register is set. Thus to read a character the processor must continually poll this receiver ready bit until it is set, and then transfer the received character from the receive register to memory. Reading from the receive register auto- matically clears the receiver ready bit in the status register.

## 7.2.2 Interrupts

Although the polling scheme for I/O, discussed in the previous section, is simple to understand and to implement it is inefficient with slow I/O devices, as the processor can spend a lot of time waiting for an I/O device to become ready. Consider the following fragment of program code:

    calculate   $x$
    print       $x$
    calculate   $y$
    print       $y$.

If the printer interface is operated by a polling technique, then the processor will have to wait after the calculation of $x$, while $x$ is being printed, before the calculation of $y$ can begin. For example, if the speed at which the characters can be printed is $10 \text{ s}^{-1}$, say, then the processor will have to wait for 1/10 s, or 100 ms, while each character is being printed. If the character string corresponding to $x$ is just 5 characters say (e.g. 1.234) then the processor will have to wait for 500 ms while the string is being printed. This time greatly exceeds the execution time of a processor instruction, which is typically a few μs, and is time wasted which might have been usefully used performing the next calculation. What is required then is a system which allows the calculation of $y$ to be started immediately that of $x$ is completed, and for $x$ to be printed when the printer is ready.

One way in which this can be done is as follows. If the calculation of $y$ contains a number of intermediate steps then the printer interface can be polled at the end of each intermediate step to see if it is ready, and as soon as it is $x$ can be output. This solution is clearly cumbersome, and is impractical to use generally. Moreover it also wastes time, as the processor has to keep having to poll the interface. A more practical solution is for the program that is calculating $x$ and $y$ to store their results in a buffer, and then for the printer interface to take a character from the buffer when it is ready to print the next character. This is achieved by stopping the main program when the printer interface is ready, and running a second program which takes a character from the buffer, transfers it to the printer interface, and then finally returns to the main program. A scheme which works in this way is known as an **interrupt scheme**.

When a peripheral device (for example, the printer interface discussed above) requires servicing it outputs a special signal known as an interrupt signal. This signal goes from the peripheral to a pin on the processor, often labelled **INT**, as on the 8085 processor. When such an interrupt signal occurs the processor has three basic actions to carry out:

1.  It must recognize that an interrupt has occurred, and if there is more than one interrupt possible it must determine which of the peripheral devices generated the interrupt.
2.  Stop the program that is currently being executed, and start running the program that is associated with the interrupt. This program is usually known as an **interrupt handler**, or an **interrupt service routine**. Each peripheral device that is able to generate an interrupt has its own interrupt handler associated with it.
3.  When the interrupt handler has finished, the execution of the main program must be re-started at the point at which it was interrupted.

In section 5.1 it was shown that a processor continually repeats the actions of fetching, decoding and then executing an instruction from memory, the fetch-execute cycle. To cope with an interrupt this cycle is modified to:

1.  Fetch and decode the next instruction from memory
2.  Execute the instruction

3. If an interrupt request has occurred start executing the interrupt handler, else go to step 1.

The fetch and execute phases are executed as before, but at the end of the execute phase the processor checks to see if an interrupt request has occurred, that is, if **INT** = 0. If it is then the processor must store some information about the main program, so that it knows, for example, where to go back to when the interrupt handler has finished. The minimum information that must be saved is the current value of the program counter (PC), which points to the next instruction of the main program to be executed, and the status bits, or flags, stored in the status register (SR). These values are stored in memory, and the PC is then loaded with the address of the first instruction of the interrupt handler. In the simplest systems the interrupt handler starts at a fixed address in memory. The first instruction of the interrupt handler is fetched and executed, the PC incremented to point to the next instruction, which is then fetched and executed, and so on. A special instruction, called **return from interrupt** (RTI), must be placed at the end of the interrupt handler. This instruction causes the execution of the interrupted program to be restarted. It is accomplished by re-loading the saved PC and the status register. The values of these registers are usually saved in a special area of memory, called a **stack**, which is discussed in detail in Chapter 11.

### (a)  Saving and restoring registers

When a program is executing some, or all, of the processor's registers will be used to store temporary values, pointers to tables in memory, etc. Now consider what happens when an interrupt occurs. The interrupt service routine starts executing and it will almost certainly also want to use the processor's registers. In doing so it will overwrite values stored there by the main program. However when the interrupt service routine finishes and control returns to the main program, the processor assumes that the appropriate values in the registers are still there; it is unaware that the registers may have been corrupted by the interrupt service routine. To prevent such corruption the interrupt service routine must save the contents of those registers that it is going to use at its start, and then restore their contents at its completion, just before the RTI instruction is executed. The contents of the registers are most easily saved on the stack, and most processors have special instructions for saving and restoring registers to and from the stack. The basic structure of an interrupt service routine is then:

Save registers on the stack

. . .

Body of the interrupt service routine which must contain instructions to clear the interrupt

. . .

Restore registers from the stack
RTI

### 7.2.3 Multiple interrupts

In many situations there are likely to be several I/O devices which require servicing by the processor and which are capable of producing an interrupt. For example, in the USART discussed earlier both the transmitter and the receiver sections will have separate interrupts. The transmitter produces an interrupt when it is ready to accept the next character for transmission, while the receiver will generate an interrupt when it has received a character. Each of the possible interrupts will have an interrupt handler associated with it. The interrupt situation is now more complicated. When an interrupt occurs the processor must identify which of the possible interrupting devices has generated the interrupt, and then execute the appropriate interrupt handler. When an I/O device generates an interrupt it also sets a bit (or flag) in its own status register to indicate that it is the device that has produced the interrupt, and so requires to be serviced. The processor then has to respond to the interrupt by polling the I/O devices to see which one produced the interrupt. As an alternative to polling a scheme which is frequently used is one in which the interrupting I/O device automatically places the address of its interrupt handler onto the data bus. This scheme gives a faster response to an interrupt, although the I/O device is more complicated. Indeed many special-purpose I/O devices, such as floppy disk controllers, for example, are more complex than the processor, but their availability greatly simplifies the task of designing a computer system.

In a system with interrupts there will be occasions when the processor does not want to respond immediately to a given interrupt, such as when it is dealing with another higher-priority time-critical interrupt. All processors contain a facility for enabling and disabling interrupts under program control. Modern processors, such as the 68000 series, contain a number of different levels of interrupt priority, which may be selectively enabled and disabled.

### 7.2.4 Direct memory access

Transfers of data between a peripheral and memory frequently involve blocks of characters and take place on a character-by-character basis. Each character transfer involves the intervention of the processor to control and monitor the transfer. This is a waste of processor time, even using interrupts. An improvement on this technique is to use direct memory access (DMA). In this scheme, the peripheral interface includes a control which is able to act as a bus master and to transfer information between memory and the peripheral without the intervention of the central processor. The CPU initiates the transfer by writing the address in memory from or to where the transfer is to take place into a register in the controller, together with the direction and number of transfers. The controller then controls the transfer of information, incrementing the memory address and decrementing the count after each individual transfer.

In a system with only one bus or where the path between peripheral and memory is shared with the central processor, there is potential conflict on the bus. In order to avoid this, the processor and controller have to synchronize their use of the bus. On simple systems the processor idles whilst the DMA transfers take place, but on more complex systems the DMA device 'cycle steals', that is, it uses the bus in preference to the processor when there is contention. This requires more complex arbitration logic but is more efficient.

On the Intel 8085 system a DMA controller will gain access to the bus by asserting the CPU HOLD signal and awaiting HLDA, the signal that the processor has released the bus. On completion of the DMA operation the controller de-asserts the HOLD signal. The CPU idles until DMA finishes and HOLD is de-asserted.

There are a number of DMA controllers available for the 68000 processor, including the Motorola standard MC68450 four-channel controller. Although these devices are complex, often with many features, they all functionally similar. DMA data transfers between a peripheral device and memory, or vice versa, are initiated by the DMA controller in response to an external request (usually from a peripheral device). The DMA signals the processor that it requires use of the 68000's address, data and control buses by asserting the bus request signal $\overline{BR}$ (see Fig. 5.15). The DMA controller then waits for the bus grant signal, $\overline{BG}$, from the processor to be activated, indicating that the processor has released the use of the buses, and acknowledges by asserting the bus grant acknowledge signal, $\overline{BGACK}$. Data transfer between a peripheral device and memory now proceeds under the control of the DMA controller. This data transfer may be programmed to take place either in 'burst mode', where several data words may be transferred, or in 'cycle stealing mode', where only a single data word is transferred at a time. In the cycle stealing mode DMA data transfers are shared, or interleaved, with normal processing, that is, the processor and the DMA controller share the processor's buses.

DMA controllers are relatively expensive and hence it is not feasible to provide them for all peripherals. In order to lower the cost, a DMA controller may be shared among a group of peripherals. This type of facility is called a channel by IBM. The DMA controller is a small processor and the programming of this controller becomes very complex when the channel is shared between many peripherals.

## Exercises

7.1 Discuss the advantages and disadvantages of memory-mapped I/O versus separate I/O memory.

7.2 Data is transferred between computers as 8-bit ASCII code with one start bit, one stop bit and no parity at a baud rate of 9600. What is the effective data rate?

7.3 Estimate the time taken to transfer 10 Kbytes of data between a peripheral device and a processor's memory using (1) a polled I/O system and (2) a DMA system. Why are DMA devices usually given a higher priority for using the system bus than the processor?

7.4 In a given microcomputer system the time taken for the processor to recognize and acknowledge an interrupt is 4 μs, while the time taken to save or restore the program counter and status registers is 10 μs. If the execution time of an interrupt handler associated with a peripheral device is 70 μs, estimate the highest interrupt frequency that may be used. Assume that there are no other interrupts.

# 8

# Control and microprogramming

Earlier it was shown that a computer is effectively a collection of registers, an ALU, and a connection to external memory, all of which are interconnected by buses. Data are transferred from one register to another, possibly undergoing a transformation on the way via the ALU, by connecting the registers onto the appropriate buses with control signals. This flow of information is controlled by the control unit, the most complex part of the CPU design. All the actions of the control unit are concerned with the decoding and execution of instructions, i.e. the fetch and execute cycles. In this chapter the design of a control unit will be considered, and in particular the concept of microprogramming will be introduced.

## 8.1 The fetch cycle

The fetch cycle involves the reading of the next instruction to be obeyed, from memory into an internal register of the CPU, the instruction register. The instruction is then decoded so that it is ready to be executed. To explain these actions in more detail a simple computer system will be used for illustrative purposes, as shown in Fig. 8.1. The computer consists of a number of registers, three internal buses, and an ALU.

For simplicity, all registers and buses will be assumed to be 16-bits wide. The three buses marked bus1, bus2 and bus3 are internal to the CPU and are used to route data between registers and the ALU. The memory address register (MAR) acts as a buffer between the CPU and the external address bus. The memory buffer register (MBR) acts in the same way between the CPU and the external data bus, and is bidirectional, that is, data is transferred to and from external devices. Each register contains 16 D-type flip-flops with tristate outputs and control lines similar to the register bank design discussed in section 4.8. The ALU has two inputs, bus1 and bus2, and a single output

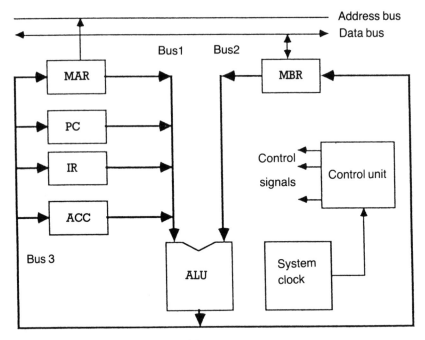

**Fig. 8.1** A minimal processor architecture.

connected to bus3. The only input to bus2 in this design is the output from the MBR register.

For an instruction to be fetched from memory the following sequence of operations has to be performed:

1. Load the contents of the program counter register (PC) into MAR, which results in the value appearing on the address bus,
2. instruct the memory to perform a read operation by asserting the read control signal. This results in data being placed on the data bus,
3. store the value on the data bus in the MBR, and transfer this value from the MBR to the instruction register (IR), and finally
4. increment the contents of the PC so that it points to the next instruction in memory.

For operation 1, transfer of the contents of the PC to the MAR, there must be a path between the two registers. In this architecture the only such path is via the ALU, so the ALU must have a transfer operation, which directly connects bus1 to bus3.

The five steps listed above are a description, or specification, of the register transfer operations that correspond to the fetch cycle. It is very useful to have a language that can be used to describe such operations, partly so that such operations can be described concisely, and partly to prevent ambiguities. There are a large number of such high-level hardware-description languages in use (e.g. ELLA and VHDL) but a simple register-transfer notation will be used here. It is best described by examples.

The fetch cycle, described above, written in a register transfer notation is:

1. **PC → MAR**
2. **READ**
3. **MBR → IR**
4. **PC + 1 → PC**

The notation is self-explanatory. In (1) the contents of the PC are transferred to the **MAR**. A **READ** cycle is then initiated in (2) which will result in the contents of the addressed memory being placed in the **MBR**, and so on. What we have written is a program, with each program statement taking the same fixed time to execute. This time will be called a **minor cycle**. Thus the fetch cycle consists of four minor cycles. During each minor cycle one or more control signals is asserted at the start of the cycle, and de-asserted at the end of the cycle. The minor cycles for the fetch cycle will now be considered in more detail.

*Minor cycle 1;* **PC → MAR**

As discussed above the only connection between the output of the PC and the input to the MAR is from bus1 to bus3 via the ALU, so that the ALU requires a transfer operation to transfer its input from bus1 to the output on bus3. Two control signals are required, one to enable the tristate outputs of the PC to connect the contents of the PC onto bus1 at the beginning of the minor cycle, and the other to latch bus3 into the MAR at the end of the minor cycle. In addition the operation code for 'transfer' must be sent to the ALU.

*Minor cycle 2;* **READ**

The only control signal required is **READ** which tells the external memory to perform the read cycle. This signal is also used by the MBR to latch data from the external data bus at the end of the minor cycle.

*Minor cycle 3;* **MBR → IR**

Again the only data pathway between the MBR and the IR is from bus2 to bus3 via the ALU. Two control signals are required, one to enable the tristate outputs of the MBR onto bus1, and the other to latch the contents of bus3 into the IR. In addition an ALU operation is required to transfer the contents of bus2 to bus3.

*Minor cycle 4;* **PC** + 1 → **PC**

The contents of the PC must be routed onto bus1, the value '1' placed onto bus2, the operation code for 'add' sent to the ALU, and finally the contents of bus3 latched into the PC. The value '1' is most easily organized by having a special read-only register, which can be connected to bus2, containing the binary pattern 00 ... 1.

Each minor cycle must last long enough for the actions required to be completed. For example, in minor cycle 1, **PC** → **MAR**, this cycle time must be at least equal to the time taken for the contents of the PC to be output onto bus1 and for the contents of bus1 then to be transferred by the ALU onto bus3. Minor cycle 2 will take the longest time since it involves a read from external memory, whereas the other minor cycles only involve register-to-register transfers within the CPU. It is usual to make all minor cycle periods the same, and, for simplicity, equal to that of the longest minor cycle. However, if speed of execution is important then a more complicated clocking scheme can be used in which each minor cycle is given a variable time just sufficient for its required control actions to complete.

## 8.2   The execute cycle

Although the fetch cycle is the same for every instruction, the execute cycle will differ from instruction to instruction. Execute cycles also differ between computers as the architecture of a computer will greatly influence how an operation is performed.

As an example of an execution sequence consider the minor cycles required to perform an 'add immediate' instruction with the simple architecture shown in Fig. 8.1. With this architecture an 'add immediate' instruction is defined as adding the contents of the next location in memory to the contents of the accumulator register (ACC), and leaving the result in ACC. In a typical assembly programming language this instruction might be written as

**ADD #x**

where x stands for a number, and # means use immediate addressing mode (see Chapter 11 for a fuller explanation of assembly code). It is assumed that the **ADD** instruction is stored in one word, and the value x in the next word.

In the fetch cycle just completed the instruction 'add immediate' has been fetched from memory, and is in the IR. Before the addition can be carried out a second fetch cycle must be performed to fetch the value x from memory into the MBR. If an unmodified fetch cycle, as described earlier, is used then the value of x will also have been transferred into the IR. However, this does not matter as the 'ADD' instruction itself is no longer required. The addition can now be carried out; using the simple register transfer language it is

1. **MBR** → **ALU**
   **ACC** → **ALU**
2. **ADD**
3. **ALU** → **ACC**.

In 2 the control signals necessary to get the ALU to perform the add operation must be sent to the ALU. The minor cycles are then:

*Minor cycle 1;*

Issue control signals which output the contents of ACC to bus1 and MBR to bus2.

*Minor cycle 2;*

Send **ADD** command to the ALU.

*Minor cycle 3;*

Issue a control signal which latches the contents of bus3 into the ACC.

## 8.3   The control unit

The task of the control unit, which is the most complex part of the CPU, is to issue the appropriate control signals for the minor cycles of both the fetch and execute cycles. There are two design implementation techniques, namely hardware and microprogramming. The first, the hardware approach, treats the control unit as a piece of sequential logic, implemented with gates and flip-flops, with each minor cycle being a state. The design method closely follows that discussed in Chapter 2.

The second solution is to use a technique known as microprogramming. Using this technique, the register transfer programs for the fetch and execute cycles are actually the instructions for a simpler processor. These instructions are known as micro-instructions, to differentiate them from the instructions of the higher-level machine. The outline structure of a simplified micro-programmable control unit is shown in Fig. 8.2. It is explainable in terms similar to those used to define the higher-level machine. It consists of a set of registers and a memory (usually called the control or microprogram memory) in which the sequences of micro-instructions that correspond to the fetch and execute cycles of the higher-level machine are stored. This ROM has $n$ address lines so that $2^n$ words are addressed, and each word is $m$ bits long. The output from the ROM is latched into the $m$-bit wide micro-instruction register. Some of the bits are used as control bits, controlling individual signals, while others are grouped into fields for particular actions (see below).

Consider the fetch cycle:

1. PC → MAR
2. READ
3. MBR → IR
4. PC + 1 → PC

These four register transfer statements translate directly to four micro-instructions, stored within the microprogram ROM, as follows.

### PC → MAR

Two control signals are required: PC-to-bus1 and bus3-to-MAR as described earlier. These control signals are shown as bits 5 and 10 of the micro-instruction word in Fig. 8.2. In addition a code to transfer bus1 to bus3 has to be sent to the ALU. A control field assumed to be 4 bits, labelled wwww, is set aside for this function, and occupies the least significant four bits of the micro-instruction word. Thus the micro-instruction is

0 0 ... 0 0 0 0 0 1 0 0 0 0 1 0 w w w w

It is assumed here that the contents of bus3 are latched into the MAR on the falling edge of the control signal, at the end of the micro-instruction (or minor) cycle.

### READ

Bit 15 of the control field is used as the **READ** signal to external memory, so the micro-instruction is

0 0 ... 1 0 0 0 0 0 0 0 0 0 0 0 0 0 0

Note that all other bits must be set to zero.

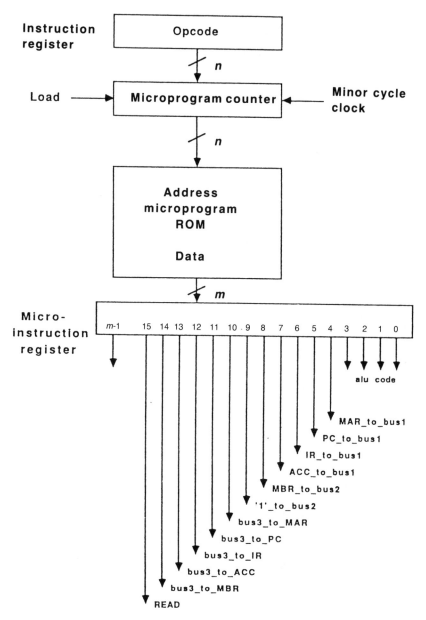

**Fig. 8.2**  Outline structure of a simplified microprogrammable control unit.

MBR → IR

This is very similar to **PC** → **MAR**. Two control signals are required: MBR-to-bus2 and bus3-to-IR, so the micro-instruction required is

0 0 ... 0 0 0 1 0 0 0 1 0 0 0 0 w w w w.

Again wwww is the code required to transfer bus1 to bus3.

**PC** + 1 → **PC**

This is the most complicated micro-instruction in the fetch cycle. It requires a control bit in the control field to output the contents of the PC to bus1 (PC-to-bus1), a control bit to output the register containing 1 to bus2 (1-to-bus2), the code for **ADD** to be sent to the ALU, and a control bit to latch the result of the addition from bus3 into the PC. The micro-instruction is

0 0 ... 0 0 0 0 1 0 0 0 0 0 1 0 w w w w

where wwww is the four-bit pattern code for **ADD**.

This set of four micro-instructions completes the microcode for the fetch cycle.

Note that at the completion of the fetch cycle the opcode for the present high-level machine instruction is in the instruction register. This opcode is then transferred into the microprogram counter by activating the **load** control signal. The microprogram counter is an ordinary binary counter, with its output acting as the address into the control ROM. Thus the opcode is actually the starting address of the micro-instruction sequence in ROM that corresponds to that opcode. The ROM acts in the usual way: the word corresponding to that address is output from the ROM to the micro-instruction register. This word is made up of the $m$ bits of the control field, and consists of the register control bits and the ALU operation code.

At the start of the next minor clock cycle the microprogram counter is incremented to point to the next micro-instruction. In this way a sequence of micro-instructions is executed, in an analogous way to the execution of a sequence of machine code instructions. When the micro-instruction sequence for an execute cycle has finished the microprogram counter must then be set to the start of the fetch sequence again. This cannot be done with the present simple architecture as there is no means for the microprogram counter to branch to an address which is out of sequence. In addition there is no control path for the load signal.

These deficiencies are corrected with the modified architecture shown in Fig. 8.3. An extra bit, known as the **load control** bit, is allocated in the micro-instruction register and is connected to the load signal. In Fig. 8.3 this bit is

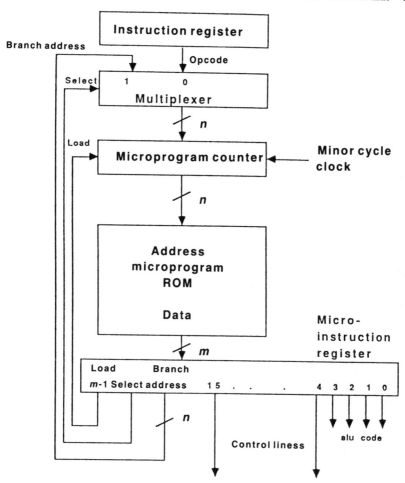

**Fig. 8.3** Modified architecture of Fig. 8.2.

the most significant bit, i.e. bit $m$-1. When this bit is '1' the microprogram counter is loaded with a new address; when it is '0' the microprogram counter is incremented on each minor clock cycle to point to the next micro-instruction in a sequence. The last micro-instruction of the fetch cycle will be to load the microprogram counter, so this micro-instruction will have the load control bit set to '1', and all other bits to '0'.

The ability to branch to an arbitrary address in the microprogram ROM is achieved by adding a multiplexer in front of the microprogram counter, together with an **address select** bit and a **branch address** field in the instruction register. When the address select is '0' the microprogram counter is loaded from the instruction register when load is activated as before. However, when the address select bit is set to '1' the microprogram counter is loaded, via the multiplexer, with the branch address contained in the current micro-instruction. This causes execution to continue at that address. The micro-instruction register has now become very wide. In the architecture of Fig. 8.1 each register was assumed to be 16 bits wide. If this is the case, the $n$ in Figs 8.2 and 8.3 is also 16 so that the microprogram ROM has $2^{16}$ (i.e. 64K) registers each with a word width of at least 32 bits (4 for the ALU code, 16 for the branch address, and 12 control bits). However, this ROM size is much too large since a typical CPU will probably only have of the order of 100–200 separate instructions, and each instruction will require no more than 10–20 micro-instructions. These figures lead to a maximum microprogram ROM size of about 4K words. Moreover the size of the opcode need only be sufficient to give a unique binary pattern for each instruction, which for 200 instructions is 8 bits. Consequently in a 16-bit machine only 8 bits will be used for the opcode, leaving 8 bits available for address information. This topic is covered further in Chapter 11.

Now a 4K ROM requires an address of 12 bits, so if an 8-bit opcode is used a further 4 bits are required to completely specify an address within the ROM. In the simplest system each micro-instruction sequence will start on a 256 word boundary. The starting address of a sequence is then given by concatenating the 8 bits of the opcode with 4 least significant bits which are all zero. However, the branch address field in the micro-instruction register must contain all 12 bits if a jump to any arbitrary address within the ROM is required.

## 8.4   Horizontal and vertical microcoding

In the scheme discussed above each bit in the micro-instruction register is used to control a single register control line, either to gate data from a bus into a register, or to output data from a register onto a bus. The micro-instruction register rapidly becomes very wide; even in the simple example discussed there are 32 bits. In a more realistic design the number of bits may easily exceed 100. This method of coding is simple, and is known as horizontal microcoding. An alternative scheme is to group control signals into fields, and then to use additional decoding circuits to generate the control signals. For example, examination of Fig. 8.1 shows that only one register can output at a time onto bus1, so that any one of the four control signals ACC-to-bus1, IR-to-bus1, PC-to-bus1 and MAR-to-bus1 can be high. Consequently these four signals could be grouped together, and controlled by just two bits from the instruction register $i$ and $j$, say. The truth table for the decoding circuits is then given by:

| i | j | ACC-to-bus1 | IR-to-bus1 | PC-to-bus1 | MAR-to-bus1 |
|---|---|---|---|---|---|
| 0 | 0 | 1 | 0 | 0 | 0 |
| 0 | 1 | 0 | 1 | 0 | 0 |
| 1 | 0 | 0 | 0 | 1 | 0 |
| 1 | 1 | 0 | 0 | 0 | 1 |

Note that with this simple scheme one register is always connected to bus1. This is acceptable for output onto a bus, but not for input since there will be many minor cycles when no input from a bus is required. In a more realistic scheme more control signals will be grouped together. For example, seven control signals can be controlled by three micro-instruction register bits; when all three bits are '0' none of the registers is active.

This second scheme is known as vertical microcoding. There is a trade-off between the width of the micro-instruction register, and the amount of additional decoding circuitry required. A horizontal encoding scheme will give the fastest speed of operation, while a vertical scheme may well give more compact hardware with a smaller microcode ROM, but will be slower due to the additional propagation delays through the decoding circuits. In most real microcoded computers a mixture of the two encoding schemes is used.

## 8.5  Emulation

One advantage of the microprogramming approach to control unit design is that because it is programmable it is always possible to add additional micro-instruction sequences by reprogramming the ROM. This means, for example, that users can be given a limited ability to add new micro-instructions tailored to a particular task. Another advantage is that standard software development techniques can be used.

An interesting feature of microprogrammed control is the ability to emulate another computer's instruction set. Suppose, for example, that we have a program written for a computer X, say, but we want to run it on a different computer Y, say (i.e. Y has a different instruction set to X). One possibility, of course, is to re-write the program using Y's instruction set. However this may well be a time-consuming and error-prone process, and must be repeated for every program. Another possibility is to re-write the micro-instruction program for Y, so that it 'understands' the original instructions of computer X. This technique is known as emulation, in this case Y is said to emulate X. Emulation is a widely used technique in the computer industry. Clearly once an emulator has been written for Y to emulate X, then it can be used for any program that runs on computer X.

## 8.6 Summary

The design of the control system for a processor has been discussed. A processor is a complex synchronous finite-state machine, and the job of the control unit is to generate all the control signals required in the correct timing sequence. The control system may be implemented in hardware.

---

### Exercises

8.1 Write out the micro-instruction sequences for the following assembler instructions, using the architecture given in Fig. 8.1 and the controller scheme of Fig. 8.2:

(a) **CLR**
(clear the accumulator)

(b) **LDA #10**
(load the accumulator with the number that immediately follows the load instruction)

(c) **ADD 20**
(add to the accumulator the number whose address (20 in this case) immediately follows the add instruction, and leave the result in the accumulator).

8.2 The controller scheme shown in Fig. 8.3 is very simple. In particular there is no means for executing different micro-instruction sequences depending on the value of the accumulator flags (zero, carry, etc.). Investigate how you would add this facility to the controller scheme of Fig. 8.3.

8.3 As an extension to the previous question investigate how you would add a subroutine facility to the microprogrammable controller.

---

# 9

# Design of a small computer system

In the previous chapters the principal components of a computer system have been discussed, namely the CPU, memory and input–output devices. This chapter shows how these components are connected together to make a computer system, and discusses the design of two simple microcomputer systems, one 8-bit and the other 16-bit, built up from the type of components already described.

## 9.1 Connecting the components together

The interfacing of memory and input–output interfaces to a processor requires that the address, control and data lines from all the components are connected together. When connecting circuits from the same family, interfacing the control signals is usually very simple since the circuits are designed so that they are compatible. Connecting circuits from different families can be more complex since, not only may the sense of the signals be inverted, but the control signals may also not be used for exactly the same purpose. However, for the sake of the discussion here, compatible circuits are assumed.

Interfacing the data and address buses together is less straightforward, especially in the case of memory, because the size of the address and data buses from the processor almost certainly will not match those of the other components.

### 9.1.1 Decoding

In a typical 8-bit microprocessor the address bus is 16 bits wide giving an address space of 64K words. This address space is usually populated by several memory chips, some being ROM and some RAM. In addition, the address space is frequently not fully populated since a particular application may not need the maximum amount of memory. Individual memory circuits usually contain less memory than the total memory space and so will have less address pins than the processor. In this case, the memory circuits are connected to the lower-order address lines from the processor and the higher-order address lines are decoded to generate the chip select signals.

## ☐ Example 1

To connect a 2K word ROM at address 0-2047 and two 256 word RAMs at addresses 2048-2303 and 4096-4351 to the 16-bit address bus of a processor.
   The memory map required is:

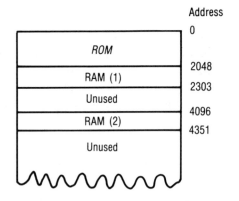

or, in terms of bit patterns, with x = 0 or 1:

| $A_{15}$ | $A_{14}$ | $A_{13}$ | $A_{12}$ | $A_{11}$ | $A_{10}$ | $A_9$ | $A_8$ | $A_7$ | $A_6$ | $A_5$ | $A_4$ | $A_3$ | $A_2$ | $A_1$ | $A_0$ | |
|---|---|---|---|---|---|---|---|---|---|---|---|---|---|---|---|---|
| 0 | 0 | 0 | 0 | 0 | x | x | x | x | x | x | x | x | x | x | x | ROM |
| 0 | 0 | 0 | 0 | 1 | 0 | 0 | 0 | x | x | x | x | x | x | x | x | RAM (1) |
| 0 | 0 | 0 | 1 | 0 | 0 | 0 | 0 | x | x | x | x | x | x | x | x | RAM (2) |

To implement this memory system, $A_0$–$A_{10}$ from the processor are connected to the ROM chip and $A_0$–$A_7$ to both the RAM chips. The memory chip select lines have to be driven from a decoding of address lines, and $A_{11}$ and $A_{12}$ are used in this example to specify which chip is being addressed. The simplest method is to use a decoder as described in Chapter 2. In this case, a 1

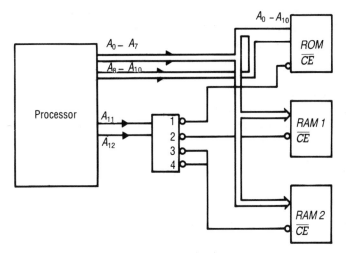

**Fig. 9.1**    Decoding memory addresses.

to 4 decoder is required with the inputs connected to $A_{11}$ and $A_{12}$ and the outputs connected to the ROM chip, the first RAM chip, the second RAM chip and left unconnected, respectively. The required circuit is then as given in Fig. 9.1.

□ *Example 2*

In the example above, if the ROM was not required then the circuit could be simply modified by removing the ROM and leaving the chip enable signal unconnected. However, decoding of the chip enable signals to the RAMs could be provided much more simply in this case by connecting the appropriate address line directly to the RAM chip. Since RAM chips normally have a $\overline{CE}$ input, RAM 1 could be connected to $A_{12}$ and RAM 2 to $A_{11}$.

The decoding described above can lead to a number of problems. In the first example, address lines $A_{13}$–$A_{15}$ are not used at all. For any address generated by the processor only the bottom 13 bits are significant, which means that eight different addresses generated by the processor will all map to a single memory address. For example, 0, 8192, 16384, 24576, 32768, 40960, 49152 and 57344 will all map to memory address 0. Since the system is configured with the given memory map, presumably the addresses, other than 0, should never be generated except in error. However, this does mean that finding errors in programs can be difficult. In example 1 above, to be completely safe, a 1 of 32 decoder should be used with inputs $A_{11}$–$A_{15}$ and only the three required outputs connected. In this case, for the example above, any address other than 0 would not access a memory location. This is frequently not done, in order to save circuitry, and the example given is typical of what would be found in practice. Another problem which can occur is in the use of the partial decoding of address bits as used in the second example. As well as suffering from the same problems as example 1, this circuit also suffers from the fact that it is difficult to expand since the addition of more memory may involve the addition of a decoder.

The problem of decoding does not occur with data lines but it is frequently the case that memory chips have a smaller number of data inputs and outputs than that of the processor. To overcome this, it is necessary to group the memories together and connect them in parallel to provide the necessary data width. For example, to produce an 8K memory system to connect to the 8-bit data bus of a processor using 8K×1-bit memory chips, requires eight memory chips to be connected in parallel, one to each bit of the data bus. This would produce a memory system 8K in size. All the control signals, for example $\overline{RD}$, $\overline{WR}$, $\overline{CS}$, would be connected in parallel to all the memory chips.

The problem of matching the size of the address and data lines between memory and processor can give rise to interesting trade-offs when designing a complete system. For example, if an 8K×8 memory system is required, then a single 8K×8 memory chip would be ideal. However, if a large memory system is required which is not available as a single integrated circuit, the designer may have the choice between circuits with the required number of address bits but fewer data bits and circuits with the required number of data bits but fewer address bits. The circuit with the required number of address bits is often preferred because it requires no address decoding. For example, to produce a 64K×8-bit memory system the designer might have the choice of using eight 64K×1 or eight 8K×8-bit memory chips. In the former case, the address lines could be routed to all the memory chips without decoding, while in the latter case, a 1 of 8 decoder would be required. The former would be preferable since it uses fewer components and so needs less space to implement.

The discussion above, although using memory as the example, also applies to input–output. In this case, the data route is usually the same size as the processor, but decoding is normally required on the address lines since the interface contains only a few registers, which may be memory mapped or part of a separate input–output address space. The exact method of decoding required depends on how the input–output system is to be operated.

## 9.2 A minimal Intel 8085 system

Fig. 9.2 shows a simple microcomputer system comprising 2K bytes of ROM, 256 bytes of RAM, six parallel ports and one serial port all attached to an Intel 8085 microprocessor. Although the basic operation of the devices has

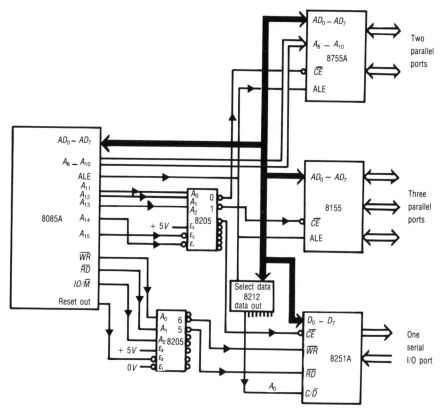

**Fig. 9.2**   Small Intel 8085 microcomputer system.

been considered previously there are some comments to be made on the particular components chosen here. First, the ROM and RAM chips, 8755A and 8155, respectively, which also provide parallel input–output interfaces, were specifically designed for the 8085 processor and hence interfacing these components is simple; the data and address lines are connected as required together with some of the control lines as discussed below. The serial interface chip, 8251A, was not designed for this microprocessor and hence interfacing is slightly more complex.

Remembering that the bottom 8 lines of the address bus are multiplexed with the data bus, these pins on the processor are connected directly to the equivalent pins on the RAM and ROM chips. The 8251A serial interface only has a data port and the common address and data lines are connected to this 8-bit wide data port. The ROM is 2K ($2^{11}$) bytes in size and hence requires 11 address lines. Thus, address lines $A_8$–$A_{10}$, inclusive, are connected from the processor to the ROM to provide the three additional address lines. The RAM being 256 bytes in size only requires eight address lines, which have already been connected. The ALE, WR, RD, and IO/M control signals are directly connected to the 8755A and 8155 but cannot be directly connected to the 8251A. Instead the IO/M and RD and WR signals are combined using an 8205 decoder which produces an output WR and RD signal when either of the input read or write is asserted together with the IO signal. The serial interface requires a C/D (control/not data) signal to allow the control and data registers in the chip to be assessed. Since the data bus is shared with the bottom eight bits of the address bus an 8212 latch has to be added to the bus to latch the address using the ALE signal. This latched address is then used to generate the C/D signal, in this case by discriminating on the lowest bit, $A_0$. Thus the control register of the 8251A is at an even address and the data registers at odd addresses.

The remaining problem with the interfacing is to provide the CE signals to the three peripheral chips. In the example given, one Intel 8205 decoder is used to generate the chip-select signals and another to generate the input–output read and write signals for the USART. When the enable inputs $A_1$ and $E_2$ are low and $E_3$ high on these decoders, the output corresponding to the binary value on the input is set low and all the other outputs set high. Since all the inputs of the chip select decoder are connected to the $A_{11}$, $A_{12}$ and $A_{13}$ address lines each output corresponds to a different 2K ($2^{11}$) address space. For example, output 0 will be set low for an address in the range 0–2K. Hence the EPROM memory is at address 0–2047 and the RAM memory at address 2048–4095. Here we have a problem of partial decoding since the RAM only contains 256 bytes, and hence only addresses 2048–2303 are valid. Because of the partial decoding addresses with different values of $A_8$–$A_{10}$ but with the same values in $A_0$–$A_7$ will all map to the same address in RAM. For example, access to addresses 2049 and 2305 would map to the same RAM location. To overcome this problem a further stage of decoding on address $A_8$–$A_{10}$ would be required, but for simple systems this is often ignored. The parallel ports on each chip are accessed by putting the appropriate addresses on the data bus with the chip enabled and the IO/M signal set at IO. Since, on the IO instructions, the data on the data bus are duplicated on the upper eight bits of the address bus, addresses 0–3 access the data and control registers of the ROM chip whilst addresses 08–0B hexadecimal are used to access the parallel ports on the RAM chip. The 8251A USART is selected via the decoder and so it may be addressed via the binary pattern 00010xx0 (where x = don't care) for control, or 00010xx1 for data.

The reason why the address and data signals are multiplexed in this design is due to limitations of technology. At the time that this processor was designed the most widely used package for integrated circuits had 40 pinouts. This is not enough to dedicate a pin to each data, control and address signal, hence some have to be multiplexed. This causes problems since the signals have to be demultiplexed before they can be used, but if special support chips are designed then the demultiplexing can be performed internally rather than externally. However, if chips of a different family are used, as the 8251A in this example, or from a different manufacturer, external latching is required.

## 9.3  A Motorola 68000-based microcomputer

Fig. 9.3 shows a simple microcomputer consisting of a Motorola 68000 processor, 8K words of ROM, 8K words of RAM, a Motorola 6821 parallel interface adapter (PIA) and a Rockwell R6551 asynchronous communications interface adapter (ACIA) or UART. The 6821 PIA is functionally similar to the Intel 8255 programmable peripheral interface discussed in Chapter 7. The 68000 has a 23-bit address bus, labelled $A_1-A_{23}$, so that it can address $2^{23}$ or 8M words of data. However, memory is actually byte addressable. As discussed in Chapter 5 the 68000 has two control lines labelled $\overline{\text{UDS}}$, upper data strobe, and $\overline{\text{LDS}}$, lower data strobe to facilitate byte addressing. When a word is being accessed both $\overline{\text{UDS}}$ and $\overline{\text{LDS}}$ are asserted (that is, taken low); when a byte is being accessed $\overline{\text{UDS}}$ is asserted if the byte is on the upper half of the data bus ($D_8-D_{15}$), and $\overline{\text{LDS}}$ if it is on the lower half of the data bus ($D_0-D_7$). In order to provide 8K words of RAM two 6264 RAM chips are required, connected to the upper and lower halves of the data bus, respectively. Similarly, the 8K words of ROM are provided by two 2764 EPROMs. No multiplexing is used on the buses of the 68000, so the connection between the memory chips and the processor is straightforward. The memory chips require 13 address lines (to select between their internal memory locations) and so the low-order address lines $A_1-A_{13}$ are connected directly to the chips. Address lines $A_{14}-A_{16}$ are then used to select between the various memory and peripheral devices, and to allow for future expansion. Note that address lines $A_{17}-A_{23}$ are not used in this simple design. The address map for the system is then:

| | | | | *Address* | | | | | | | | | | | | *Device* |
|---|---|---|---|---|---|---|---|---|---|---|---|---|---|---|---|---|
| *16* | *15* | *14* | *13* | *12* | *11* | *10* | *9* | *8* | *7* | *6* | *5* | *4* | *3* | *2* | *1* | |
| 0 | 0 | 0 | x | x | x | x | x | x | x x x x | | | | x x x x | | | | ROM |
| 0 | 0 | 1 | x | x | x | x | x | x | x x x x | | | | x x x x | | | | RAM |
| 1 | 0 | 0 | | | | | | | | | | | x | x | | PIA |
| 1 | 0 | 1 | | | | | | | | | | | x | x | | ACIA |

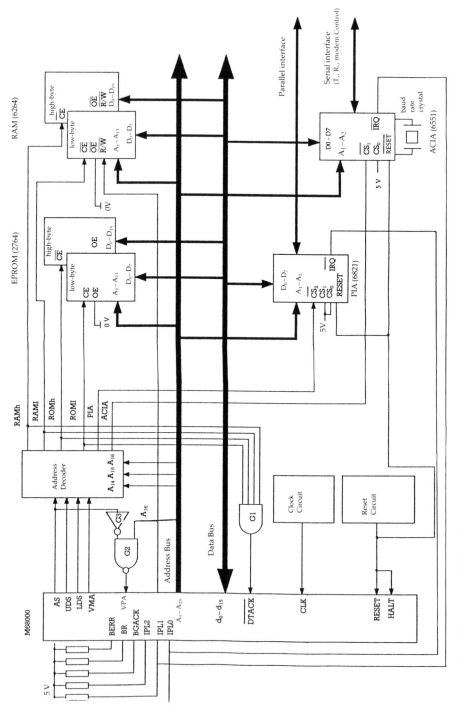

**Fig. 9.3** Small Motorola 68000 microcomputer system.

The ROM is placed at the bottom of the address range because when the system is started up, or a reset is performed, the processor expects to find initializing information in the bottom 1K bytes of memory. This information is most easily placed in the ROM. The RAM is then placed immediately above the ROM's address space. The chip select signals for the four ROM and RAM chips are generated by the combinatorial address decoder by combining $A_{16}$, $A_{15}$ and $A_{14}$ with the address strobe signal $\overline{\text{AS}}$, and the $\overline{\text{UDS}}$ and $\overline{\text{LDS}}$ data-strobe signals as shown in Fig. 9.3. The address strobe signal is used so that the memory chips are only selected when there is a valid address on the address bus. The address decoder circuit must generate the following signals:

$$\text{ROMh} = \overline{A_{16}}.\overline{A_{15}}.\overline{A_{14}}.\overline{\text{AS}}.\overline{\text{UDS}}$$
$$\text{ROMl} = \overline{A_{16}}.\overline{A_{15}}.\overline{A_{14}}.\overline{\text{AS}}.\overline{\text{LDS}}$$
$$\text{RAMh} = \overline{A_{16}}.\overline{A_{15}}.A_{14}.\overline{\text{AS}}.\overline{\text{UDS}}$$
$$\text{RAMl} = \overline{A_{16}}.\overline{A_{15}}.A_{14}.\overline{\text{AS}}.\overline{\text{LDS}}$$
$$\text{PIA} \quad = A_{16}.\overline{A_{15}}.\overline{A_{14}}.\text{VMA}.\overline{\text{LDS}}$$
$$\text{ACIA} = A_{16}.\overline{A_{15}}.A_{14}.\text{VMA}.\overline{\text{LDS}}$$

The address decoder can be built either from discrete TTL gates and a decoder chip, or from a single PLA. The latter is usually preferred as it reduces the number of chips required to implement the logic.

The only 'novel' part of the circuit is the data acknowledge $\overline{\text{DTACK}}$ generator. The four memory chip select signals from the address decoder are ANDed together (gate G1) to form the input to $\overline{\text{DTACK}}$. When the memory is not being addressed the chip-select signals are high, and so $\overline{\text{DTACK}}$ is high. Whenever one of the memory select signals goes low $\overline{\text{DTACK}}$ goes low immediately, signalling to the 68000 that the memory has responded. (Note that the AND gate here is actually being used to implement an OR function, since the memory select signals are all active low!) This is the simplest possible data acknowledge scheme, but it has two disadvantages. First, fast ROM and RAM must be used, and secondly the generator cannot cope with the case, frequently met in practice, in which a mix of devices having widely different access speeds are used. Referring back to the 68000 read timing diagram (Fig. 5.16) it can be seen that the memory devices must have access times of less than two clock cycles (that is, they have to respond between the end of state $S2$ and the beginning of state $S7$). With a clock frequency of 8 MHz this is just $2 \times 125 = 250$ ns. RAMs with these access times are available; for example, the Hitatchi HM6264 has a quoted access time of 150 ns, and faster devices are available. EPROMs are generally slower than RAMs, with access times typically in the region of 300–500 ns. However, there is a fast Hitatchi 8K EPROM available, the HN482764G-2 with an access time of 200 ns. Clearly, if a faster clock speed is used then either faster memories, or a more complicated data acknowledge generator which introduces a suitable delay must be used. The output enable, $\overline{\text{OE}}$, pins of all the chips are tied low, and the R/$\overline{\text{W}}$ control signal is taken from the 68000 to the write enable, $\overline{\text{WE}}$, pins of RAMs.

Consider now the peripheral devices, the 6821 PIA and the 6551 ACIA. The PIA contains two parallel 8-bit input–output ports, a control register and a status register. The ACIA is a standard serial receiver–transmitter and has a built-in baud-rate generator, and modem control signals. Both these devices are synchronous, and must be controlled by the 68000's synchronous bus control signals. The address decoding scheme is as follows. Synchronous devices are selected by address line $A16$. A high signal on $A16$ is used to indicate that a synchronous bus transfer is required. This address line, ANDed with the address strobe signal $\overline{\text{AS}}$, is returned to the 68000's $\overline{\text{VPA}}$ input to inform the processor that it has to perform a synchronous bus cycle (gates G2 and G3). Note that the chip select signals for the peripheral devices use the synchronous control signal $\overline{\text{VMA}}$ (valid memory address). Both of the peripheral devices have a number of internal registers which are selected by $RS_0$ and $RS_1$. These register select lines are connected to address lines $A_1$ and $A_2$, respectively. Finally, both these peripheral devices are able to generate interrupts, via their $\overline{\text{IRQ}}$ pins. These are connected to $\overline{\text{IPL0}}$ and $\overline{\text{IPL1}}$, respectively, on the processor. To complete the microcomputer, a clock-oscillator module, and a reset circuit are required. Finally, note that all unused inputs on the 68000, such as the external bus request input BR, are tied high using 4k7 pull-up resistors. This section has only given a very brief introduction to a simple 68000 microcomputer system; readers requiring further information on how to design and build 68000 systems are referred to the book by A. Clements in the bibliography.

## 9.4 Summary

The design of a small microcomputer system involves the connection of the processor to memory and to input–output devices. This requires the connection of appropriate signals, such as the data and address buses, and the generation of extra control signals such as the chip-enable signals. The design of systems based on 16-bit processors is no more difficult than 8-bit systems, except that the data and address buses are wider.

# Exercises

9.1  Modify the Intel 8085 system design given in Fig. 9.1 to add an extra 512 bytes of RAM at addresses 8192–8703, and 2K bytes of ROM at addresses 9216–11263.

9.2  Modify the 8085 system design given in this chapter for full decoding of the addresses for RAM access.

9.3  Modify the Motorola 68000 system design of Fig. 9.2 to change the RAM size to 4K words using Hitachi 6116 RAM chips.

# 10

# Data representation and manipulation

## 10.1 Introduction

The bit patterns in the memory of a computer represent two different types of information: instructions, and data to be manipulated by the instructions. There is no distinction in the memory between these two types of information; they are all bit patterns. The difference only manifests itself in the way the bit patterns are used. In fact it is likely that the same bit pattern can represent either a number or an instruction depending on how it is used.

In $n$ bits $2^n$ different bit combinations are possible and thus the size of the bit pattern determines the number of different instructions or data which can be stored. The basic unit of storage is a word and, on modern computers, this is a multiple of eight bits. Instructions are normally stored in one or more words, whereas the data types supported are often an integral number of bytes. Several data items may be packed into a word or a data item may require several words.

Since much of the data stored in computers are numbers we will examine number systems before considering data representation and manipulation. Instruction representation will be considered in the following chapters.

## 10.2 Number systems

In the decimal number system 10 different symbols are used to represent numbers and each digit in a number is 10 times more significant than the digit to its right and 10 times less significant than the digit to its left. This figure of 10 is known as the **radix**, or base, of the number system. Thus a number such as 1372 is shorthand for $1\times1000 + 3\times100 + 7\times10 + 2$ or $1\times10^3 + 3\times10^2 + 7\times10^1 + 2\times10^0$. The radix of the binary system used in computers is 2 and thus two symbols, 0 and 1, are sufficient to represent any number. Each digit in a binary number is twice as significant as the digit on its right and half as significant as the digit on its left. Using the notation $(\ldots)_n$ to represent a number in the radix $n$ number system, some examples of binary numbers and their corresponding decimal equivalents are given below.

$$(1011)_2 = (1\times2^3 + 0\times2^2 + 1\times2^1 + 1\times2^0)_{10} = (11)_{10}$$
$$(011)_2 = (0\times2^2 + 1\times2^1 + 1\times2^0)_{10} = (3)_{10}$$
$$(101010)_2 = (1\times2^5 + 0\times2^4 + 1\times2^3 + 0\times2^2 + 1\times2^1 + 0\times2^0)_{10} = (42)_{10}.$$

To convert a number from decimal to binary one method is to continually divide the number by 2 until the quotient is zero. The remainders, in reverse order, give the binary representation of the number, as illustrated by the example below.

$$
\begin{array}{ll}
 & \text{remainder} \\
2\,|\,\underline{23} & 1 \\
2\,|\,\underline{11} & 1 \\
2\,|\,\underline{\;5} & 1 \\
2\,|\,\underline{\;2} & 0 \\
2\,|\,\underline{\;1} & 1 \\
\quad 0 &
\end{array}
$$

so $(23)_{10} = (10111)_2$

To convert from binary to decimal the scheme outlined previously could be used, that is to multiply the digits by the correct power of two and then to sum them. An alternative method is the reverse of the decimal to binary conversion outlined above, that is starting with the top bit multiply it by two and add the next bit in sequence, then multiply this result by two and add the next bit in sequence and so on for all the bits, as shown in the example below.

$(111001)_2$

$$2 \times 1 + 1 = 3$$
$$2 \times 3 + 1 = 7$$
$$2 \times 7 + 0 = 14$$
$$2 \times 14 + 0 = 28$$
$$2 \times 28 + 1 = 57$$

so $(111001)_2 = (57)_{10}$

It is very tedious to write out a long string of binary digits and so they are often shortened to an octal (radix 8) or hexadecimal (radix 16) number. For the octal system the eight symbols used to represent the digits are

0,1,2,3,4,5,6,7. The hexadecimal system requires 16 symbols, and uses the digits 0–9 and the letters A–F, with A representing the eleventh and F the sixteenth symbol. The conversions between numbers in these number systems and decimal numbers can be performed as outlined above for binary except that the twos in the algorithm are replaced by eight or sixteen as appropriate. For example,

$$(7A2)_{16} \quad = 7 \times 16^2 + 10 \times 16^1 + 2$$

which may be computed as follows:

$$7 \times 16 \; + 10 = 122 \text{ (since } A_{16} = 10_{10})$$
$$122 \times 16 + 2 = 1954$$
so $(7A2)_{16} = (1954)_{10}$.

The conversion between binary and octal or hexadecimal is, however, very much easier since $8 = 2^3$ and $16 = 2^4$. To convert from binary to octal the binary digits are grouped into sets of three starting from the right hand end and padding the left most group with zeros if necessary. Each group of three binary digits is then converted to its equivalent octal value and the string of resulting octal digits is the octal representation of the original binary value. To convert from binary to hexadecimal the same procedure is applied except that the binary digits are grouped into sets of four. The example below illustrates this octal and hexadecimal conversion process.

|  |  |
|---|---|
| 1 0 1 1 0 1 1 0 0 1 1 1 0 0 1 1 | 16 bit binary no. |
| (0 0 1)(0 1 1)(0 1 1)(0 0 1)(1 1 0)(0 1 1) | |
| 1   3   3   1   6   3 | octal equiv. |
| (1 0 1 1)(0 1 1 0)(0 1 1 1)(0 0 1 1) | |
| B   6   7   3 | hexadecimal equiv. |

so $(1011011001110011)_2 = (133163)_8 = (B673)_{16}$

The reverse coding is simply a matter of writing the binary equivalent of each octal or hexadecimal digit and concatenating the resulting bit patterns.

Another type of coding used is called Binary Coded Decimal (BCD) where each separate decimal digit is encoded into a pattern of four bits; for example,

2     4     8     1     in decimal
is   (0 0 1 0)(0 1 0 0)(1 0 0 0)(0 0 0 1)   in BCD.

The reason for using such a representation, rather than the straight binary representation presented earlier, is concerned with the trade-off to be made between converting between internal and external representations, which are usually different, and the ease of computation. We will see this in more detail later in this chapter.

So far we have only been concerned with whole numbers (integers). Computers also have to store and manipulate real numbers, that is numbers including a decimal point. There is a basic difference between these two types of numbers which affects the way in which they are represented and manipulated in a computer. Between any pair of integers there is a finite number of integers, for example, between 3 and 6 there are the two integers 4 and 5. Thus if we decide what range of integers we wish to represent in a computer we immediately know how many different integers we have to represent and hence how many different bit patterns are required. Between any pair of real numbers there is an infinite number of real numbers, for example, between 1.0 and 1.1 are all the real numbers which start 1.0 and there are an infinite number of these since a real number can have any number of digits after the decimal point. Because a computer has finite memory it cannot represent all possible real numbers between two bounds. Instead, the number of real numbers between two bounds which can be represented is limited by limiting the accuracy to which real numbers are stored. Obviously the greater the number of decimal places and the greater the range the more storage required. Whilst it would be feasible to represent and manipulate numbers of differing accuracy this would cause problems for the hardware architect in designing the ALU circuitry, and hence real numbers are usually stored in a common format. As is the case for integers, real numbers have to be converted from the normal user format into their internal format and vice versa. Because of the limitations of the range and format of the internal representation, approximations may be introduced in this conversion. Also, manipulating real numbers in a computer system can lead to predictable and consistent errors since the numbers are stored in a standard internal representation. For example, if two very small numbers are multiplied together then the result may be too small to be represented, in which case it will be represented by zero. In cases where small numbers are being manipulated this can mean that care has to be taken to perform operations in the order which best preserves the accuracy. This problem is of great importance in numerical analysis and has to be taken into account when considering the accuracy of numerical computations.

## 10.3  Data representation

In this section the representation of three different types of data in a computer, characters, integers and real numbers, are considered.

### 10.3.1   Characters

Computers often have to manipulate textual information and thus require a method for storing characters. The most widely used code for storing characters is the American Standard Code for Information Interchange (ASCII), shown in Fig. 10.1. This is a 7-bit code allowing $2^7$ (or 128) different characters to be represented. Among the characters represented are upper and lower case letters, the digits 0–9 and the standard punctuation characters such as the colon, semicolon and comma; in other words, all the characters which can be typed on a typewriter keyboard. There are less than 128 of these characters and the extra codes available are used for special control purposes which will not be discussed here. A character is normally stored in a byte (eight bits) of memory and the corresponding ASCII code for the character is stored in the bottom seven bits with the top bit often being ignored but sometimes being used as a parity check. When parity is being used the eighth bit is set to 0 or 1 to make the number of 1 bits in the byte odd, for odd parity, or even, for even parity. Thus single bit errors may be detected as mechanisms are often provided for checking the parity of a byte. On the 8085 this is done via the parity condition code which is set via the result of some arithmetic operations. Character codes are often used to represent data in computer-readable form outside the computer and the process of inputting and outputting information is comparatively error prone; hence the need for error checking on characters.

### 10.3.2   Integers

An integer is typically represented in a computer in 16 or 32 bits, often the word size of the machine. In $n$ bits $2^n$ different bit patterns are possible, each one representing a different integer. These patterns have to be shared out between positive and negative integers, assuming that negative values are required. Although there are many different mappings possible between the integers and the bit patterns representing them, only the two common ones are discussed here. The simplest method is to regard one bit as the sign bit and the rest of the bits as the unsigned number. This is known as sign-magnitude representation and is shown in Fig. 10.2.

However, for a reason which will become apparent later, the most popular scheme, called two's complement, uses a less obvious encoding scheme. Representations of positive integers start with a zero and are the binary encodings of the integer. Negative numbers are represented by bit patterns which when added to the corresponding positive number representation produce the representation of zero. The negative representations may be produced from the corresponding positive representation by inverting all the

| code | | character |
| decimal | hex | |
|---|---|---|
| 0–31 | 0-1F | control codes |
| 32 | 20 | space |
| 33 | 21 | ! |
| 34 | 22 | " |
| 35 | 23 | # |
| 36 | 24 | $ |
| 37 | 25 | % |
| 38 | 26 | & |
| 39 | 27 | ' |
| 40 | 28 | ( |
| 41 | 29 | ) |
| 42 | 2A | * |
| 43 | 2B | + |
| 44 | 2C | , |
| 45 | 2D | - |
| 46 | 2E | . |
| 47 | 2F | / |
| 48–57 | 30-39 | 0 to 9 |
| 58 | 3A | : |
| 59 | 3B | ; |
| 60 | 3C | < |
| 61 | 3D | = |
| 62 | 3E | > |
| 63 | 3F | ? |
| 64 | 40 | @ |
| 65–90 | 41-5A | capital A to Z |
| 91 | 5B | [ |
| 92 | 5C | \ |
| 93 | 5D | ] |
| 94 | 5E | ^ |
| 95 | 5F | note arrow to be inserted |
| 96 | 60 | ` |
| 97–122 | 61-7A | lower case a to z |
| 123 | 7B | { |
| 124 | 7C | \| |
| 125 | 7D | } |
| 126 | 7E | ~ |
| 127 | 7F | DEL |

**Fig. 10.1** The ASCII code.

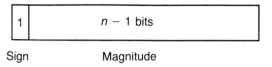

Fig. 10.2   Signal-magnitude representation.

bits and then adding one. Illustrating this scheme using four bits the integers which can be represented and their corresponding bit patterns are

| | |
|---|---|
| 0111 | +7 |
| 0110 | +6 |
| 0101 | +5 |
| 0100 | +4 |
| 0011 | +3 |
| 0010 | +2 |
| 0001 | +1 |
| 0000 | 0 |
| 1111 | −1 |
| 1110 | −2 |
| 1101 | −3 |
| 1100 | −4 |
| 1011 | −5 |
| 1010 | −6 |
| 1001 | −7 |
| 1000 | −8. |

Thus the range of values which can be stored in $n$ bits using two's complement representation is $(+2^{n-1} - 1)$ to $(-2^{n-1})$.

One of the problems with having a fixed amount of storage for an integer is that the range is limited. This can cause problems with arithmetic operations as we show below. (Note that binary arithmetic may be performed in the same way as decimal arithmetic using the rules below).

$$0 + 0 = 0 \qquad\qquad 0 - 0 = 0$$
$$0 + 1 = 1 \qquad\qquad 0 - 1 = 1 \text{ borrow } 1$$
$$1 + 0 = 1 \qquad\qquad 1 - 0 = 1$$
$$1 + 1 = 0 \text{ carry } 1 \quad 1 - 1 = 0$$

$$0 \times 0 = 0$$
$$0 \times 1 = 0$$
$$1 \times 0 = 0$$
$$1 \times 1 = 1.$$

Using these rules an example of binary addition is given below.

```
0010              (  2  )
0101 +            (  5+)
0111              (  7  )
```

However, problems can arise, as illustrated below.

```
0101              (  5  )
0011 +            (  3+)
1000              (-8  )
```

The problem here is that the correct answer, +8, cannot be represented in four bits using two's complement representation. In order to stop incorrect results being computed the hardware has to detect faults such as this, called overflow, and report them to the programmer. A similar condition can be produced by subtraction as shown below.

```
1001              (-7  )
0011 −            (  3−)
0110              (  6  )
```

Multiplication can also produce overflow. The normal way for overflow to be reported to the programmer is via a bit in the condition code register used specifically for this purpose.

One reason for using two's complement representation is that subtraction can be performed more cheaply than by sign-magnitude representation. To perform subtraction using the two's complement system the subtrahend – the value being subtracted – is first complemented, that is all the bits are inverted. The result of adding this complemented value to the other operand with an initial carry in of 1 is exactly the same as would have been obtained by subtracting the original value; see the arithmetic of the example below.

```
0101              0101
0011 −            1100 +
0010              0001 +
                  10010 = 0010 in four bits
```

Thus subtraction may be performed by the use of an adder and a complementer. The circuit to invert a bit pattern is cheaper and less complex than a subtraction circuit and is also required for other purposes.

## 10.3.3   Real numbers

Real numbers can be stored in the same way as integers, as shown below, with the decimal point being explicitly stored or implied by its position;

123.4375 may be stored as
1111011.0111

where the digits after the point represent contributions of 1/2, 1/4, 1/8 and 1/16, respectively, to the value. This representation creates problems with the storage of very small and very large numbers. In decimal arithmetic the problems are overcome by the use of scientific notation; for example, $1.4 \times 10^6$ to represents one million four hundred thousand. This allows very large and very small numbers to be represented with only a few digits. The same technique can be used for binary numbers. Numbers are represented in floating point form, $a \times 2^b$ where $a$ is known as the mantissa and $b$ the exponent. Separate fields are used to store the values of $a$ and $b$ and the value of $b$ is adjusted before storing to ensure that $a$ is in a specified range, typically between +0.5 and −0.5. This process of adjustment is known as normalization. In many representations the exponent is stored in a biased form, that is a fixed value, called the bias, is subtracted from the value stored in the exponent field to obtain the true exponent. Also, it is common practice for the mantissa to assume that there is an implied 1 and a binary point before the digits stored, thus saving storage space. This is actually how the representation given in Fig. 10.3 is stored. In spite of using this compact representation, most computers require at least twice as much storage space for a real number as an integer. On some computers more than one floating point representation is used depending on the accuracy and range required. There are now a number of standards, for example, IEEE 754, for the storage of floating point numbers. The format for one of the representations defined in IEEE 754, that for single-precision numbers, is given in Fig. 10.3.

As indicated above, real numbers are normally stored in a computer using floating-point format. The mantissa and exponent are stored in a given number of bits giving an accuracy and range, respectively, for the number. In the same way that integer arithmetic can give rise to overflow, so the same operations on floating-point numbers can also give rise to overflow. Additionally, a condition called underflow can occur with floating point numbers. This happens when the result of a computation is smaller than the smallest value, positive or negative, which can be represented. Underflow and overflow conditions are shown in Fig. 10.4. In addition, floating point numbers are only kept to a certain accuracy, as defined by the size of the mantissa field. Hence floating point arithmetic can lose precision due to the effect of rounding a computational result to the nearest representation value. The complexities

| 1 | 8 | 23  bits |
|---|---|---|

Sign exponent          Mantissa

where sign $= 0$ for positive and 1 for negative; exponent is an unsigned
8-bit integer; mantissa is the 23 bits after an initial 1

Thus   number $= (-1)^{sign} \, 2^{(exp-127)} \, (1.\text{mantissa})_2$

*Examples*

(a)  1.0 is represented as

| 0 | 01111111 | 00000000000000 |
|---|----------|----------------|

i.e.  $(-1)^0 \times 2^{(127-127)} \times (1.0000)_2 = 1 \times 1 \times 1.0000 = 1.0000$

(b)  0.5 is represented as

| 0 | 01111110 | 00000000000000 |
|---|----------|----------------|

i.e.  $(-1)^0 \times 2^{(126-127)} \times (1.0000)_2 = 1 \times 2^{-1} \times 1.0000 = 0.5$

(c)  2.0 is represented as

| 0 | 10000000 | 00000000000000 |
|---|----------|----------------|

i.e.  $(-1)^0 \times 2^{(128-127)} \times (1.0000)_2 = 1 \times 2 \times 1.0000 = 2.0$

(d)  $-2.5$ is represented as

| 1 | 10000000 | 01000000000000 |
|---|----------|----------------|

that is,
i.e. $(-1)^1 \times 2^{(128-127)} \times (1.0100)_2 = -1 \times 2 \times (1.0100)_2 = -2 \times 1.25 = -2.50$

**Fig. 10.3**   IEEE single precision standard for floating point numbers and some
examples.

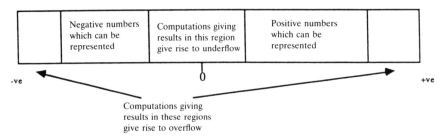

**Fig. 10.4** Underflow and overflow in floating point number computations.

of real-number arithmetic are beyond the scope of this book. The interested reader is referred to one of the books quoted in the bibliography for more details.

## 10.4 Differing representations

An external symbol may be represented in more than one way internally, depending on the type of information it represents. For example, the symbol 1 can represent either a character or an integer and the representation in the computer will depend on which one is intended; 0110001 is the ASCII character code for 1 and 0000000000000001 is the representation of the integer 1 on a 16-bit computer. Conversely, the bit pattern 01000111 could represent a character, integer or instruction on an 8-bit computer; the interpretation depends on the context.

A further complication is that the number 1.0 is not stored in the same representation as the integer 1 since the former will be stored as a floating-point representation with separate mantissa and exponent, whilst the latter will be stored as the integer representation, probably in two's complement form. In order for the computer to be able to manipulate data it must be aware which type of data it is handling. The arithmetic operations that need to be performed to add two integers together are different from those required to add two floating-point numbers together. Hence different machine instructions are required to perform the same operation on different data types. For example, there might be an integer add instruction which operates on integers, and a floating-point add operation which operates on real numbers. The range of data types supported directly by the hardware differs from processor to processor. Virtually all processors provide instructions to manipulate integers but few provide instructions to manipulate floating-point numbers. For example, the 8085 and 68000 both provide instructions to manipulate integers but not floating-point values. In the case of the 68000 an extra chip, called a co-processor, is available which directly supports floating-point arithmetic.

The character representation is most often used externally. For example, information sent to a computer from an input device and sent by the computer to an output device will normally be represented in the ASCII code. Few computers provide arithmetic and logical operations on character representations and hence if arithmetic or logical operations have to be performed on input data, that data must first be converted into internal integer or real-number format. Similarly, most computers insist on output data being in character-string form so that if integers or real numbers are to be output they first have to be converted into the equivalent character representation. The conversion to and from character form is straightforward in the case of integers – the addition or subtraction of a constant – although it is more complicated in the case of floating-point numbers. Appropriate conversion software is normally provided if the user is using some language other than machine code.

The conversion from integer or floating-point to character form and *vice versa* imposes an overhead on processing numbers. Whilst this does not matter if substantial computations are involved, simple operations, such as those involved in electronic scales, benefit from a simpler method. Instead of using integer arithmetic, the processors in such equipment use BCD arithmetic. As described previously, each decimal digit is stored in four bits; half a byte. Addition is carried out by adding bytes together using normal-integer arithmetic and then adjusting the result to the appropriate BCD representation, as in the example below.

```
0110    0010      (62 )
0010    1000 +    (28+)
1000    1010
     1 + 1010 −
1001    0000      (90 )
```

The adjustment involves subtracting decimal 10 from any group of bits which are greater than 10 and adding 1 to the group of bits to the left. Since BCD digits are stored two to a byte, one adjustment is performed internally and the other adjustment has to be performed across a pair of bytes. This is done using the carry flag in the condition code register. The process of adjusting the pair of BCD digits in a byte is normally performed by a special machine operation; this is what the 8085 DAA instruction does. Hardware is available to directly connect seven-segment displays to the output of computers and the displays may be driven directly from BCD output. Similarly, hardware is available to encode a set of keys into BCD for direct input to a computer.

## 10.5   Summary

The operand of an instruction is data and the simplest forms of data are integers, characters and real numbers. All data are represented in memory by bit patterns, so numbers may be represented in several different ways. Integers are typically represented in either two's complement form or sign magnitude. Characters are represented in most computers using the 7-bit ASCII code. There are a multitude of representations for floating-point or real numbers but many recent computers use the IEEE 754 standard.

Computers generally use the character representation for external representation of all data and hence numbers have to be converted from internal to external representation and *vice versa* on output from and input to the computer. Also, programmers use several different number systems when writing programs so the number system as well as the representation has to be considered on conversion.

Manipulation of real numbers can give rise to problems in accuracy since the numbers are not stored exactly, but only to some given accuracy. This does not arise with integers. Arithmetic operations on integers can give rise to overflow and on real numbers to overflow and underflow.

## Exercises

10.1 Convert the following values from decimal to binary, octal and hexadecimal.
(a) 27
(b) 96
(c) 1032
(d) 1111

10.2 Convert the following decimal numbers to two's complement form in six bits.
(a) 27
(b) −27
(c) 0
(d) −32

10.3 Perform the following decimal arithmetic in binary. Indicate any computations which give rise to overflow if the computations are performed to 6 bits accuracy. Can you suggest any way of avoiding overflow in any of the cases without increasing the number of bits required?
(a) 5 + 7
(b) 12 − 3
(c) 20 + 16 − 5
(d) −30 + 7 − 12
(e) 12 × 5

10.4 Perform the computations given in Exercise 10.3 in BCD arithmetic.

10.5 Convert the following decimal values into the IEEE standard single-precision floating-point representation (Fig. 10.3).
(a) 0.0
(b) 8.0
(c) −10.5
(d) 123.4375

# 11

# Instruction sets and addressing modes

## 11.1 Instruction sets

A computer executes instructions which have been preloaded into its memory. Each instruction comprises one or two fields, one of which is known as the operation code, or opcode, which defines the operation to be carried out, and another field, which defines the values upon which the operation code executes. The operand field is further subdivided into source fields, which define where the values to be operated on are located, and a destination field which specifies where the result of the operation is to be stored. This structure is shown in Fig. 11.1.

The set of different operation codes provided by a particular processor is known as its **instruction set** and the ways in which the operands can be specified are known as the **addressing modes**.

The opcode and operands of an instruction have to be encoded into bit patterns which reside in memory. Whilst in theory any number of bits can be used for storing the instruction, in practice instructions are represented in a whole number of words since transfers between memory and processor use the word as their unit of transfer. Some instructions need more operands than others; for example the instruction to halt execution needs no operands whilst the instruction to add two values together needs at least two operands. Thus there is often more than one format for instructions, and opcodes and operands can occupy a different number of bits in different formats. The ramifications of this are discussed below.

Just as with any other information, instructions are stored in the memory of a computer as bit patterns. Before a program is executed the bit patterns, the **machne code** corresponding to the instructions in the program and the constant data accessed by the instructions have to be loaded into the memory of the

| Operation code | Operands | |
|---|---|---|
| | **Operands** | |
| | Source(s) | Destination |

**Fig. 11.1**   Structure of an instruction.

computer. This loading is performed by a program which is described in the next chapter. However, specifying the program in terms of the appropriate bit patterns is not very convenient for the programmer. Instead, the programmer can use a notation called **assembly code** which is a simple mnemonic encoding of the bit pattern. Some examples are given in Fig. 11.2, and more are to be found later in this chapter.

Also in this chapter the types of instructions which exist on a typical processor and the way in which operation codes and their operands are expressed both at the machine-code and assembly-code levels are considered. Examples are given from both the 8085 and 68000 computers; however, this chapter is not intended to be used as a programming guide for either of these computers as there is not enough space to deal with this task adequately. Readers who require detailed information to program either of these processors should consult the manufacturer's literature or one of the books quoted in the bibliography.

## 11.1.1   Opcode

The set of instructions provided by the designer is known as the **instruction set** of that computer. It is defined by the designer and determined by the lower-level abstractions, the implementation, of the processor. It defines the combinations of operatons of the ALU and operands which can be activated by the control unit in a single instruction cycle. Restrictions on the number of different operations and the combinations of operations and operands are imposed by the designer for a number of reasons. First, the designer is often

```
ADD       B            ; add the contents of register B to the accumulator

ADD       D0,D1        ; add the contents of the register D0 to the contents
                         of the register D1 and store the result in D1

L: MOVE   D0,D4        ; L is a label so the statement can be referred to
                         from elsewhere in the code. The instruction
                         moves the contents of register D0 to register D4
                         overwriting any information stored there
```

**Fig. 11.2**   Examples of assembly code instructions.

working against a limit on the size of the integrated circuit used to implement the processor and so it is not possible to include all the combinations of operations and operands or, sometimes, the number of opcodes the designer wishes. A second reason for restricting the number of operations and combinations with operands is that the processor is aimed at a particular application or set of applications and these do not need the complete set of possible instructions.

One of the first tasks of the computer designer is to decide how to encode the operation code in each instruction. The simplest method is to encode the opcode in the minimum number of bits, so that $n$ bits can represent $2^n$ different operations. However, as explained above, not all operations require the same number of operands and hence the number of bits required to store a field of an instruction can vary. Thus it may not be necessary for all opcodes to be fully encoded, that is, to use the minimum number of bits. This makes it easier to design and implement the decoding hardware within the processor. In fact, it is often the case that the amount of memory taken to store an instruction is mainly dependent on the storage needed for the operands and the space occupied by the opcode is whatever is left to make the instruction length an integral number of words.

A processor provides operations on a range of different data types. The range of types supported will depend on the complexity of the processor but even the simplest processors will normally support operations on characters (8-bit quantities) and integers (16 bits or more) as part of the standard instruction set. Processors intended for numerical computation will also include operations on floating-point numbers (see Chapter 10). The 8085 supports operations on 8-bit quantities and a limited range of operations on 16-bit quantities, whereas the 68000 supports operations on 8-, 16- and 32-bit quantities. Neither of these processors supports floating-point operations directly. For each of the different representations, different instructions are required to perform the same function, since the internal operations required will be different in each case. For example, the internal operations to be performed to add two integers together are different from those required to add two floating-point numbers together, hence the need for two different types of **ADD** instruction. A simple way of distinguishing, in the coded form of the operation, between the different forms of an instruction is to use one or more bits to signify the data type involved. This is reflected in assembly code by the use of a qualifier to the instruction, for example, the 68000 has many different forms of **MOVE** instruction and some of which operate on bytes (8 bits), some on words (16 bits) and some on long words (32 bits). These instructions are differentiated by the use of .B after the opcode for the byte instructions, .W after the opcode for word instructions and .L for long word instructions. The 8085 only supports operations on 8- and 16-bit quantities and different mnemonics are provided for the different data types.

## 11.2   The programmer's models

Before considering instructions in more detail, the model of the processor which the programmer has to keep in mind in mapping the algorithm to solve the problem is considered. Two processors are considered in this chapter, the 8085 and 68000, and simplified versions of the programmer's models for both these processors are given in Figs 11.3 and 11.4.

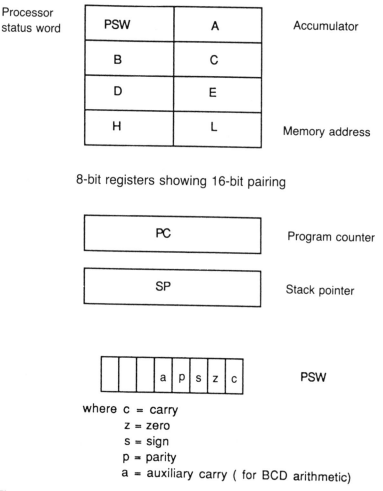

**Fig. 11.3**   Programmer's model of the 8085.

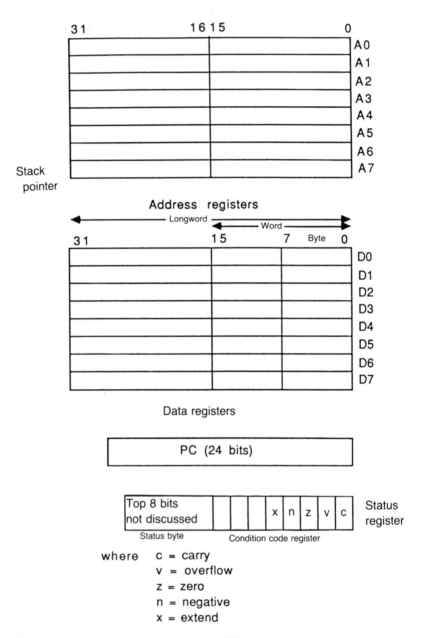

**Fig. 11.4** Programmer's model of the 68000.

## 11.2.1    8085

The 8085 has seven 8-bit registers which are immediately accessible to the programmer: A, B, C, D, E, H and L. Of these, six can be used as register pairs and therefore act as 16-bit registers: B and C, D and E and H and L. A is the accumulator, source and destination of many instructions. H and L act as the memory address register, that is memory reference instructions assume the memory address required is to be found in these registers. In addition to these registers there is a 16-bit stack pointer register SP and an 8-bit status register which contains flag bits, such as the zero bit, denoting the result of the last operation performed by the processor. Operations on the stack work on 16-bit quantities and for this purpose the status register is combined with the accumulator so that, for example, **PUSH PSW** puts the contents of the accumulator and the status word on the stack. There is also a program counter but this cannot be directly accessed by the programmer. Thus the register structure of the 8085 can be depicted as shown in Fig. 11.3.

## 11.2.2    68000

The 68000 has a programmer's model which is far more complex than the 8085 (Fig. 11.4). First, there are 16 general-purpose registers, each 32 bits wide, called $A0-A7$ and $D0-D7$. The set $D0-D7$ are called data registers and are generally used for storing intermediate results of calculations. They are completely general in that any operation on one of the set could equally well take place on any other one; there are no restrictions. Each register may be operated on by three groups of instructions; long-word instructions, word instructions and byte instructions, denoted by .L, .W and .B, respectively, in assembly code. The long-word instructions manipulate the complete 32 bits of the register, the word instructions only the bottom 16 bits and the byte instructions only the bottom 8 bits, with the bits which are not manipulated being unaffected.

The registers $A0-A7$ are known as address registers because they normally act as pointers to locations in memory. They may also be used to hold data, but word and long-word operations affect all the bits and byte operations are not allowed. $A7$ is used as a pointer to a stack on which subroutine return addresses are held. In actual fact there are two registers called $A7$ and hence two stacks, and it depends on the context which one is referred to; this complication will be ignored in this discussion.

In addition there are two special-purpose registers. There is a status register, similar to the 8085, except that as well as keeping the condition codes it also stores a status byte which will be ignored in the discussion here. The other special register is the program counter which keeps the address of the next instruction to be obeyed. Like the 8085 this register cannot be explicitly addressed by the programmer.

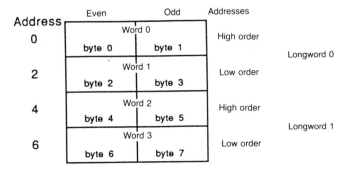

**Fig. 11.5** Memory addressing on the 68000.

Although not strictly part of the programmer's model, the addressing structure of memory is important to the programmer and it can differ from processor to processor. On the 68000, memory is byte addressable and words have even addresses. The high-order bits of the word, bits 8–15, take the word address and the low-order bits the word address +1. Long words are mapped in a similar way, that is the 16 high-order bits are stored in the lower address word and the 16 low-order bits in the higher address word. These addressing conventions are shown in Fig. 11.5.

## 11.3   Instruction types

Each type of processor provides its own unique set of instructions but the types of instruction provided by processors can be classified into a number of classes.

### 11.3.1   Data-movement instructions

Probably the most extensive class of instructions provided on all present day computers are the data-movement instructions. These instructions allow the programmer to move data between registers, between registers and memory and to move data about in main memory.

The instructions on the 8085 to perform data-movement of bytes are called move (**MOV**) instructions. The name move is something of a misnomer since they are really copy operations, that is the source operand still retains its original value after the completion of the operation. There are a large number of different move instructions, some of which accomplish moves between any pair of registers (**MOV r,r**), some of which transfer information between a register and memory (**MOV r,M** or **MOV M,r**) and others which move constant values to a register or memory (**MVI r,val** or **MVI M,val**). In addition, since the 8085 supports some register pair operations ([B,C],[D,E],[H,L]) and some 16-bit registers (program counter, stack pointer), there are some data-movement instructions which move 16 bits of data. For example, the **LXI** instructions load a 16-bit constant into a register pair. There are a number of other data-movement instructions on the 8085 which move information about using the indirect addressing mode described later in this chapter.

The 68000 similarly has a large number of move (**MOVE** and its derivatives such as **MOVEQ**) instructions, to accomplish transfers between any pair of registers, between any register and a memory address and to load a constant embedded in the instruction to a register or memory address. Many of the move instructions operate on the three sizes of data which the 68000 can manipulate; bytes (8 bits), words (16 bits) and long words (32 bits). The 68000 is also able to move data between memory locations directly rather than having to go via the accumulator, which is the case on the 8085, since the 68000 has multiple address registers whereas the 8085 has only one. There are a large number of **MOVE** derivatives on the 68000 concerned with moving the contents of special registers, moving multiple registers and the like, but they will not be described here.

□ *Examples*

| 8085 | MOV | A,B | move the value in register B to register A, the accumulator |
|---|---|---|---|
| | MVI | D,5 | move the value 5 to register D |
| | LXI | H,2000 | move the value 2000 to the register pair HL – assuming 2000 hexadecimal means 20 in H and 00 in L |
| 68000 | MOVE.B | D0,D1 | move the bottom 8 bits of $D0$ to the same position in $D1$ |
| | MOVE.L | D0,D1 | move the 32 bits in $D0$ to $D1$ |
| | MOVEQ | #3,D0 | move (quick) the constant 3 to the 32 bits of $D0$: note that for this instruction the constant must be $\leq$ 8 bits. |

## 11.3.2   Arithmetic and logical operations

Another class of instructions are the arithmetic and logical operations. The main arithmetic and logical operations available on the 8085 and 68000 are shown in Fig. 11.6. In a single accumulator computer such as the 8085 the arithmetic instructions assume that one operand is in the accumulator and that the result is put back into the accumulator, overwriting the value stored there. Thus arithmetic operations such as addition which require two operands

| 8085 | | 68000 |
|---|---|---|
| ADD | add + variants | ADD |
| SUB | subtract + variants | SUB |
| INR | increment (by 1) | |
| DCR | decrement (by 1) | |
| | negate + variants | NEG |
| | | |
| ANA | logical AND | AND |
| XRA | exclusive OR | EOR |
| ORA | inclusive OR | OR |
| | | |
| RLC | | ROL |
| RRC | rotate and | ROR |
| RAL | shift | ASL |
| RAR | | ASR |
| | | |
| DAD | double length ADD | |
| INX | double length INR | |
| DCX | double length DCR | |
| | | |
| | divide + variants | DIVS |
| | multiply + variants | MULS |

**Fig. 11.6**  Arithmetic and logical operations available on the 8085 and 68000.

usually assume that one is in the accumulator and that the other is in a register specified in the instruction. The **ADD** instruction of the 8085 has several different forms depending on whether the operand is in one of the registers or in the main memory pointed to by registers H and L. A form of the add instruction, **ADI**, is provided for the case where the operand is specified as a constant in the instruction. The operations which only require a single operand, such as increment, specify a single operand, a register or memory address, in the instruction. Since the 8085 supports some 16-bit operations, some instructions operate on register pairs.

The 68000 has a conventional set of arithmetic and logical operations. It has a full set of addition and subtraction operations which operate on 8-, 16- and 32-bit operands. In addition, unlike the 8085, it has multiply and division operations, but these only operate on particular types of operands. Similar to the 8085, it has a set of operations to facilitate BCD arithmetic but it has no operations to manipulate floating-point values. Its logical operations are also similar to the 8085 as it provides logical operations for **AND**, **OR**, **XOR** and **NOT**.

| BTST | test bit, if bit = 0 set Z condition code |
|------|-------------------------------------------|
| BSET | set the addressed bit to 1 |
| BCET | set the addressed bit to 0 |
| BCHG | invert the addressed bit i.e. $1 \rightarrow 0$ or $0 \rightarrow 1$ |

**Fig. 11.7**   Bit operations on the 68000.

□ *Examples*

| 8085 | ADD | *D* | add the contents of register *D* to the contents of the accumulator (register *A*) and store the result in the accumulator |
|------|-----|-----|---|
| | ADI | 3 | add the constant 3 to the contents of the accumulator and leave the result in the accumulator |
| | DAD | *D* | perform a 16-bit add operation on the value in registers *D* and *E* with the value in registers *H* and *L*. Store the result back in registers *H* and *L* |
| 68000 | ADD.W | *D*0,*D*1 | add the bottom 16 bits of *D*0 to the bottom 16 bits of *D*1 and store the result in the bottom 16 bits of *D*1 |
| | ADD.L | *D*0,*D*1 | same as above but with 32-bit operands. |

## 11.3.3  Bit-manipulation operations

The 8085 does not provide any bit-manipulation operations directly, rather it assumes that they can be performed by **AND** and **OR** instructions with the appropriate immediate operands. For example, **AND**ing an 8-bit operand with $(11110000)_2$ results in the bottom four bits of the operand being set to zero and the top four bits being left as they were and thus this could be used to test if any of the top four bits were non-zero in combination with a conditional test as described below.

The 68000 provides four instructions which operate on single bits in an operand. There are operations to test the value of a single bit, to set the value of a single bit to 1, to set the value of a single bit to 0 and to change the value from 1 to 0 or *vice versa*, as shown in Fig. 11.7. These operations are very useful if a set of Boolean values is packed into a single location since they can be individually manipulated.

□ *Examples*

| 68000 | **BSET** *D*1,*D*5 | the value in *D*1 is taken as an integer mod 32 and this bit of *D*5 is set to 1 |
|-------|--------------------|---|

BTST *D3,D6* the *D*3th bit of *D*6 is tested and if zero the Z condition code is set to 1.

## 11.3.4   Program-control instructions

An important property of any processor is the ability to change the program-execution sequence depending on the input data, either directly or indirectly. Without this facility a set of instructions could only be executed once. To change the execution sequence requires two types of instruction: ones which can test the value of some item of data and ones which can jump to an instruction out of sequence depending on the result of a previous data test. There is also a requirement for an unconditional transfer of control to implement loops in the code. Most processors store information about the result of the last instruction executed in a set of flag bits, sometimes called condition codes, which are usually grouped together in a status register. The test instructions set or clear the appropriate condition codes and the conditional jump instructions test the values in one or more of these condition codes to decide whether or not to perform the jump. Whilst most processors update the condition codes as the result of the execution of most instructions in the instruction set, it is often necessary to perform specific tests or comparisons before a conditional jump.

The condition codes provided on most processors are similar but not identical. For example, the 8085 provides flags for the conditions zero, carry, sign, parity and auxiliary carry, whilst the 68000 provides flags for carry, overflow, zero, sign and extend.

### (a)   Condition tests

The 8085 and the 68000 provide compare instructions which set the condition code registers depending on the result of the comparison, as shown in Fig. 11.8. Since the 8085 is a single-accumulator machine, the compare instruction takes a single operand which is compared with the contents of the accumulator. The compare instruction on the 68000, which can take a number of forms, takes two operands and similarly sets the values of the condition codes. There is also a test instruction on the 68000 which takes a single operand and sets the condition codes according to its value.

□ *Examples*

| | | | |
|---|---|---|---|
| 8085 | **CPI** | 5 | set the condition codes on the result of subtracting 5 from the contents of the accumulator. The accumulator contents are not changed |
| | **CPM** | B | subtract the contents of register *B* from the con- |

tents of the accumulator and set the condition codes on the result. The contents of the accumulator do not change

68000    CMP.L  *D0,D4*  subtract the 32-bit value stored in *D0* from that in *D4* and set the condition codes on the result. Neither the contents of *D0* or *D4* are changed

CMPI.B  #7,*D5*  subtract 7 from the least-significant 8 bits of *D5* and set the condition codes on the result. *D5* is not altered.

TST.W  *D1*  set the condition codes depending on the value stored in the least-significant 16 bits in *D1*.

### 8085

CMP          compare register or memory contents with accumulator, set condition codes on result

CPI          compare constant with value in accumulator, set condition codes on result

### 68000

CMP + variants          compare two values stored in memory or registers, set the condition codes on result

TST          set the condition codes depending on the value in the single address specified

**Fig. 11.8**   Conditional tests.

## (b)   Branch instructions

Both the 8085 and 68000 have an extensive set of conditional jump instructions as shown in Fig. 11.9. Each of these instructions uses the value of one or more of the condition codes or flags to determine whether the next instruction to be obeyed is the next one in sequence or the one at the address specified as the operand of the conditional jump. Both 8085 and 68000 include an unconditional branch instruction which causes control to be transferred to the specified address unconditionally.

## ☐ *Examples*

8085    JZ    LAB1    jump to the statement labelled LAB1 if the zero condition code is set, that is the result of the last operation was zero. If not take no action

|         |         |         |
|---------|---------|---------|
|         | JMP CC  | unconditional jump to the statement labelled CCi |
| 68000   | BEQ LAB | jump to the statement labelled LAB if the result of the last instruction was equal to zero, that is, the zero condition code was set, otherwise take no action |
|         | BPL THERE | jump to statement labelled **THERE** if the result of the last instruction was positive, otherwise take no action. |

| Jump condition | Condition code tested | 8085 | 68000 |
|----------------|-----------------------|------|-------|
| carry clear    | c                     | JC   | BCC   |
| carry set      | c                     | JNC  | BCS   |
| last ins = 0   | z                     | JZ   | BEQ   |
| last ins ≠ 0   | z                     | JNZ  | BNE   |
| last ins +ve   | n                     | JP   | BPL   |
| last ins -ve   | n                     | JM   | BMI   |
| last ins >     | z, n, v               |      | BGT   |
| last ins <     | n, v                  |      | BLT   |
| parity odd     | p                     | JPO  |       |
| parity even    | p                     | JPE  |       |
| always jump    |                       | JMP  | JMP   |
|                |                       |      | BRA   |

**Fig. 11.9**   Some of the branch and jump instructions on the 8085 and 68000.

## (c)   Subroutine call and return

Another class of transfer of control instructions is the subroutine entry and exit instructions, often called call and return instructions. There are frequent cases in programming where the same sequence of instructions is required in more than one place in a program. Instead of writing the code in both places, it may be written once as a subroutine or procedure and special instructions inserted in the code at the appropriate place to cause transfer of control to the appropriate routine. At the end of the routine control has to be returned to the instruction following the call. This is illustrated in Fig. 11.10. In order for this action to be possible the return address has to be stored when the routine is called and this address restored to the program counter by the return instruction at the end of the routine. Frequently subroutines call other sub-routines to perform part of the calculation, and the return address mechanism must be able to work over a set of subroutine calls nested hierarchically. The most common way of providing this facility is to store the return addresses in

Main program                    Subroutine

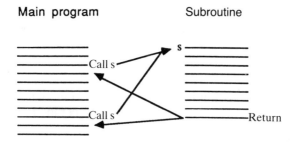

**Fig. 11.10**   Subroutine call and return.

a data structure called a stack where the last value inserted is the first value retrieved. Using this data structure a set of routines can call one another and the return instructions will cause control to be returned in the correct order, that is in the opposite order to the calling sequence. Stacks are explained in more detail later in this chapter. The instruction to branch to a subroutine on the 8085 is called a **CALL** instruction and the return a **RET**. On the 68000 the equivalent instructions are **JSR** and **RTS**. In addition the 8085 has a set of conditional call instructions which only transfer control to the specified address if the condition is met. The conditions refer to the condition codes in the condition code register. The call and return instructions available on the 8085 and 68000 are shown in Fig. 11.11.

|  | 8085 | 68000 | |
|---|---|---|---|
| Unconditional | CALL | JSR<br>BSR | only differ in<br>addressing modes |
| Return | RET | RTS<br>RTR | normal<br>restore condition<br>codes as well |
| Conditional<br>calls | CZ<br>CNZ<br>CC<br>CNC<br>CPE<br>CPO<br>CP<br>CM | | zero<br>non zero<br>carry set<br>carry not set<br>parity even<br>parity odd<br>plus<br>minus |

**Fig. 11.11**   Call and return instructions for the 8085 and 68000.

□ *Examples*

| | | | |
|---|---|---|---|
| 8085 | **CALL SUB1** | | jump to the statement labelled **SUB1** having saved the program counter value (the address of the next instruction) on the stack |
| | **CZ** | **SR** | jump to the statement labelled **SR**, saving the program counter, if the zero condition code is set, that is, the result of the last operation was zero, otherwise no effect |
| | **RET** | | place the value at the top of the stack into the program counter, that is, return from where this subroutine was called |
| 68000 | **JSR** | **SUB** | jump to the statement labelled **SUB** having stored the return address on the stack |
| | **RTS** | | return from subroutine, that is, restore the program counter value from the stack. |

## 11.3.5   Input–output instructions

Every computer needs some mechanism to input data and output the result of computations. Input and output peripherals are treated like registers by the programmer and these registers are normally accessed by one of two different mechanisms. One method called **memory mapped input–output** maps the input–output registers into the normal memory address space of the processor and so the standard data movement instructions of the computer may be used for input and output; no special instructions are necessary. This is the case with the 68000. The other technique is to provide special instructions, called **IN** and **OUT** on the 8085, which are solely used to input and output data, usually to/from a particular register, the accumulator in the case of the 8085. The **IN** and **OUT** instructions contain a port number as an operand to identify which peripheral is involved in the transfer. There are advantages and disadvantages of both techniques, for example, the use of extra input–output instructions complicates the instruction set but memory mapping reduces the address space available for real memory. Although both methods are still used, memory mapping is likely to become dominant since the use of a few memory addresses for input–output will not seriously affect the amount of memory which can be addressed with the ever-increasing address space provided in new processors.

□ *Examples*

| | | | |
|---|---|---|---|
| 8085 | **IN** | 6 | input an 8-bit value from the peripheral attached to port 6 into the accumulator |

| | OUT | 3 | output the contents of the accumulator to the peripheral attached to port 3 |
|---|---|---|---|
| 68000 | MOVE.B | $D0$,ad | output the least significant 8 bits of $D0$ to the peripheral memory mapped at address ad |
| | MOVE.B | ad,$D3$ | input the 8-bit value from the peripheral memory mapped at address ad to the least significant 8 bits of $D3$. |

### 11.3.6   Other instructions

As well as the different types of instructions mentioned above there are a number of extra instructions provided on most processors. All processors include an instruction to halt the processor, and most processors, including the 68000 and 8085, have an instruction which has no effect, a no-operation. This latter type of instruction can be useful in debugging a program and also in cases where timing is critical, for example when controlling a mechanical device. Most processors also provide some form of arithmetic shift instruction which provides a quick method of multiplying or dividing an integer by a power of 2. Other instructions are provided but there is insufficient space in this brief discussion of instruction sets to detail them; some examples are given in Fig. 11.12. Interested readers are referred to the appropriate books mentioned in the Bibliography.

## 11.4   Operands

Consider an **ADD** instruction. The information required when the instruction is obeyed is:

1. the addresses of the two values to be added;
2. the address in memory where the result is to be placed;
3. the address of the next instruction to be obeyed.

This information may be given explicitly in the instruction or it may be implied. As seen above, the **ADD** instruction on the 8085 assumes implicitly that one of the operands is in the accumulator whilst on the 68000 the instruction contains the address of both operands. The task of the designer of the processor is to decide how this information is to be represented in the computer under consideration.

If an operand can reside anywhere in the address space of the processor then the address fields in an instruction must be the same size as the address bus. For a typical 8-bit microcomputer, the address bus is 16 bits wide, implying that an **ADD** instruction, which requires four addresses (the address of the two source operands, the destination address and the address of the next

8085

| | | |
|---|---|---|
| decimal adjust accumulator (for BCD arithmetic) | DAA | |
| complement accumulator | CMA | |
| exchange the contents of the accumulator and HL | PCHL | |
| store A in memory at address in register pair BC | STAX B | plus other register pairs |
| put the value in the register pair on the stack | PUSH B | plus other register pairs |
| take the value off the top of the stack and put in the register pair | POP B | plus other register pairs |

68000

| | | |
|---|---|---|
| decrement the register and branch to the labelled statement if the condition on the register is true | DBcc Dn,label | where cc is any of the branch condition codes and Dn is any data register. Used for end of loops. |
| checks the lower order word of the data register against two bounds | CHK addr,Dn | |
| tests the addressed byte, sets the condition codes accordingly and the byte to 10000000 | TAS addr | |

**Fig. 11.12**   Some of the other instructions on the 8085 and 68000.

instruction), would require about 9 bytes of memory if all this address information were given explicitly. For a 16- or 32-bit microcomputer the figures would be proportionally larger. This leads to excessive memory requirements so the designer has to find some way of reducing the storage required for each instruction. This can be done by reducing the number or size of the operand fields.

## 11.4.1   Reducing the number of operand fields

The information required on instruction execution cannot be reduced; hence the only scope for the designer is either to make one or more operands implicit rather than explicit or to combine some of the operand fields.

In a typical program, instructions are obeyed in sequence most of the time with only infrequent jumps out of order. If the instructions are stored in sequence in memory, the address of the next instruction will, most frequently, be a few words further on in memory, the exact number of words depending on the length of each instruction. This being so, a register, the program counter, can be used to store the address of the next instruction. The addition of a small constant to the program counter will then give the address of the next instruction. In fact the operation of updating the program counter is not as complex as it might appear. The requirement is simply that the program counter is incremented after each word of an instruction has been fetched. The inclusion of a program counter removes the need for a next instruction address field, but means that the Branch Instruction class has to be provided to change the value of the program counter when the next instruction to be executed is not the next one in sequence.

With the above modification, an **ADD** instruction still requires three operand fields. A common method of reducing this still further is to amalgamate one of the source fields with the destination field, so that the result of the operation overwrites one of the source operands. This reduces the number of operand fields to two, at the expense of requiring a copy instruction to save the source operand before it is overwritten, if necessary.

To reduce the number of operands still further, one or more of the operands must be implied. A common technique, employed on the 8085, is to provide a special register called an **accumulator**, to and from which all **ALU** operations take place. Hence an **ADD** instruction only requires a single operand on such an architecture since, by implication, one operand will be found in, and the result placed back in, the accumulator.

This technique can be taken to its logical conclusion and all the operands implied so that the **ADD** instruction would require no explicit operands. It would be possible to do this assuming that the operands and results were always in fixed registers or memory locations, but this creates problems since information has to be moved from place to place to satisfy the requirements of different instructions. A better solution is to use a stack architecture. A stack may be thought of as a last-in-first-out (LIFO) memory structure. The two operands of the **ADD** instruction would have to be loaded onto the stack by previous instructions. The **ADD** instruction would remove these two operands from the stack, compute the result and place it back on the stack. All instructions in this type of architecture obtain their operands from and put the results back on the stack. Hence the stack acts as a communication area between instructions. For this type of architecture extra instructions are required to load data on to the stack and to store information from the stack at particular positions in main memory. The possible options for the designer in reducing the number of address fields are shown in Fig. 11.13.

Although the techniques outlined above greatly reduce the size of an instruction the computer designer is also concerned with the size of the

```
4 address instruction
   e.g.  ADD A,B,C, next instruction address
         operands in A and B
         result placed in C
         next instruction at stated address
3 adddress instruction
   e.g.  ADD A,B,C
         operands in A and B
         result placed in C
         next instruction next in sequence
2 address instruction
   e.g.  ADD A,B
         operands in A and B
         result overwrites B
         next instruction next in sequence
1 address instruction
   e.g.  ADD A
         operands in A and accumulator
         result overwrites accumulator
         next instruction next in sequence
0 address instruction
   e.g.  ADD
         operands on the stack
         result placed back on stack
         next instruction next in sequence
```

**Fig. 11.13**   Instruction classes using **ADD** as an example instruction.

program and the speed at which it operates. There is no simple correlation between all these factors, hence the range of different architectures found in processors. In fact most modern computers cannot be classified as falling into any one of these categories; they encode different instructions using a mixture of zero, one and two addressing forms. The Intel 8085 is basically a single accumulator machine and in many instructions one operand is found in, and the result placed in, the accumulator. The 68000, on the other hand, is a multiple register machine and its instructions are mainly of the two-address format.

## 11.4.2   Reducing the size of operand fields

As well as reducing the number of operand fields the computer designer can also consider reducing the size of operand fields. The problem here is that to address $2^n$ words of memory a minimum of $n$ bits are required. This would appear to indicate that there is a limit to the reduction in the size of the operand fields if the complete addressing range of the processor is to be supported. However, there is a technique which the designer can use and this is to specify the address indirectly rather than directly. If a register can hold any address in main memory then instead of quoting the memory address

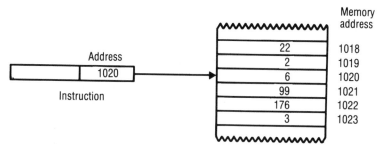

**Fig. 11.14**  Direct addressing.

required for an operand the instruction could hold a register address assuming that the register had been preloaded with the required memory address. Since the number of registers in a processor is generally very much smaller than the number of words in main memory, typically 8 or 16 as opposed to 64K for an 8-bit processor, the size of the operand field in an instruction can be reduced, from 16 to 3 or 4 bits in the example quoted. There is, of course, a penalty for doing this. Instead of the operand address being obtained from the instruction the actual address required has to be read from the register specified in the instruction and this imposes a time penalty as an extra memory read has to be performed. Also the address has to be placed in the register before the instruction is executed and this may require an extra instruction to be obeyed. However, in spite of these time penalties, this technique is frequently used and examples are given later in this chapter.

## 11.5  Addressing modes

The method by which an operand is encoded into an instruction is known as its addressing mode. There are many different modes and several of these are described below.

### 11.5.1  Direct or absolute addressing mode

The simplest way of encoding the address information is to directly encode the address as a bit pattern in the opcode field. This is known as **direct** or **absolute addressing**, see Fig. 11.14. For example, if the address 1020 decimal was to be encoded in a 16-bit field then the bit pattern in the instruction would be 0000001111111100. The size of the address field determines the largest address which can be stored and hence the amount of memory which can be addressed by that instruction.

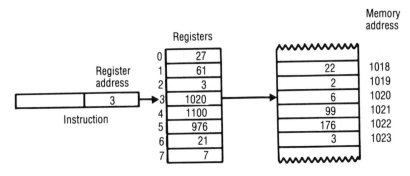

**Fig. 11.15** Indirect addressing.

□ *Examples*

8085    **LHLD**     **2000**    load H and L with the contents of memory location 2000 and 2001

68000   **MOVE.W**  **122,D5**  move the 16-bit contents of memory location 122 to register $D5$.

## 11.5.2   Indirect addressing mode

The designer may wish to use indirect addressing to reduce the number of bits needed to specify an operand. In **indirect addressing**, shown in Fig. 11.15, the address quoted in the operand field is not the address of the required operand but the address of the memory location containing the address of the required operand. In general the actual address of the required operand is called the **effective address** and, for this addressing mode, is obtained by performing a read operation on the address specified in the operand field. One reason for using indirect addressing is to save bits in an address; the address quoted in an instruction is not usually a memory address but a register address which requires fewer bits. Since there are now two different ways of interpreting the address in an operand field there has to be some way of specifying which one is required in any particular situation. The way in which this is done in most computers is to split the operand field into two subfields, one defining the addressing scheme to be used to calculate the effective address of the operand and the other used to specify the address to be used in the effective address calculation, that is a register address. If the computer only contained the two addressing schemes, or modes, as discussed so far then only a single bit would be required to differentiate between them. However, most modern-day computers support a wide range of addressing modes and hence more bits are required to differentiate between them. The 8085 being an old design only supports direct and indirect addressing and then only in a limited form. The Motorola 68000 supports both types of addressing.

☐ *Examples*

| | | | |
|---|---|---|---|
| 8085 | **ADD** | **M** | add the contents of the memory location whose address is in the register pair HL to the contents of the accumulator |
| 68000 | **MOVE.B** | (*A*0),*D*6 | move the byte from the memory address contained in *A*0 to the least significant bits of *D*6 |
| | **MOVE.W** | *D*3,(*A*4) | move the least-significant bits of *D*3 to the memory word whose address is in *A*4. |

The two addressing modes discussed above are sufficient to enable the programmer to specify any type of addressing required but some more complex types of addressing occur so frequently that it is more convenient for the programmer and more efficient for the implementation if special addressing modes are provided at the machine code level. Some of these additional addressing modes are now described.

## 11.5.3 Autoincrement mode

The action when using this addressing mode is the same as for indirect addressing except that the register used is incremented after the effective address has been calculated as shown in Fig. 11.16. The action of this addressing mode could be simulated by using the required instruction with indirect addressing and then an extra instruction to increment the register contents if autoincrement is not supported on a particular processor. Note that the register contents are incremented by a constant which depends on the size of the data item being accessed by the instruction. On the 68000 the increment is 1 for byte operands, 2 for word operands and 4 for longword operands. This is to align the pointer value in the register to point to the next item of data which is 1, 2 or 4 bytes away, respectively.

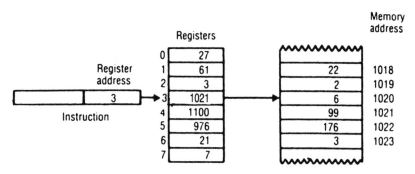

**Fig. 11.16** Autoincrement addressing.

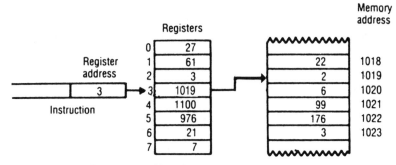

**Fig. 11.17**   Autodecrement addressing.

☐ *Examples*

68000   **MOVE.W (A0)+,D2** move the contents of the memory word whose address is in *A*0 to *D*2 and then increment the contents of *A*0 by 2

   **MOVE.B   D1 (A1)+** move the least-significant 8 bits of *D*1 to the memory location whose address is in *A*1 and then increment the contents of *A*1 by 1.

### 11.5.4   Autodecrement mode

The action when using this addressing mode is the same as indirect addressing except that the register used is decremented before the effective address is calculated as shown in Fig. 11.17. The amount by which the register is decremented is determined in exactly the same way as for autoincrement addressing.

☐ *Examples*

68000   **MOVE.L – (A2),D3** subtract 4 from the contents of *A*2 and then move the longword at the memory location whose address is contained in *A*2 to *D*3

   **MOVE.B – (A1),D4** subtract 1 from the contents of *A*1 and then move the byte at the address contained in *A*1 to *D*4.

### 11.5.5   Index mode

Using this mode both a register and an offset are specified. The effective address is the sum of the contents of the register and the offset as shown in Fig. 11.18. The offset required in this addressing mode is normally stored in the instruction thus making the instruction longer when this mode is used.

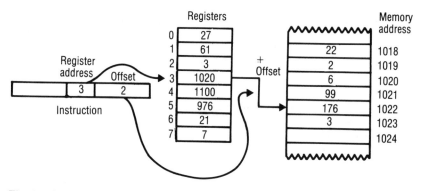

**Fig. 11.18**   Indexed addressing.

The 68000 has two different forms of indexed addressing called register indirect with displacement and register indirect with index.

☐ *Examples*

| 68000 | **MOVE.W  4(*A2*),*D1*** | register indirect with displacement move the word whose address is the contents of *A2* + 4 to *D1* |
|---|---|---|
|  | **MOVE.B  3(*A0*,*D0*.B),*D1*** | register indirect with index move the byte whose address is the sum of 3, the 32 bit contents of *A0* and the contents of the least-significant 8 bits of *D0* to the least-significant 8 bits of *D1*. |

## 11.5.6   Relative mode

The address in the operand field is an address relative to the position of the instruction. The effective address is the sum of the content of the address field and the current contents of the program counter as shown in Fig. 11.19.

☐ *Examples*

| 68000 | **MOVE.W  1000(PC),*D1*** | move the word whose address is the sum of 1000 and the contents of the program counter to *D1*. |
|---|---|---|

## 11.5.7   Immediate mode

The contents of the address part of the operand field are regarded as a constant to be used as the operand. The effective address is the address of the operand itself, that is an address of part of the instruction. This is the addressing mode used to manipulate constants.

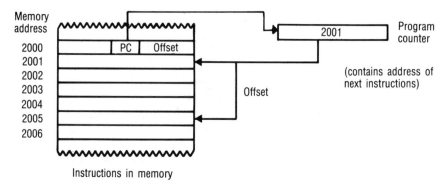

Fig. 11.19 Relative addressing.

□ *Examples*

| | | | |
|---|---|---|---|
| 8085 | **MVI** | *E*,2 | move the constant 2 to register E |
| | **LXI** | H,2000 | load the constant 2000 into the HL register pair; 20 in H and 00 in L |
| 68000 | **MOVE.B** | #2,*D*2 | move the constant 2 to the least-significant 8 bits of *D*2 |
| | **MOVE.L** | #10000,*A*2 | move the constant 10000 into the 32 bits of *A*2 filling the most-significant bits with zeros. |

## 11.5.8   Other addressing modes

In addition to the addressing modes described above there are also many more modes possible although not common. For example, there are indirect forms of many of the modes described above, such as indirect autoincrement, where the effective address is the content of the location whose address is specified in the location given in the operand field of the instruction; it is simply one level of indirection more than autoincrement mode. As stated above, these are not strictly necessary as they can all be formed by combination of the other modes. The more complicated the addressing mode the longer the execution time of the instruction but it is usually quicker to use a complicated addressing mode rather than to use simpler modes and extra instructions.

## 11.6   Instruction encoding

Before considering the use of the addressing modes just described, some comments on the way in which an instruction is actually encoded in the memory of the computer are in order. Remembering that all information is coded in memory as a pattern of bits the question arises as to how the instructions and addressing modes described above are coded on the processors under consideration. As already pointed out, the instruction set and therefore the encoding is unique to a particular processor: however, some general guidelines are used by many designers in producing the encoding. For example, in most architectures, but not all, instructions occupy a whole number of words of memory. Also, the bits representing the opcode are frequently separated from and occur before those representing the operands. In general, the encoding is designed to minimize the number of bits required to represent the instruction whilst making the decoding of the opcode and operands as simple as possible.

☐ *Examples*

|  | assembly code | bit encoding | hex |
|---|---|---|---|
| 8085 | **MOV B,C** | 01000001 | 41 |
|  | **ADD D** | 10000010 | 82 |
|  | **JMP L1** | 11000011 | C3 |
|  |  | xxxxxxxx | XX low order byte of address |
|  |  | xxxxxxxx | XX high order byte of address |
|  | **MVI L,3** | 00101110 | 2E |
|  |  | 00000011 | 03 immediate value 3 |

68000   **MOVE.W** *D0,D1* 0011001000000000 3200
which is coded as

| 15 | 13 | 11 | | 6 | 5 | 0 |
|---|---|---|---|---|---|---|
| 0 | 0 | size | destination<br>mode  register | | source<br>mode  register | |

**MOVEQ** #3,D2  0111010000000011  7403
which is coded as

| 15 | | | 11 | 9 | 8 | 7 | 0 |
|---|---|---|---|---|---|---|---|
| 0 | 1 | 1 | 1 | register | 0 | data | |

**BRA L1**        01100000xxxxxxxx 60xx xx is address offset which is coded as

| 15 | | | | | | | | 8 | 7 | | 0 |
|---|---|---|---|---|---|---|---|---|---|---|---|
| 0 | 1 | 1 | 0 | 0 | 0 | 0 | 0 | | 8-bit displacement | | |

Notice that the 68000 has the more regular decoding structure in so far as the opcode bits are distinct from the operand addressing mode bits. Since the 8085 does not have so many addressing modes it does not need to make the distinction so clearly.

## 11.7   Use of addressing modes

The reader may now be wondering why a computer designer would provide such a wide range of addressing modes. To understand this it is necessary to consider the types of data structure that programmers use and how they are accessed since it is this which necessitates the range of addressing modes. There are two basic types of operand which occur in operations; constants and variables. As the name implies constants are values which remain constant during the execution of a program. They are also known as literals, and examples are the number 2 and the character string abc. Operands which change during execution are called variables, and instances of these are given symbolic names, called identifiers, to differentiate between them. Thus the identifier $A$ could represent a variable whose value could change from, say, 0 to 5 and then 8 during the execution of a program.

### 11.7.1   Table

Constants and variables can be organized into structures where each item in the structure bears a relationship to other items in the structure. The simplest type of structure is a **table** and the simplest form of table is a sequence of items of the same type, for example, integers. Each item may be accessed by an index denoting its position in the table, assuming the start of the table is known. A table is normally stored in the memory of a computer in consecutive memory locations. The table is characterized by a start address, sometimes called the base address, and each item is characterized by an index or offset from this start address. The address of any item may then be obtained by adding its index in the table to the starting address of the table in memory, assuming that each data item occupies a single memory location. This arithmetic is exactly that which is performed in the case of indexed addressing. In recent 16- and 32-bit microcomputers indexed addressing modes are present

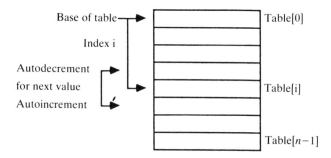

**Fig. 11.20** Table structure and accessing.

which take into account the number of words occupied by each data item, since characters typically take 8 bits each whilst integers take 16 or 32 bits. Frequently, a table has to be searched to see if it contains a particular item. The simplest way of performing this search is linearly, that is, item by item starting at the first entry. This type of access uses autoincrement or auto-decrement addressing depending on whether the table is stored in ascending or descending address order in memory. Initially the start address is placed in a register and this value used to access the first data item. If this is not the required data item the contents of the next address have to be examined and so on. This address incrementing is exactly what autoincrement addressing performs. Two-dimensional table structures, **matrices**, are very common in mathematical applications and these are normally stored in memory either by row or by column. Accessing an individual item now requires two indices, one for the row and one for the column, and the address calculation is slightly more complex although indexed addressing is still required. Since this structure is so common in many applications, some processors have extra addressing modes to simplify the address calculation. This is the purpose of the register indirect with index addressing on the 68000.

So far we have only considered the table as having a start address and each item having an index into the table. The table also has length and this is some-times used to check that access to the table is within the limits of the table size. Each address calculation then additionally has to check the calculated address against a predefined constant. Some more recent architectures allow this checking to be performed as a separate instruction.

Fig. 11.20 shows some methods of accessing a table and matrix in memory.

## 11.7.2 List

Another method of storing a set of items is in a data structure called a **list**. In this structure the separate items are stored anywhere in memory and each

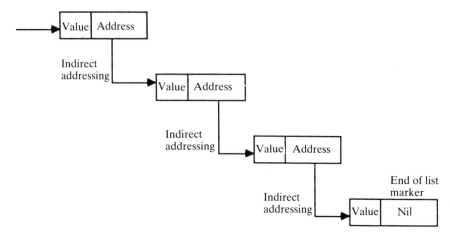

**Fig. 11.21**   List structure and list accessing.

item includes a pointer which contains the address of the next item in the list (see Fig. 11.21). The start of the list is pointed to by a standard header and the end of the list is signified by a special marker called nil. The main difference between a list and a one-dimensional array is in the method of access. Whereas in an array access to any item takes the same amount of time, in a list access to any item is sequential through the header and thus the access time depends on the position of the item in the list. The standard operations allowed on a list rely on being able to manipulate the address pointers and hence on indirect addressing.

## 11.7.3   Stack

A **stack** is a form of data structure which has the property that the last item written is the first item to be read, that is, the stack acts as a last-in first-out (LIFO) structure. It may be thought of as a stack of plates where the only access is to the top plate. The operations allowed include adding another plate to the stack (pushing), taking the top plate from the stack (popping) and testing whether there are any plates on the stack. A stack may be represented by a contiguous block of memory with a pointer indicating the current top of the stack (see Fig. 11.22). The operation of pushing a value on to the stack then involves moving the stack pointer upwards and then writing the value to the top of the stack using indirect addressing via the stack pointer. Similarly, the operation of popping a value off the stack involves reading the top value indirectly via the stack pointer and then moving the stack pointer value downwards. Notice that the operations of adjusting the value of the pointer

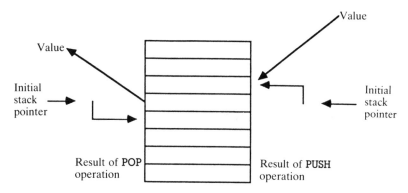

**Fig. 11.22**    Stack and stack operations.

occur before the stack access in one operation and after the access in the other operation. The operations of push and pop may be accomplished by the use of the autoincrement and autodecrement addressing modes. Note that for the way in which the autoincrement and autodecrement addressing modes were defined previously either the stack has to work downwards in memory, that is pushing a value is performed using the autodecrement mode, or the stack pointer points to the next position to insert on the stack rather than the top of stack if pushing is performed using autoincrement mode. The definitions of autoincrement and autodecrement mode given above are those most frequently used but some computers define the pointer arithmetic to take place in the opposite order to that give here. The 8085 provides special instructions to put values on and off the stack, called **PUSH** and **POP**, respectively. The 68000 does not have special instructions but the user may use autoincrement and autodecrement addressing modes to access a stack.

The stack provides an orderly method for storing procedure or subroutine return addresses as described before which is another reason why autoincrement and autodecrement modes are common on computers.

## 11.7.4    Queue

A **queue** is a similar data structure to a stack except that access for reading and writing is to opposite ends of the data structure, as shown in Fig. 11.23. Thus a queue corresponds to the normal informal idea of a queue. A queue is represented by a contiguous block of memory with two pointers, one pointing to the head of the queue and the other to the tail. Access to the head and tail of the queue uses the same addressing mode, either autoincrement or autodecrement depending on the direction in which the queue grows. As data are added and removed from the queue the data structure moves through memory

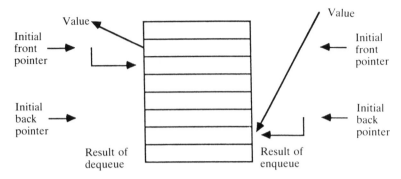

**Fig. 11.23**   Queue and queue operations.

since both types of access move the pointers in the same direction. This is obviously inconvenient, so a queue is normally mapped on to a fixed block of memory and the pointers wrap around when they reach the block boundary. Checking is required to detect the pointers reaching the boundary and also for the conditions of underflow, trying to read a value when the structure is empty, and overflow, trying to write a value when the structure is full.

Both a stack and a queue may also be implemented as linked lists as described earlier, in which case they require indirect addressing to access the structures.

These are just some of the data structures provided in high-level programming languages and used by assembly-code programmers. As can be seen from the foregoing discussion, the implementation of these structures requires a number of different addressing schemes and this is why most modern processors support a wide range of addressing modes. As has been shown the only addressing modes which are strictly necessary are the direct and indirect modes; the other modes can be simulated by just these two modes and more instructions. However, the provision of the extra addressing modes makes for more efficient implementation, both in terms of memory and execution time.

## 11.8   Examples to illustrate assembly code and addressing modes

So far, in this chapter, the types of instruction which are provided to the programmer at the machine-code level and the range of addressing modes that more recent processors such as the 68000 provide have been discussed. In this section we give a small program in 8085 and 68000 assembly code and the equivalent machine code to show what such programs look like and to show how some of the instructions and addressing modes are used. The examples are extensively documented so that they should be understandable, even though the instructions have not been explained in great detail above. Readers who experience any difficulty or require more information should consult one of the relevant texts mentioned in the Further Reading section.

The code below contains some assembler directives, such as org and end. These directives provide information to the program which translates the assembly code into machine code. More details are given in the next chapter.

## 11.8.1  Program to count the number of occurrences

These programs count the number of times a given item, lookup, occurs in the table and leaves the result in a register. The algorithm (method) used is simply to scan the table from top to bottom, incrementing the count whenever the desired item is found. The code is not the shortest or most efficient which could be written for this problem but it is simple to understand.

*8085 code*

| addr code (hex) (hex) | | label | opcode | operands | comments |
|---|---|---|---|---|---|
| | | | org | 0 | code to be loaded into memory from location 0 |
| | | lookup | equ | 2 | symbol lookup is equated with the value 2 |
| 000 | 05 | length | db | 5 | length of table in location length |
| 001 | 0703090106 | table | db | 7,3,9,1,6 | table contains 7,3,9,1 and 6 |
| 006 | 210000 | start: | lxi | h,length | address of length loaded into register pair hl. Start represents the address of this instruction |
| 009 | 46 | | mov | b,m | move the contents of length into register b |
| 00A | 3E02 | | mvi | a,lookup | put the value searched for into the accumulator |
| 00C | 0E00 | | mvi | c,0 | initialize register c used to store item count |
| 00E | 210100 | | lxi | h,table | load the base address of the table into the hl register pair |
| 011 | BE | loop: | cmp | m | compare next element in table with the value searched for which is in the accumulator |
| 012 | C21600 | | jnz | eol | if they are not the same go to the statement labelled eol |
| 015 | 0C | | inr | c | otherwise increment the count |
| 016 | 23 | eol: | inx | h | increment the contents of hl to point to the next table entry |
| 017 | 05 | | dcr | b | b contains the number of items left to scan in the table so decrement it |
| 018 | C21100 | | jnz | loop | if still more to compare in the table (b > 0) then go back to the statement labelled loop |
| 021 | 76 | | hlt | | otherwise halt the processor |
| | | | end | start | end of program and execution starts at statement labelled start. |

*68000 code*

| addr code<br>(hex) (hex) | label | opcode | operands | comments |
|---|---|---|---|---|
| | | . = 0 | | code and data start at location 0 |
| | lookup | equ | 2 | symbol lookup equated to 2 |
| 0000 05 | length | dc.b | 5 | length contains 5, the length of the table |
| 0001 0703090106 | table | dc.b | 7,3,9,1,6 | table contains 7,3,9,1 and 6 |
| 0006 207C<br>0000<br>0001 | start | move.1 | #table,a0 | put the address of the base of the table into address register a0 |
| 000C 1239<br>0000<br>0000 | | move.b | length,d1 | put the length of the table into data register d1 |
| 0012 303C<br>0000 | | move.w | #0,d0 | initialize the register holding the count, d0, to zero. |
| 0016 0C18<br>0002 | loop | cmp.b | #lookup,(a0)+ | compare the next entry in the table with the value required |
| 001A 6602 | | bne | eol | if not the same go to the statement labelled eol |
| 001C 5240 | | addq | #1,d0 | otherwise increment the count by 1 |
| 001E 5341 | eol | subq | #1,d1 | d1 contains the count of no. of items to search so decrement it |
| 0020 66F4 | | bne | loop | if still more of table to search go back to the statement labelled loop |
| 0022 4E72 | | stop | | halt execution |
| | | end | start | end of program and execution is to start at the statement labelled start. |

## 11.8.2 Program to add two single-digit integers

These programs illustrate the conversion required between internal and external representations when values are input and output and some numerical manipulation has to be performed on the values. The 68000 program could be optimized but a simple version is given here. The 68000 code also illustrates the use of subroutines.

*8085 code*

| addr code<br>(hex) (hex) | label | opcode | operands | comments |
|---|---|---|---|---|
| | | org | 0 | code and data start at zero |
| 0000 310020 | start: | lxi | sp,2000H | initialize stack pointer to 2000 hex |
| 0003 DB0A | | in | 10 | input first value to accumulator |
| 0005 DE30 | | sbi | 48 | convert from char code to int code |
| 0007 47 | | mov | b,a | save value in register b |

| | | | | | |
|---|---|---|---|---|---|
| 0008 | DB0A | | in | 10 | input second value into accumulator |
| 000A | DE30 | | sbi | 48 | convert to integer code |
| 000C | 80 | | add | b | add the two values input |
| 000D | FE0A | | cpi | 10 | compare result with 10 |
| 000F | F21700 | | jp | mto | if greater go to mto |
| 0012 | C630 | | adi | 48 | convert to char code |
| 0014 | D30B | | out | 11 | output the result |
| 0016 | 76 | | hlt | | and finish execution |
| 0017 | DE0A | mto: | sbi | 10 | convert to single last digit |
| 0019 | 4F | | mov | c,a | save in register c |
| 001A | 3E31 | | mvi | a,49 | char code for first digit (1) to accumulator |
| 001C | D30B | | out | 11 | output it |
| 001E | 79 | | mov | a,c | restore second digit to accumulator |
| 001F | C630 | | adi | 48 | convert to char code |
| 0021 | D30B | | out | 11 | output digit |
| 0023 | 76 | | hlt | | halt execution |
| | | | end | start | end of program and start execution at statement labelled start |

## 68000 code

| addr code (hex) (hex) | | label | opcode | operands | comments |
|---|---|---|---|---|---|
| | | | . = 0 | | code and data start at 0 |
| 0000 | 2E7C 0000 0BB8 | start | move.l | #3000,a7 | initialize stack pointer to 3000 |
| 0006 | 7000 | | moveq | #0,d0 | clear d0 |
| 0008 | 7200 | | moveq | #0,d1 | clear d1 |
| 000A | 6128 | | jsr | input | jump to subroutine to get first int into d0 |
| 000C | 1200 | | move.b | d0,d1 | save in d1 |
| 000E | 611E | | jsr | input | jump to subroutine to get second int into d0 |
| 0010 | D041 | | add.w | d1,d0 | add two integers together |
| 0012 | B07C 000A | | cmp.w | #10,d0 | is total greater than 10? |
| 0016 | 6A04 | | bpl | mto | if so go to mto |
| 0018 | 6120 | | jsr | output | otherwise output total |
| 001A | 4E72 | | stop | | and stop execution |
| 001C | 90BC 0000 000A | mto | sub.l | #10,d0 | get lowest digit of total |
| 0022 | 2200 | | move.l | d0,d1 | and save in d1 |
| 0024 | 7001 | | moveq | #1,d0 | first digit to output |
| 0026 | 6112 | | jsr | output | and output it |
| 0028 | 2001 | | move.l | d1,d0 | restore second digit to d0 |
| 002A | 610E | | jsr | output | and output it |
| 002C | 4E72 | | stop | | stop execution |
| 002E | 4E4F | input | trap | #15 | software interrupt |
| 0030 | 0010 | | dc.w | $10 | parameter meaning input |
| 0032 | 90BC | | sub.l | #48,d0 | convert char to int code |

|        |       |        |        |         |                          |
|--------|-------|--------|--------|---------|--------------------------|
| 0000   |       |        |        |         |                          |
| 0030   |       |        |        |         |                          |
| 0038   | 4E75  |        | rts    |         | return from subroutine   |
| 003A   | D0BC  | output | add.l  | #48,d0  | convert from int to char code |
| 0000   |       |        |        |         |                          |
| 0030   |       |        |        |         |                          |
| 0040   | 4E4F  |        | trap   | #15     | software interrupt       |
| 0042   | 0011  |        | dc.w   | $11     | parameter meaning output |
| 0044   | 4E75  |        | rts    |         | return from subroutine   |
|        |       |        | end    | start   | end of program and start execution from statement labelled start |

Note that this program uses a software interrupt instruction, **TRAP**, to perform input and output. The software interrupt is a call to the operating system, see Chapter 12, to perform the input or output as specified by the following word of memory.

## 11.8.3 Program to search a table for a given input value

The algorithm used here is a sequential search through the table, comparing each value with the given input value. If a match is found then the code for 'found' is output but if all the table is searched and no match is found then the code for 'notfound' is output.

### 8085 code

| addr (hex) | code (hex) | label | opcode | operands | comments |
|------------|------------|-------|--------|----------|----------|
|        |            |           | org | 0 | code to be loaded into memory from location 0 |
|        |            | found:    | equ | 49 | symbol found represents char code for 1 |
|        |            | notfound: | equ | 48 | symbol notfound represents char code for 0 |
| 0000   | 05         | length:   | db  | 5 | location called length contains length of table |
| 0001   | 0703090106 | table:    | db  | 7,3,9,1,6 | table represents the address of the start of the table which contains the data items shown |
| 0006   | 210000     | start:    | lxi | h,length | start represents the address of the first instruction in the program. This instruction loads registers h and l with the address of the location length |
| 0009   | 46         |           | mov | b,m | move the contents of length into register b |
| 000A   | DB0A       |           | in  | 10 | input the required match value from the peripheral attached to port 10 into the accumulator |
| 000C   | DE30       |           | sbi | 48 | convert to integer code |

| 000E | 210100 |        | lxi | h,table    | load the start address of table into registers h and l |
|------|--------|--------|-----|------------|--------------------------------------------------------|
| 0011 | BE     | loop:  | cmp | m          | compare the first value in the table with the value in the accumulator |
| 0012 | CA1D00 |        | jz  | match      | if they match go to the instruction labelled match |
| 0015 | 23     |        | inx | h          | add 1 to the contents of h and l so that it now contains the address of the next item in the table |
| 0016 | 05     |        | dcr | b          | subtract 1 from (decrement) the count of the number of items in the table left to be searched |
| 0017 | C20F00 |        | jnz | loop       | if there are still some left (jump if be non-zero) go back to check the next one |
| 001A | 3E00   |        | mvi | a,notfound | put the code for notfound into the accumulator |
| 001C | D310   |        | out | 12         | output from the accumulator to the peripheral attached to port 12 |
| 001E | 76     |        | hlt |            | halt execution |
| 001F | 3E01   | match: | mvi | a,found    | put the code for found into the accumulator |
| 0021 | D310   |        | out | 12         | and output to the peripheral attached to port 12 |
| 0023 | 76     |        | hlt |            | halt execution |
|      |        |        | end | start      | denotes end of the program text and the address from which execution is to start. |

## 68000 code

| addr (hex) | code (hex) | label    | opcode | operands    | comments |
|------------|------------|----------|--------|-------------|----------|
|            |            |          | . = 0  |             | code to be loaded into memory from location 0 |
|            |            | found    | equ    | 49          | symbol found represents char code for 1 |
|            |            | notfound | equ    | 48          | symbol notfound represents char code for 0 |
| 0000       | 05         | length   | dc.b   | 5           | location called length contains the byte constant 5 |
| 0001       | 0703090106 | table    | dc.b   | 7,3,9,1,6   | table is the starting address of the table containing the byte data items shown |
| 0006       | 307C 0001  | start    | move.w | #table,a0   | start is the address of the first instruction of the code which puts the value of table – the start address of the table – into the address register a0 |
| 000A       | 7000       |          | moveq  | #0,d0       | clear register d0 |
| 000C       | 7200       |          | moveq  | #0,d1       | clear register d1 |
| 000E       | 1239 0000 0000 |      | move.b | length,d1   | the length of the table (a byte) – stored in length – is moved into data register 0 |
| 0014       | 4E4F       |          | trap   | #15         | software interrupt |
| 0016       | 0010       |          | dc.w   | $10         | parameter meaning input |

| 0018 | 903C | | sub.b | #48.d0 | convert to integer code |
| | 0030 | | | | |
| 001C | B018 | loop | cmp.b | (a0)+,d0 | compare the input value in d1 with the current table value. Autoincrement mode used with a0 containing an address in the table |
| 001E | 670E | | beq | match | if a match found – values equal – go to the instruction labelled match |
| 0020 | 5341 | | subq.b | #1,d1 | subtract 1 from the count of items left to search in the table |
| 0022 | 66F8 | | bne | loop | and jump to loop if still some left – loop non-zero |
| 0024 | 103C | | mov.b | #notfound,d0 | put notfound code into d0 |
| | 0030 | | | | |
| 0028 | 4E4F | | trap | #15 | software interrupt |
| 002a | 0011 | | dc.w | $11 | parameter meaning output |
| 002C | 4E72 | | stop | | stop execution |
| 002E | 103C | match | move.b | #found,d0 | move code for found to d0 |
| | 0031 | | | | |
| 0032 | 4E4F | | trap | #15 | software interrupt |
| 0034 | 0011 | | dc.w | $11 | parameter meaning output |
| 0036 | 4E72 | | stop | | stop execution |
| | | | end | start | end marks end of the program text and start is the address where instruction execution is to start. |

Comparing the two programs it is obvious that the 68000 is shorter and if the details of the programs are compared it will be seen that the 68000 code is more straightforward. This is not surprising given that the 68000 is much newer and can process 16- and 32-bit operands, whereas the 8085 is basically an 8-bit processor with a few 16-bit instructions. Also the 8085 suffers from only having a single accumulator and limited addressing modes, whereas the 68000 can use any of its registers as accumulators and has a wide range of addressing modes. The 8085 was expected to be programmed in assembly code and used as a simple controller whereas the 68000 is expected to be programmed in a higher-level language and is a general-purpose computer.

## 11.9  Summary

An instruction consists of an operation code and, usually, one or more operands. The operands define addresses of memory locations where the data manipulated by the operation code is to be found and where the results are to be placed. Both the operation code and the operands are stored in memory as sets of bits and the operands are frequently represented by two separate fields called the mode and register. The mode field specifies how the register field is to be used.

Most processors, including the 8085 and the 68000, have a number of different classes of instructions – data movement, arithmetical and logical, bit manipulation, program control, input–output and miscellaneous. The two basic forms of addressing mode are direct addressing and indirect addressing. Indirect addressing specifies the address of a location containing the required address. Many other addressing modes are possible and the Motorola 68000 contains a large number. These modes are included mainly in order to make the translation of data structures and their accessing operations in high-level languages easier and execution of the resulting programs faster.

## Exercises

11.1  How many general-purpose registers are available to the programmer and what length are they

(a) on the 8085,
(b) on the 68000?

11.2  In each of the following cases state which addressing mode would be used and give example code:

(a) to write a value to a given position in a table,
(b) to push a value on to the stack,
(c) to add an item to a queue,
(d) to access an item in a list.

11.3  Write sequences of instructions for the following English descriptions:

(a) 8085
  (i)   Add the contents of register H to the accumulator,
  (ii)  Add the contents of register B to the contents of register C,
  (iii) Put the contents of location 2000 into the accumulator,
  (iv)  Put the contents of word 5 of the table whose address is in registers HL into the accumulator,
  (v)   Put a zero in register B if the accumulator contains 6, otherwise put a 1 in register B,
  (vi)  Jump to the subroutine labelled **SUB** if register B contains 2. The subroutine should put zero in register B and return.

(b) 68000
  (i)   Add the longword contents of register $D1$ to register $D0$,
  (ii)  ADD the contents of word 2000 to register $D0$,
  (iii) Add the contents of byte 2000 to register $D0$,
  (iv)  Put a zero in register $D1$ if $D0$ contains 3; put 1 in $D1$ otherwise.
  (v)   Jump to the subroutine labelled **SUB** if register $D1$ contains 6. The subroutine should set the contents of $D1$ to zero and return.

11.4   Write sets of instructions for the 8085 to imitate the action of the bit manipulation operations on the 68000 given in Fig. 11.7.

11.5   Write a program for the 8085 which puts 0 into the accumulator if register B contains an even value and 1 otherwise. Repeat the program for the 68000 assuming that the value is in $D1$ and that the result is to be placed in $D0$.

11.6   Write a program to sort a table of integers, each occupying a word of memory, into ascending order,

(a) in 8085 assembly language,
(b) in 68000 assembly language.

Compare and contrast the two programs.

(Hint: one algorithm to sort a table of items is to search for the smallest item and interchange that item with the first one in the table. This process is repeated, each time omitting the new item placed at the front of the table, until the complete table is searched.)

# 12

# Introduction to system software

## 12.1  Introduction

In order for a user to make efficient use of a computer a set of tools is required. These tools include design tools, implementation tools and execution tools. In this chapter we are concerned with the implementation and execution tools which a user might expect to be available on most computer systems. In order for a user to write a program for a computer a language is needed in which to express the algorithm. Since the computer will normally only recognize its own machine code the user would appear to have to express the algorithm in machine code. However, this is not very convenient for the user; it would be preferable to write programs in a higher-level language. In order to do this the program has to be translated into a form the computer understands before execution can commence. The two options here are translation or interpretation, as was explained in Chapter 1. Hence some of the possible tool requirements are a **compiler**, **assembler** and **interpreter**. Having written a program the user wishes to test and run it. This involves a number of stages such as translating the program into machine code, loading the machine code into memory and starting it at a particular memory location. Whilst this could be done by hand it is not very efficient to do so and most computers provide the user with an **operating system** which, among other tasks, organizes the work flow.

It is this collection of software tools which is known collectively as system software.

## 12.2  Assembly language and assemblers

As discussed in the previous two chapters, an instruction at the machine-code level consists of a bit pattern, some of the bits representing an operation code and some representing operands or addresses of operands. It is not convenient for the programmer to program at this level because it is easy to make mistakes and there is little correspondence between the bit patterns and the objects and operations of the application being programmed. Higher-level languages were invented so that the programmer's job was easier and so that there was a closer correspondence between the objects and operations of the language and of the application. There is therefore a hierarchy of higher-level languages, from those close to machine code to those close to a particular type of application. At the level of language immediately above machine code is assembly language. This language is very close to machine code, the main difference being the use of symbols instead of bit patterns. In fact an assembly language is one in which there is normally a small ratio, typically 1:1, between statements in the language and the equivalent machine-code instructions. We have already seen the use of this type of language earlier in the book, for instance, the use of **ADD** to specify the add instruction and B to represent an operand rather than bit patterns. These symbols are usually called **mnemonics** as they are an aid to memory. The use of a higher-level language means that the program cannot be directly executed by the computer since it only 'understands' bit patterns – the machine code defined by the designer. Hence the program in the higher-level language has to be translated into the equivalent machine code before it can be executed. This translation can be performed by a computer, given a suitable algorithm coded as a machine-code program to do the translation. The program which translates from assembly code to machine code is called an **assembler**. Since different computers have different machine codes, each computer has its own assembly language which requires its own assembler. The assembler is relatively simple to produce since assembly code is so close to machine code. The major operation is one of changing mnemonics to the bit patterns they represent.

The advantage of using an assembler as opposed to a higher-level language is that the programmer has available the complete range of machine facilities, whereas in a higher-level language some features of the machine are often not accessible. However, it requires an experienced programmer to make efficient use of assembly code and it is relatively easy to make mistakes. The chances of producing an error-free program decrease rapidly with the length and complexity of the program; assembly code is therefore not suitable for producing large programs, especially with inexperienced programmers. Typical figures for debugged code production are 10 instructions per programmer per day for assembly code in a large-scale project.

An assembly code instruction typically consists of an opcode and zero, one or more operands, just like machine code, except that each of these quantities is represented by a symbol rather than a bit pattern. The symbols representing the opcodes are usually defined by the manufacturer, whilst those used for the operands are defined by the programmer. The fields of the instruction are delimited by special characters which are specific to the particular assembly code, but a typical assembler might use the following scheme:

label:opcode operand1,operand2 ;comments.

It is usual to allow the operand fields to be expressions rather than simply symbols but these expressions are often limited in the operators they allow, for example only allowing the use of plus, minus and some logical operators.

All assemblers allow a label to be attached to an instruction or data item in the language so that reference may be made to that item symbolically from elsewhere in the program. The label represents the address of the instruction or data item to which it is attached. One common use of a label on a statement is to enable a jump or call instruction elsewhere in the program to specify the address of that statement as the operand of the jump. But the label and the comment field are removed in the process of translation to machine code; they generate no machine code.

All assemblers allow the programmer to intersperse **assembly directives** or pseudo-operations with the code to be translated. These assembly directives allow the programmer to give information and to control the operation of the assembler. Two of the most common pseudo-operations are those to tell the assembler the starting address of the assembled code (or subsection of code) and those that tell the assembler that the end of the code to be assembled has been reached. Neither of these directives generates any code; they just control the operation of the assembler. Other types of directives do generate code. A typical example is the 'data' directive which allows the user to load a vector of constants or expressions into the code. This directive would normally be labelled so that its associated data can be referred to symbolically by instructions in the program. Normally, the user can also associate a symbol

| Meaning | 8085 | 68000 |
|---|---|---|
| Define position of code or data | ORG addr | |
| Define constant - byte<br>word<br>longword | DB val,val...<br>DW val,val... | DC.B val,val...<br>DC.W val,val...<br>DC.L val,val... |
| Define storage block | DS size | DS.B size<br>DS.W size<br>DS.L size |
| Equate symbol with constant | lab: EQU constant | lab: EQU constant<br>expression |
| End of assembly code | END | END |

**Fig. 12.1**  Some assembler directives for typical 8085 and 68000 assemblers.

with a value and more comprehensive assemblers even allow macro facilities as described below. Some examples of directives available on 8085 and 68000 assemblers are shown in Fig. 12.1.

It is normal for the translation of the assembly code to be performed on the computer for which the code is destined. However, this is not necessary; it is possible to perform the translation on another computer and then transfer the code to the target computer. This is known as **cross-assembly** and is frequently used when the target machine is an embedded microprocessor which does not have the requisite resouorces, for example discs and a printer, for performing the assembly process.

As stated above, an assembler is a relatively simple translator to write since the input language is very similar in structure to the output language. The main problem to be overcome in the translation is known as the **forward referencing problem**. Consider the following fragment of 68000 code:

```
        jmp    loop
         . . .
         . . .
loop:   add    #1,d0
```

When the assembler comes to the jmp statement on a sequential pass through the code it cannot translate the statement into machine code since it has not encountered the statement labelled loop and thus it does not know what address to generate for the jump. The solution to this problem is for the assembler to make two passes through the assembly code. On the first pass the assembler collects the definitions of the user-defined symbols and on the second pass the translation is performed. An outline of the assembly process is given in Fig. 12.2. The assembly location counter keeps track of the position of the code in memory after it has been translated. Thus on the first pass when a label is discovered its value, which is the present contents of the assembly location counter, is stored in the user symbol table together with the symbol name. On the second pass the assembler uses the **permanent symbol table** which contains the standard assembler mnemonics for the operation codes together with the machine code template for that instruction, and the **user symbol table** which contains the user defined symbols and their values to translate the assembly code into the corresponding machine code. There are a few assemblers, called one pass assemblers, which only scan the input once and thus cannot fill in the forward references. These assemblers output a table containing the position of the forward references and the values to be filled in. It is a task for the loader in these systems to fill in the forward references when the program is loaded to be run.

## 12.3   Macros

A macro facility gives the user a method of performing simple text substitution at translation time. For example, if the programmer wishes to insert a section of code in his program in several different places the macro facility allows him to define this code once, in the form of a macro, and to insert calls to the macro at appropriate points in the code. An example is given in Fig. 12.3. At translation time the section of code defined in the macro will be substituted for the macro calls, normally as a preliminary to the main translation. Note that in this example the parameters in the macro definition start with the special symbol ' so that it is easy to pick them out in the macro body at macro substitution time. The macro facility appears to give the programmer a similar facility to subroutines – for example, both can have parameters – but there is a crucial difference: in most languages macro substitution occurs at translation time, whereas subroutines are called at execution time. Macro facilities are often found in assemblers but their use is not confined to these systems. There are stand-alone systems called macro processors which allow macro processing with any input language. Macro-processing systems offer many sophisticated features which allow complicated text substitution but they are outside the scope of this book. The interested reader is referred to the book by Brown given in the section on Further Reading.

## 12.4   Link editors

Another common facility of many translators allows the programmer to specify the program as a set of modules or segments. These segments are translated separately and a further program, usually called a linker or link editor, is used to link the separately assembled segments into a single program. This linking facility allows the user to set up a library of standard segments and to use these in appropriate programs. For example, a library of input–output routines or a library of mathematical procedures could be set up. In some systems the user is allowed to write different segments in different languages and to combine these to form a single program as shown in Fig. 12.4. This mixed language facility can be useful if an application requires features of several different languages to solve different parts of the problem. It is also useful for libraries since they can be written in the most appropriate language but can be used from any other language; the library does not have to be implemented in different languages. The reason why this special program, the link editor, is necessary is that inter-segment references can only be resolved when all the segments are combined; the translator only

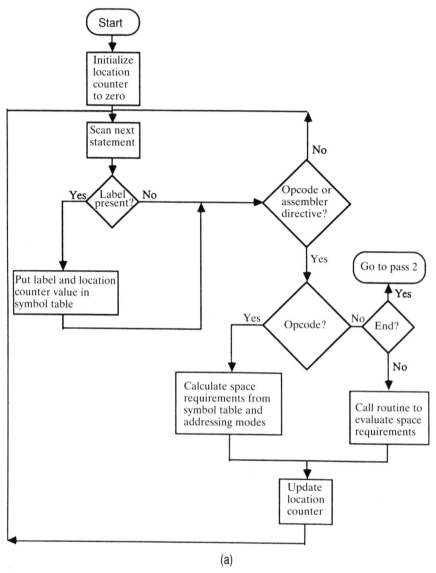

(a)

**Fig. 12.2** (a) Pass 1 of an assembler.

knows about a single segment at a time and cannot know the address of symbols defined in another segment. This leads to another problem. Since the assembler only knows about a single segment at a time then it cannot know where each segment will be loaded since this will depend on the length of the preceding segments as well as the start address of the code. This leads to the

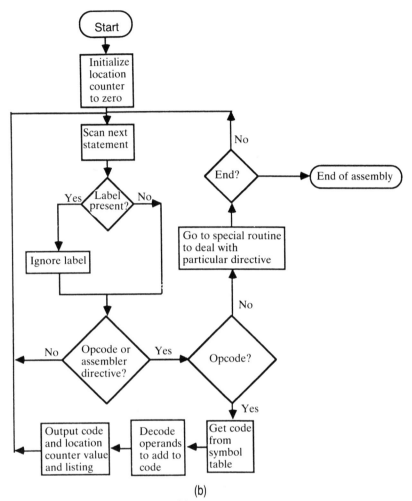

(b)

**Fig. 12.2**    (b) Pass 2 of an assembler.

requirement that segments should be written in **relocatable code**, that is code which is position-independent or in which addresses can be modified if the code has to be moved. Typically, all segments are assembled assuming they are to be loaded into location 0 onwards in memory and the relocation necessary to make the separate segments of code contiguous is performed by the link editor. The provision of relative, as well as absolute, addressing in the instruction set facilitates this relocation. A further advantage of using a link editor is that, during testing, only those segments with errors have to be reassembled, not all segments, which reduces the program development time by a significant amount in large programs.

(a) MACRO SWAP 'X,'Y,'Z
      MOV 'Z,'X
      MOV 'X,'Y
      MOV 'Y,'Z
   ENDMACRO

(b) initial code                             code with macros expanded

    ......                                                ......

    ......                                                ......

    ......                                                ......

   SWAP B,C,A   ;exchange B and C                  MOV A,B
    ......                                                MOV B,C
    ......                                                MOV C,A

    ......                                                ......

    ......                                                ......

   SWAP D,E,B   ;exchange D and E                  MOV B,D
    ......                                                MOV D,E
    ......                                                MOV E,B

    ......                                                ......

**Fig. 12.3** (a) An example macro of code to swap the contents of two registers, using a third as workspace; (b) A typical example of the use of the macro given for the 8085.

The algorithm used to perform the linking is very similar to that used by the assembler, that is it is a two-pass system where the definitions are collected into a symbol table on the first pass and the second pass performs the linking. To facilitate the linking process extra statements are added to the program, or are implied by the language notation, to specify the symbols which are defined in the current segment but may be referred to in other segments and

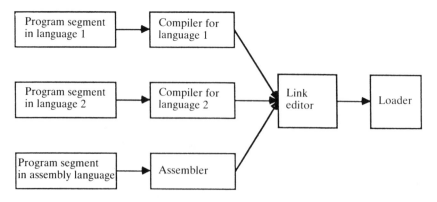

**Fig. 12.4** Combining segments from different languages using a link editor.

to specify the symbols used in the current segment but defined elsewhere. Problems arise as to what combinations of types of quantities are allowed in expressions and what actions need to be taken if the expression has to be relocated. For example, an expression including both an externally defined symbol and a local label will have to be modified if either the current segment or the segment in which the external symbol is defined is moved. This involves keeping tables of which locations have to be updated by what values if the segments are moved.

## 12.5  Loading

Most link editors send their output to a file. To run the program the output from the link editor, called an object file, has to be loaded into memory first. This task is performed by a loader. The loader's task is usually quite simple; it has to take the code produced by the link editor and load it into memory at a given specified position. However, the position in memory at which the code is to be executed is frequently only known at load time and not at link time and hence it is the loader which has to perform the relocation task. Thus the linker must output a table containing information on how the code has to be modified on relocation as well as the linked code. Some link editors also perform the loading task, in which case they are known as **linking loaders**.

## 12.6  High-level languages

As discussed previously the level of the language to be used in developing software depends on a number of factors. Basically the higher the level of language which can be used to develop software the cheaper the development costs in terms of programmer's time and program maintainability. The reason why programmers use lower-level languages is because the facilities they need are not available in a high-level language or because the high-level language implementation is too slow or uses too much memory for their requirements. High-level languages are more application-oriented and necessarily further away from the machine architecture and therefore more portable than lower-level languages. Since much of today's programming is concerned with reimplementing a given application on a different computer, portability has a high priority in present-day applications.

Conventional high-level languages provide the user with a set of control and data structures. The control structures typically include assignment, conditional and repetition statements. An assignment statement allows the user to assign the value of an expression to a variable. In Pascal, a common high-level language, an assignment statement would look like:

TOTAL:=ITEM1 + ITEM2;

where **TOTAL** is an identifier representing a variable which will hold the sum of the contents of the variables identified by **ITEM1** and **ITEM2**. The symbol := is the assignment symbol, and the expression on the right-hand side of this can be formed from variables, constants and arithmetic operators. A typical conditional statement is the **IF** statement which specifies the actions to be taken depending on whether a specified condition is true or false. An example in Pascal is:

**IF X < 2 THEN X:=X − Y ELSE X:=X + Y;**

On execution the conditional expression is evaluated, in this case the value of the variable named **X** is compared with the constant 2, and one of two actions taken. If the condition is true then the statement following the **THEN** is executed, otherwise the statement following the **ELSE** is executed. An example of a repetitive statement is the **WHILE** statement which specifies that the following statement is to be executed while the condition is true. An example of a **WHILE** construct in Pascal is given below:

**WHILE X < Y DO X:=X + Z;**

On execution the condition is tested and, if it is true, the statement following it is executed and control returns to the condition which is re-evaluated and so on. If the condition is false, control passes to the next instruction after the **WHILE** construct. High-level languages usually have several different forms of conditional and repetitive statements.

Just as at the machine-code level, high-level languages have mechanisms for procedure call and return. These mechanisms are more elaborate than those at the machine level, allowing the programmer to specify parameters to the call. These parameters allow the programmer to tailor a particular call by giving values which are specific to the particular call, and hence make it possible to write more general procedures.

High-level languages provide the programmer with a range of data structures. Some of the data structures which are provided in high-level languages have been described in Chapter 11. Pascal, for example, supports all the data structures described there and some others. For example,

**VAR X,Y:INTEGER;**

in Pascal declares two variables named $x$ and $y$ which hold values of type integer. Thus **X** and **Y** refer to memory locations which are large enough to store an integer and

Z:ARRAY[1 .. 20]OF CHAR;

declares a table or vector of characters of size 20 elements called **Z**. Individual items in the table are referred to by subscripting **Z**; for example **Z[3]** refers to the third item in the table, and **Z[3]** := 'C' assigns the character **C** to the third position in the table.

The structures supported in any language depend on the use to which the language is intended to be put, and hence different languages will support different data structures.

The question of which high-level language to use to develop software for a given computer is a difficult question to answer since it depends on a large number of factors. The reason why there are so many different high-level languages in existence is that different applications require different features in a language; there is really no general-purpose high-level language which is suitable for all applications. Also, with more experience, language designers have produced languages which are more efficient to execute and which contain more application-oriented features. However, languages which were designed several decades ago are still in very frequent use simply because of the amount of investment made in programs in those languages. One classification of high-level languages is to divide them into scientific, commercial data processing and non-numeric classes. Perhaps the best examples in the first category are FORTRAN and ALGOL 68. FORTRAN was first designed in the 1950s but has been modified a number of times since then. The main data structures required in numerical work are the vector and matrix and these are the only data structures provided in the language. The program-control structures provided in the language are very standard and mirror those available at the machine-code level. In effect, FORTRAN acts as a high-level assembler although later modifications have tried to raise the level of the language by adding extra control constructs and data types. ALGOL 68 is the latest variant of the ALGOL language which similarly had its roots in the 1950s. It has the same facilities available as FORTRAN but also includes a number of the features of non-numeric languages, such as string manipulation.

Typical members of the commercial data processing languages include COBOL and PL/1. COBOL is a language which was developed about 30 years ago and has been updated several times since. The main requirements of data processing applications are to handle structured files efficiently. COBOL therefore devotes a great deal of effort to file processing and allows the user to manipulate record structures which contain related items of different type and size, for example address lists. PL/1 was an attempt by IBM to produce a language which was equally good for both numerical and data processing applications. However, the language has been mainly used for commercial applications in the data processing area.

Non-numeric applications cover a broad spectrum. Generally these languages require a larger set of data structures to be provided and a more extensive set of control structures. No one language is suitable for all types so we shall consider some subsets here. On small computers the efficiency of the language becomes important and it is for this reason that languages such as C and Pascal have become popular on these computers. One class of applications is the so-called string-processing languages, typified by SNOBOL. These languages, as the name implies, are intended to manipulate strings of characters very easily so that operations such as concatenating two strings and searching a string for a given substring are provided. Another class of applications concerns artificial intelligence. The leading language in this field is the logic-programming language PROLOG which is of a completely different type to the other languages described above. Whereas the other languages, called imperative languages, require the programmer to describe how to solve the problem, PROLOG allows the programmer to describe the problem and let the system decide how, or whether, the problem can be solved with the information given. The implementation depends on the mathematical technique of theorem proving. Whilst this approach is attractive for applications other than artificial intelligence it is not applicable, at the present time, to all applications.

The language to be used in the solution of a problem depends on factors other than solely which is the best language. For example, factors such as which computers have translators for which languages and the efficiency of the implementations of the languages become important.

## 12.6.1 Implementation

There are two basic methods of implementing a high-level language; interpretation and compilation. The process of compilation translates a high-level language program into an equivalent set of machine-code instructions which may then be directly executed (see Fig. 12.5). Interpretation, on the other hand, simulates the action of the abstract machine defined by the high-level language (see Fig. 12.6). The abstract machine simulator, or interpreter, then 'understands' statements in the high-level language and can execute them. Another way of considering this is to remember that the machine designer has built a machine to interpret the machine code; an interpreter is simply a machine built in software to interpret another language at a higher level.

The basic differences between compilation and interpretation is that an interpreter is relatively simple to construct, slow to execute and contains good error-detecting facilities, whilst a compiler is more complex but produces a program which runs faster than an interpreted version. Interpreter code is more compact than compiled code and this is one reason why microcomputer BASIC is often interpreted rather than compiled. Because of these differing properties some languages are implemented in several stages, by a mixture of compilation and interpretation.

(a)  IF X>Y THEN X:= X+1;

(b)
|  | | Comments |
|---|---|---|
| LDA | X | Load accumulator with contents of X |
| LXI | H,Y | Load address of Y |
| CMP | M | Compare X and Y |
| JM | L1 | Jump if minus or zero |
| JZ | L1 | |
| LXI | H,X | Load address of X |
| INR | M | Increment X |
| STA | X | Store result in X |

L1:

(c)
|  | |
|---|---|
| MOVE.W | X,D0 |
| CMP.W | Y,D0 |
| BLE | L1 |
| ADDI.W | #1,X |

L1:

**Fig. 12.5**   (a) Typical high-level language statement; (b) equivalent assembly code for 8085 produced by a compiler; (c) equivalent 68000 assembly code.

## 12.7   Documentation and debugging

Debugging is the process of removing errors from programs. Debugging and documentation are considered together since it is virtually impossible to modify or debug a program which has not been properly documented. Proper documentation does not mean just adding comments to every program statement. The aim of proper documentation is to enable someone unfamiliar with the program to understand its structure and implementation in order to be able to modify or debug that program. Adequate documentation of a program, therefore, consists of structure documentation such as flowcharts or structured pseudo-code, together with an explanation of the implementation such as the meaning of the identifiers used and the representation of the application data structures. It is also helpful to have comments attached to some statements in the code, but only to supplement the other documentation. Documentation, therefore, is concerned with the complete design process and not just the implementation phase. Computer-based documentation aids exist for all phases of the design and the use of one of the integrated documentation aids throughout the design process is very useful. These aids are essential for large projects but smaller projects can use manual methods instead.

(a) 1. Fetch next instruction from memory to register using simulated program counter
    2. Increment simulated program counter.
    3. Go to subroutine for that instruction indirectly via an address table.
    4. Return to step 1.

```
                                        simulated program counter = BC
(b) START:   LDAX  B                    get next instruction
             INX   B                    increment simulated PC
             MOV   E,A
             LXI   H,TABLEADDRESS        get table address
             DAD   D                     get position in table
             MOV   E,M
             INX   H
             MOV   D,M                    get value in table to DE
             XCHG                         to HL
             PCHL                         to PC i.e. jump


             routine for an instruction
             .
             .
             .
             JMP    START
TABLEADDRESS:  DW   INS1, INS2, INS3....   address table

                                        A0 is simulated program counter
(c) START:   MOVE.B  (A0)+,D0            get next instruction
             JMP     TABLEADDRESS(A0)    jump    on    table    address
             .

             routine
             .
             .
             .

             BRA      START               back to start of interpreter

TABLEADDRESS:  DC.L  INS1, INS2, INS3,....
```

**Fig. 12.6** (a) Typical structure of an interpreter; (b) illustrative code for interpreter structure for 8085; (c) equivalent interpreter code for 68000.

Debugging is very important. For a system to be adequately debugged a good deal of thought has to go into the planning of the debugging strategy and this has to be done as an integrated part of the design process, not as an afterthought when the program has been written. It is not sufficient to simply run the program with one set of data for which the results are known and, if the program gives the correct results, to assume that the program is correct. The test data will only have exercised one of the possible paths through the program code and only some of the possible intermediate values will have been calculated. Other test data are necessary to test other paths and to test if the calculations work for the range of values required. In most applications exhaustive testing is not possible since the number of different paths and range of values of variables is too large. Mathematical techniques for proving programs correct are still not sufficiently developed to be used in practical systems and, until they are, the programmer has to make do with extensive path testing to check for errors. Although some aids are available to the designer to highlight the paths in the program and the conditions under which they will be executed, it is still a major task for the programmer to choose an adequate set of test data. Testing, therefore, can never give the user complete confidence in the program. For this we shall have to wait for the development in the mathematical techniques of program proving. Interested readers are referred to the text by (Dowsing, Rayward-Smith and Walters, 1986) quoted in Further reading.

## 12.8   Operating systems

In the 1950s programmers writing programs were responsible for coding all the details of the programming of the input–output devices which the programs used. This coding was common to virtually all programs as they nearly all used the same peripherals. It was also error-prone code since it contained some timing constraints. It was soon realized that this code was better placed in a library, or even better, embedded inside the computer system and automatically invoked by the program when it wished to do input–output. This was really the start of the development of an **operating system**, a system present in the memory of the computer which organizes the operation of the computer.

Later developments in computing have led to more and more complex operating systems which perform more and more complex management tasks. As computing became more than simply running a machine-code program the programmer needed to perform a series of tasks in order to run the program, such as compiling, linking, loading and running it. In order to perform these tasks automatically a job-control language was used to specify the tasks to be carried out and the operating system expanded to include an interpreter for the job-control language. The next advance in computing was for the system to run multiple jobs at once, known as **multiprocessing**. This could be done because input–output processing requires little CPU time and thus input from one job could be performed at the same time as output from another job and processing of a third job. This necessitated a more complex operating system which could partition the resources of the computer so that multi-processing could take place. The next development was for **multi-access** working, where a number of users sitting at terminals connected to the computer have simultaneous access to the machine and each one appears to have the full resources of the computer. This is based on the idea of **virtual machines** which are what the users see and which have to be mapped on to the real machine when they are in execution. The operating system was made responsible for this mapping of the virtual machines to the real machine and organizing the timesharing of the real machine between the users. The main development in the last decade as far as operating systems are concerned is in the interconnection of computer systems to form computer networks. This is the subject of the following chapter.

Thus an operating system acts as the manager of a computer system and controls the running of the users' programs and the use of the machine resources. In order to understand how an operating system is organized it is necessary to understand the operating system's view of a running program. A running program is viewed as a collection of processes. A **process** may be thought of as a program or a module of a program in execution and consists of code and the environment which can be affected by execution of the code. For example, the code of a procedure or subroutine could be the code and the environment would be the variables and data structures which the code could modify. The environment would also include the input and output devices which the code could read from or write to. Since there could conceptually be many processes which could perform input–output from the same devices concurrently, which could cause problems, any shared parts of the environment are treated as virtual resources and the operating system is left with the problem of how to map these to real resources. Thus from the operating system's viewpoint the system it is controlling consists of a set of processes and a set of resources. The processes are a mixture of user processes and operating system processes, that is, processes which have been invoked by the user, for example to perform input–output, but which reside in the operating system. Not all the processes inside the operating system are in the same state. Some processes are in a state where they are able to be run when the resources required, for example, the CPU, become available. Some of the processes will be waiting for something to happen; they are waiting for an event. As an example of this, consider a user process which reads input from a terminal. When the program is started the process is created but it is then not able to continue until the user types something at the terminal; it is in a waiting state.

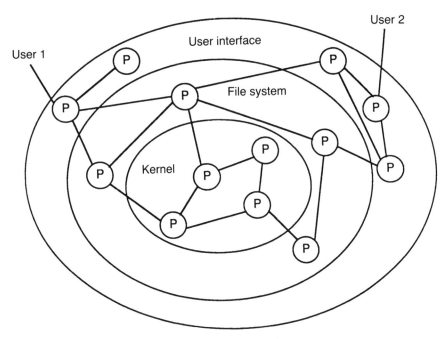

**Fig. 12.7**   Process structure of an operating system showing only three of the layers.

When the user types something at the terminal the process can be activated but this cannot be done until the resources required by the process are available, for example until it can obtain its share of the CPU. Thus processes have a temporal existence; they are created, live and die. Whilst they are alive they are in one of three states: being run, waiting to be run or waiting for an event.

The structure of an operating system is based around processes and is usually hierarchical. A number of operating systems are based on a layered approach; that of 'wrapping' the hardware of the system in successive layers of software, each one providing a higher level of services to the outer layers. This type of structure is shown in Fig. 12.7. The inner layers are concerned with process management, for example, moving processes from the 'waiting for event' state to the 'waiting to be run' state and with selecting the processes to be run. The middle layers are concerned with resource management tasks for resources such as the file system. The outer-level tasks are concerned with user interaction and hence tasks such as that of interpreting the user's requests and validating passwords.

Although there is no such thing as a standard operating system, the one which is available on the widest range of computers today is the **UNIX** operating system developed at the Bell Research Laboratories of AT&T in the USA in the early 1970s. This has been developed in a number of ways from the original system and is now implemented on most of the common computer systems, although, since there is no standard, many developers have implemented their own version and given it their own name, for example, **ULTRIX** from **DEC** and **PC/IX** from IBM. Exactly how compatible these versions are is debatable but there are now industry bodies concerned to make the program interface the same so that programs are portable between different systems. With the momentum behind **UNIX** systems at the present, it is likely that this is the operating system which will be dominant for the forseeable future, in spite of the fact that the basic structure is already 20 years old.

The books on operating systems by Peterson and Silberschatz and by Tanenbaum are useful reference books on the concepts and techniques of operating system implementation.

## 12.9  Summary

In order to use languages other than machine code on a computer some programming aids are required. The lowest-level language above machine code is assembly code. In order to run assembly code programs they first have to be translated into machine code. The program which performs this translation is called an assembler. Most assemblers are two-pass in order to overcome the forward reference problem, that is where a symbol is used before it is defined. Another way of raising the level of a language is to use a macro processor which performs simple text substitution. Thus a set of useful fragments of code can be identified and referred to in a program. A macro processor can be used to substitute the code for the references to it with the appropriate parameter substitution.

Higher-level languages require a compiler to translate them to machine code prior to execution. These languages make it easier for the programmer to write algorithms but they imply the existence of the appropriate compiler. The compiler for any language which allows the programmer to write the program as a set of segments normally outputs the code for the program segment by segment. A program called a linker or link editor is required to link the separate segments together. A loader program is used to load the linked program into memory prior to execution.

Very few programs work correctly the first time they are run and the user has to discover where the errors are; the program has to be debugged. To this end aids are provided on the computer. It is also important that the program is well documented at the design stage so that it is relatively easy to check aspects of the design.

In order for the resources of the computer to be effectively managed a piece of software called an operating system is normally resident in a computer. The task of the operating system is to interface between the user and the program and the hardware of the computer system. The operational model of an operating system and user programs is a set of processes which communicate in order to co-ordinate their activities.

## Exercises

12.1 Give an outline of the linking process indicating what happens in pass 1 and pass 2.

12.2 Indicate what would need to be changed in the code for the 68000 shown below if it was to be relocated to location 4000 onwards. What would be the difference if the data, length and table, were located at 2000 and the code at 4000?

```
                .=0              ;code and data start at location 0
        table:  dc.b    1,3,4
        endtable:

        start:  move.l  #table,A0
                cmpi.b  #1, (A0)+
                beq     found
                cmpa.l  #endtable,A0
                beq     notfound
                bra     start
        found:  move.b #3,-(A0)
                move.w# 1,D0
                stop
        notfound: move.w#0,D0
                stop
                end
```

12.3 Translate into the equivalent 68000 assembly code the following section of high-level language code to find the largest value in an array. Note any assumptions you make.

```
LARGEST:=0;
INDEX:=1;
WHILE(INDEX<LIMIT)DO
     BEGIN
         IF NUMBER(INDEX)>LARGEST THEN
```

```
                LARGEST:=NUMBER(INDEX);
                INDEX:=INDEX+1;
            END;
```

12.4  What is wrong with the following piece of 68000 assembly code to
      count the number of 3s in the table called X and put the result in
      *D0*? Modify it to make it understandable.

```
    X       DC.W    2,3,5,7,3

    ABC     MOVE.W#0,D1
            MOVE.W#0,D2
    Q       CMP.W   #5,D2
            HLT
            CMP.W   #3,X[D2]
            BNE     Z
            ADDI.W  #1,D1
    Z       ADDI.W  #1,D2
            JMP     Q
            END     ABC
```

# 13

# Data communications

## 13.1 Communication

The way in which a computer interacts with its environment is by means of various input–output interfaces, and this was described in Chapter 5. These interfaces work in a predefined way and hence define the actions required to send or receive information from the computer. **Protocol** is the term used for the set for the rules defining the actions required in order for two or more devices to communicate. Thus the protocol for **RS232** defines, amongst other things, the order in which the bits of a character are transmitted and the logic levels used to transmit binary 0 and 1. The protocol of a communication system is designed to overcome a number of problems which may arise when two entities wish to communicate. These issues are discussed in the following sections.

### 13.1.1 Synchronization

Sender and receiver need to be synchronized so that the receiver is ready to receive a communication when it is sent by the sender. To enable the sender and receiver to synchronize their actions communications must have a well-defined start and finish. However, if a communication consists of passing more than a single piece of data then loss of some of the data can cause loss of synchronization. This can cause the receiver to misinterpret the data as the order of the data in a communication is usually important. For example, if one bit of a communication on an **RS232** line is lost then the data received might be interpreted as a different character from that sent depending on the bit which was lost. In effect, this means that communicating devices need to know the state of the devices with which they are communicating at all times. Because sender and receiver do not share address space then the only way in which the receiver can know of the sender's state is by the messages it receives, and if a message is lost then the state which it believes the sender to be in may be erroneous.

## 13.1.2 Error detection and correction

To protect against erroneous messages some form of **error detection and correction**, known as error control, has to be included in the protocol. Errors are usually detected by some form of checking code, typically a parity check or cyclic redundancy check (CRC). In both of these cases, an arithmetic computation is performed by the sender on the information communicated, and attached to the end of the communication. The receiver performs the same computation on the information received and compares its result with the check code sent. If these two values are different then an error has occurred. The difference between a parity check and the more complex cyclic redundancy check is that the latter can detect more errors in the communication. For example, a simple parity check on a stream of bits can only detect an odd number of bits in error whereas a typical CRC can detect a large number of possible errors in many bits. A compromise has to be made between the amount of computation performed to produce the checking code and the number of different errors which can be detected and thus the error code used depends on the likelihood of errors occurring. There is a problem with the scheme just outlined in that corrupted messages will be detected but lost communication will not. If all of a communication is lost the receiver will not be aware that it should have received anything. To overcome this problem communications are usually given a sequence number and the receiver checks both the sequence number and the checking code to detect errors.

There are two methods of performing **error correction**. Using **forward error correction** extra information is sent with the data so that if the data is corrupted it can be reconstituted. This is expensive in terms of the extra communication time required to send the redundant information, which will not be required most of the time (unless the communication line is very unreliable). However, in situations where errors are common, or where the delay across the communication link can be long, for example in satellite links, this type of error correction may be used. The more common form of error correction is **retransmission** of the information if it is lost or corrupted. This implies a protocol which informs the sender when retransmission is required. The simplest technique is to send a communication and wait for the response from the receiver acknowledging that the communication has been received correctly or requesting retransmission. This can cause problems, however, since if a message is lost in transmission neither end will realize this but will wait for the next expected communication from the other end. This communication will never occur since both ends are waiting for each other – a classic case of **deadlock**. The solution to this problem which is universally adopted in communication systems is to impose a **time-out period** on the time any sender will wait for an acknowledgement. If no communication is received within this period it is assumed to be lost and the appropriate corrective action taken. Waiting for a response to every transaction does not make the best use of the communication system. To speed up the communications some systems allow the sender to send several communications before waiting for a response. This complicates the protocol of the receiver since communications usually have to be processed in sequence. If a previous communication has been corrupted then that one and all subsequent ones have to be re-sent if the receiver does not have space to buffer all the communications. Alternatively, if the receiver has enough buffer space then only the communication in error needs to be re-sent.

### 13.1.3  Flow control

An issue associated with error control is **flow control**. It may not be possible for sender and receiver to communicate at the same rate because, for example, the receiver has to perform some other tasks or because it does not have as large a buffer as the sender. If the receiver does not have space available then the communication will be corrupted, an error signalled and the sender will re-send the information. This is a primitive form of flow control which can be very wasteful of both the sender's time and the communication line use. More sophisticated techniques of flow control inform the sender of the amount of buffer storage available at the receiver or, when the buffer space is exhausted, tell the sender the reason for error detection so that the sender can suspend for a period of time until the receiver's buffer contents have been processed.

## 13.2  Addressing

In the discussion above it has been implicitly assumed that the sender and receiver are directly connected by point to point links, that is, that the communication line is unshared and that the sender can direct the communication to the required receiver by sending along the appropriate link. However, in most communication systems this is not the case. Consider a bus, a common communication medium connecting all the devices attached to it. How does a receiver know which communications on the bus are intended for it? The sender normally indicates the receiver's identity by adding some **addressing** information to the communication. This usually just takes the form of an address appended to the front of the communication. Thus every device is given a unique address and only responds to communications preceded by that address, although every receiver has to monitor every communication to see if it is the required destination. In this type of shared communication system sometimes an address is reserved for broadcast communication where all receivers respond to the broadcast communication. The requirement for addressing also occurs in communications systems where the sender and receiver are not directly connected. In this case the address may also be used to perform routeing, as explained below.

A problem which can arise with addressing concerns communication systems where the number of devices can change dynamically. In this case there is a problem with the allocation of addresses. Either each device is given a unique address and the protocol specifies what happens if an addressed device does not respond or else each device is given an address when it becomes available which is removed when the device becomes unavailable. Whilst the former method is by far the simpler to manage the latter technique can be useful if, for example, some devices are designated as backup devices. Thus, in some systems devices are addressed virtually and a mapping is performed between the virtual address and the physical address.

## 13.3   Communication structure

From the foregoing it can be seen that the general structure of a communication block will be as shown in Fig. 13.1. The communication block has to have a distinct start and finish. The start field is used to synchronize the receiver with the sender. The address field contains the address of the receiver so that on a shared communication medium the correct receiver can be identified. Frequently, the address field also contains the address of the sender so that the receiver can reply to the communication. The control field contains information to enable the communication to be managed. For example it may contain information about the amount of buffer space available or the number of transmissions which can be outstanding before being acknowledged. The data field contains the information to be transmitted and the error checking field contains information which allows the receiver to check for errors. Some communications may not contain all of the fields indicated, for example, the data field could be missing if only control information is to be passed and, as we have seen earlier, simple schemes such as RS232 only contain start, data and stop fields.

| Start | Address(es) | Data | Error check | End |
|-------|-------------|------|-------------|-----|

**Fig. 13.1**   Structure of a communication block.

## 13.4   Computer networks

The design of computer systems has been constantly evolving owing to improvements in construction techniques, reductions in the cost of processing and ever-increasing complexity of user requirements. This has resulted in architectural developments concerned with utilizing multiple processor systems or multiple computers in meeting user requirements.

Consider the development of the peripheral interface to a computer system. Initially, peripheral devices such as terminals were directly connected to the computer bus via a suitable interface. This was adequate for a small number of interfaces but for large numbers it was expensive, since a large number of interfaces imply large power supplies and large cabinets. Also it meant that for a large number of peripherals the central processor had to examine and control a large number of different interfaces. Since the servicing of peripheral interrupts is a time-consuming task for the processor, the direct control of multiple interfaces is not very efficient. This led to the use of a multiplexer to interface several peripherals to a computer using a single interface. This implies a fast link to the main computer since it is assumed that the single computer interface is fast enough to service concurrent input–output from all the peripherals connected to the multiplexer. From the processor's point of view it only has to control a single device rather than many devices but it still has to deal with each character to and from every peripheral. To reduce this load, multiplexers were made more intelligent by adding buffering, so that communications with the processor were in terms of blocks of characters rather than single characters. The natural extension to this was to replace the multiplexer by a small computer dedicated to handling input–output, a front-end processor (FEP). This was an improvement because the cheap front-end processor could now do simple processing tasks thus relieving the expensive central processor of these tasks and freeing it to concentrate on computation. The front-end processor communicated with the main computer through some fast intercommunication channel which transmitted blocks of data, typically tens of bytes, very rapidly. This was the standard method of dealing with much of the input–output to mainframe computers until very recently.

Over two decades ago it was realized that, in order to reduce the cost of computing, it would be advantageous if computers could be linked over large distances using the telephone network or higher-speed links, so that scarce or expensive resources could be shared. An example of a scarce resource is a large expensive graph plotter. All computer sites could be provided with a small cheap plotter but when a plot is required on a large scale or with great accuracy then the data could be sent to a central site which has the requisite specialized equipment. Another example of a scarce resource is a large, powerful computer. All sites could be provided with computers large enough to satisfy the needs of most of the workload but only a few sites could be provided with larger computers able to tackle the few very large programs. Any job which is too large to be processed at the local site could be sent to the central site for processing. Because this sharing made economic sense there has been an explosive growth in the number of networks and it is now common to find that a computer is linked over several networks to computers around the world. Having produced these worldwide networks, the main use appears to be in the transmission of mail from user to user rather than program code or data and one of the main reasons for the provision of networks now is for efficient communication between groups of people to enable collaborative projects to be undertaken. Having said this, there are a number of networks which are in common use, such as the cash dispensers installed at the banks and other locations, credit-card authorization and the recent introduction of debit cards to directly debit a bank account when a purchase is made at a retail outlet.

The way in which networking is achieved is through the use of a specialized front-end processor which is a development of the FEP mentioned previously. This processor, called a node, is used to link to other nodes, thus forming a network. The nodes are connected to their host computers by means of fast communications channels which transfer blocks of information to and from the host.

There are various properties of networks which can be used to classify them, such as the topology and switching method. Some of these classification properties are discussed in the following sections.

## 13.4.1 Topology

The topology of the network describes the way in which the nodes are connected and there are many different topologies possible, ranging from total connection to a ring. Some common network topologies are shown in Fig. 13.2. The topologies can be broadly subdivided into two categories: point to point and broadcast.

### (a) Broadcast topology

The senders and receivers in broadcast topologies share a common communication medium and therefore every receiver can see every communication sent by a sender. Thus communications have to have the address of the intended receiver appended to them so that each receiver can filter out the communications intended for it. The two most common topologies of this type are the bus and the ring. In the case of both of these types of topology there can be potential clashes with several senders attempting to send at once; thus some method of arbitration is required to serialize the transmissions.

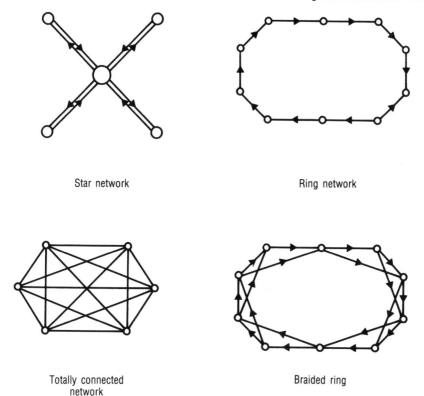

Star network

Ring network

Totally connected
network

Braided ring

**Fig. 13.2**  Some network topologies.

There are several different methods of performing this. One technique, the token passing technique, uses a special bit pattern called a token which is passed between senders. The token signifies permission to send and a sender who wishes to send must first obtain the token. Another technique used with the ring topology is to divide the available ring transmission time into slots and to allow a sender to fill any empty slots. The advantage of these broadcast topologies is that routeing is simple since every receiver automatically sees every transmission but the drawback is that a failure in the communication system means that some connections will not be possible. To overcome this drawback some rings have braids added which bypass one or more nodes and provide additional routes to circumvent node or transmission-line failure.

## (b)   Point-to-point topology

As its name implies, in this type of topology there is one or a series of communication channels between sender and receiver. Some typical examples are the star and totally connected networks. In the star network a sender sends a communication to the central node which redirects it to the appropriate node. In the totally connected configuration the sender just has to send the communication along the appropriate channel. In every configuration other than the totally connected one some form of routeing is required since the communication will have to pass through several intermediate nodes before arriving at its final destination. Therefore, the receiver address has to be included as part of the communication. Totally connected networks are not very common due to the high cost of providing all the communication channels and due to the high cost of expanding the network. Because of the irregular way in which networks tend to grow most of them do not fall into any one of the regular point-to-point topologies but have subnetworks which are regular.

## 13.4.2 Routeing

As mentioned above there is the **routeing** problem in computer networks. In a total connection topology, routeing is very simple. If nodes are not directly connected then it may be necessary for a communication to pass through some intermediate nodes to reach its destination. The problem of deciding through which links the communication should pass to reach its final destination is the routeing task. There are two different methods used to specify the route. In the first case the sender decides the route and adds the sequence of addresses of the intermediate nodes to the communication. As the communication passes through the network each node peels off its address and uses the next address to decide which is the next node on the route. In the second case each intermediate node makes its own decision on where to send the communication based on the destination address. This implies that each node in the network knows the topology of the network, whereas in the first case only the host computers have to be aware of the total network interconnections.

## 13.4.3 Circuit switching

Using the routeing techniques described above, there are two ways in which multiple communications can be sent over a point-to-point network. One method, known as **circuit switching**, is similar to that used in the telephone network. Initially a path is established through the network to connect sender to receiver. In the telephone network the dialled digits are used to form the route through the network. Similarly in a computer network an initial communication is passed through the network which sets up the path through each node. Once this route has been established data are passed between the sender and receiver. This data transmission needs no address since it will follow the path taken by the initial set-up communication. When the conversation is finished the connection is broken by replacing the handset in the case of the telephone system or by a termination communication in the case of a computer network. There are a number of disadvantages to this scheme such as the time required to set up the route and clear it down if only a short communication is required. Another disadvantage is that the utilization of the communication line may be very low since communications often result in short bursts of transmission followed by long periods of inactivity.

### 13.4.4   Message switching and packet switching

An alternative to circuit switching involves sending the address of the destination with every communication. It is the responsibility of the network to route the communication to the specified destination and several different routes may be possible from sender to receiver. The size of the communication distinguishes between **message switching** and **packet switching**. If the communication is sent as a single communication then it is known as message switching but if it is split up into a sequence of fixed size units, known as packets, then it is known as packet switching. The advantage of packet switching is that the size of the packet is known in advance so the management of memory in the network nodes is much simpler and the sharing of either communication lines or the processing power in a node is much easier. In fact, virtually no networks now use message passing as their basic switching technique but build it on top of packet switching if required.

A comparison between the three switching techniques is given in Fig. 13.3.

| *Message switching* | *Packet switching* | *Circuit switching* |
| --- | --- | --- |
| no setup time | no setup time | long setup time |
| no closedown time | no closedown time | time required to break connection |
| any size communications | fixed sized communications | any size communications |
| poor sharing of comms media | good sharing of comms media | no sharing of comms media |
| does not require compatability of code, speed and format through the network | does not require compatability of code, speed and format through the network | requires compatibility of code, speed and format through the network |
| good user response time | variable user response time | good user response time |
| suitable for message transmission, for example, electronic mail | suitable for 'bursty' traffic, for example, interactive computing | suitable for high throughput, for example, facsimile transmission |

**Fig. 13.3**   Comparison of message switching, packet switching and circuit switching.

## 13.4.5 Network services

The techniques of circuit and packet switching described above are used to provide network services to allow remote computers to communicate. There are two basic types of service provided, which should not be confused with the techniques of circuit and packet switching.

### (a)  Datagrams

With a datagram system each packet is sent around the network independently and may take a different route depending on the routeing technique employed. The packet has to include the destination address which is used to route the packet to the correct destination. Error and flow control across the network have to be implemented by the sender and receiver computers and there is no guarantee that the datagrams will be received in the same order as they are sent.

### (b)  Virtual circuit

A virtual circuit is similar to the service provided by the telephone network in that after a logical connection is established packets are routed across the network along the same connection until it is broken. Because packets flow one after another in sequence along the same route, the network provides a form of end-to-end flow control. The reason why this service is called a virtual service is because the physical communication media between the nodes may be shared between several concurrent virtual circuits.

## 13.4.6 Network protocols

As stated at the beginning of this chapter, a protocol is necessary between any two devices which communicate. If a computer which communicates with another is viewed as communicating information at a number of different levels then a number of different protocols will be required. For example, the RS232 communications standard defines a protocol for sending a character, represented by a sequence of bits, between a transmitter and receiver. The communicating entities in the networked computers, however, will probably wish to send messages composed of many characters to one another and some higher-level protocol will need to be obeyed by these entities, for example to restart a message if some of it is lost. Thus for any communicating system there needs to be a hierarchy of protocols dealing with the communication of different sized units between sender and receiver.

In addition, this hierarchy of protocols should ideally be standardized so that different manufacturers' equipment will have the same protocol and can thus be networked together.

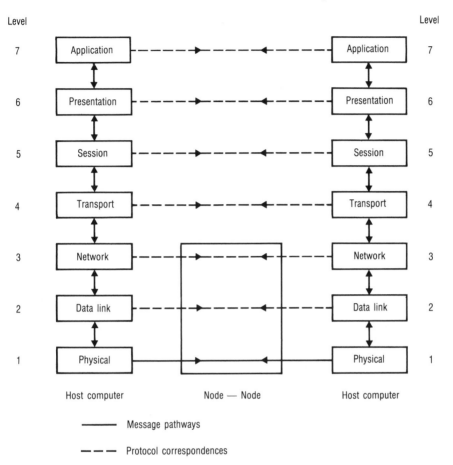

**Fig. 13.4** OSI network model.

The most widely used hierarchy of standard communication protocols is that specified by the International Standards Organisation (ISO) for its Open Systems Interconnection (OSI) reference model. An outline of the model is given in Fig. 13.4. The model consists of seven layers: application, presentation, session, transport, network, data link and physical layer. Although communication across the physical medium between the communicating computers takes place using the protocol defined for the lowest layer, the physical layer, communication logically takes place between entities in the same layer on each computer. Thus messages from the applications layer on one computer are sent to the applications layer of another computer. The simplest way to view the passage of data from the application layer on one machine to another is to imagine protocol information being added to the front and back of the data as it passes down the layers in the sending machine and removed by the corresponding layers in the receiving computer. The protocol for each layer is used for tasks such as error and flow control discussed at the beginning of this chapter. The particular division of tasks to the layers is given below.

## (a)   Physical layer

This layer is concerned with the transmission of bit patterns along a communication link. It is concerned with details such as the representation of logic 0 and 1 and the mechanical specification of the plugs, sockets and communication medium. There are some international standards for this level defined by the international telecommunications body CCITT, such as RS232.

## (b)   Data-link layer

This layer is concerned with providing an error-free link between a sender or receiver and the network. It does this by splitting data into packets, sending them sequentially and using the acknowledgement packets to provide error control. An internationally agreed standard for this layer is called HDLC, High level Data Link Control.

## (c)   Network layer

Whereas the previous two layers were concerned with communication between a sender or receiver and the network, this layer is concerned with providing the basic end-to-end communication between sender and receiver. There is an internationally agreed standard called X25, of which HDLC is a subset, which covers this and the previous two layers.

## (d)   Transport layer

The main task of the transport layer is to hide the details of the network from the higher layers. It takes data from the session layer, splits it into smaller units if necessary and sends it by the most efficient route to the destination over the network.

## (e)   Session layer

A session is the name given to the period of time for which two or more entities are logically connected. The session layer, therefore, is concerned with the setting up and management of a session.

## (f)   Presentation layer

The presentation layer is concerned with the presentation of data. Examples of the types of services provided by this layer are encryption to provide security and changes of character code where the communicating computers use different codes.

## (g)   Application layer

This is the highest level of the model and the services provided at this level are application dependent. Examples which are frequently required are a file transfer protocol and a virtual terminal protocol to allow remote terminals to interact.

## 13.4.7   Types of network

There are two basic types of network, called wide-area networks (WANs) and local-area networks (LANs), which have developed from different requirements and thus have different aims and use different techniques.

## (a)   Wide-area networks

The first type of network to be developed was the **wide-area network** (WAN). A wide-area network is a network which operates over a geographically wide area, such as a country or between different countries. The main restriction of such a network is that communication has to take place over the lines provided by the public data carriers (PTTs) in the countries concerned. In this country this means that lines provided by British Telecom, or Mercury, have to be used. These lines were not primarily designed for data traffic but rather for voice traffic. Much of the present network is analog based and this imposes some restrictions on, for example, the speed of digital communication. This situation is gradually being changed as the PTTs base their networks more and more on digital communication. The main advantage of using the services of the PTTs is that they have been aware of the problems of interworking between different telephone and telegraph networks for many years and are skilled at producing international standards. This means that networking across international borders is relatively simple. The initial need for wide-area networks was to share resources between remote sites. Thus typically a WAN would be used to interrogate a database at a remote site or to send a large program to a remote supercomputer to be run. WANs are based on point-to-point networks and some use packet switching and others use circuit switching.

|  Wide-area network | Local-area network |
|---|---|
| Operates over a geographically wide area, typically between countries | operates over a small area typically of a maximum of a few kilometres |
| uses PTT lines for communication | uses special communication lines |
| relatively slow transmission speed, typically 50 kbits/s. | relatively fast transmission speed, typically 10 Mbits/s. |
| operates as a computer network | operates as a distributed system |
| high error rates – about 1 in $10^4$ | low error rates – less than $10^9$ |
| typical topology is point to point with less than total interconnection. | typical topology is broadcast, ring or bus |

**Fig. 13.5**  Comparison of wide-area and local-area networks.

## (b)  Local-area networks

The other type of network is the **local-area network** (LAN). Local-area networks are networks which are limited to a small geographical area, such as a single building or a single site. These networks do not need to use communication lines provided by the PTT and are usually run over different communication media such as twisted pair wires, as used in the telephone system, or coaxial cable, as used for televisions. Local-area networks were initially set up so that users could share resources and also so that different computers could access the same information. The main difference between wide- and local-area networks are summarized in Fig. 13.5.

## 13.4.8  Network interconnections

Most, if not all, networks have grown in unpredictable ways. Initially networks are installed to provide particular services and gradually the networks expand and the services provided increase. Eventually the situation arises where two or more networks need to be connected. This causes problems since the dissimilarity between the networks can occur at a number of different levels. The most difficult problems occur when the two networks use completely different types of protocols. For example, if one network uses circuit switching and the other uses packet switching then interconnection becomes quite complex. The solution to the interconnection usually adopted is to link the networks via a **gateway** which is node responsible for the conversion of protocols from one network standard to another. A **bridge** is the term used for the gateway when the two networks are basically similar and use similar protocols. In this case the only task of the bridge, apart from acting as a node, is to ensure correct addressing.

## 13.5   Distributed computing

In parallel with the growth of networks, there has been an increasing interest in multiple processor computing systems due to the reduction in the cost of processing power. The simplest way to use multiple processors is to connect them to common memory as they can then share the workload, but this rapidly leads to a degradation in performance as the number of processors increases owing to memory contention. Instead of this tight coupling between processors and memory, the trend has been for loosely coupled systems, often called distributed systems, where processors and associated memory are connected by a local-area network (LAN).

Although there are a number of similarities between a network of computers and a distributed computer system there is one basic difference. A distributed computer system is thought of as a single computer with the collection of processors and memories acting together to provide the services given by a mainframe of a few years ago. It is programmed as a single computer. The network of computers, on the other hand, acts as a set of computers, each one running its own programs. A distributed system uses the underlying network to provide the communication services and builds on these basic services to provide higher level ones such as remote procedure call (RPC) and other bidirectional communication primitives.

Although distributed systems tend to be specialized to a particular application area there is one model of computation which is common to a number of these systems; the **client server model**. In this model of computation, processes are divided into clients and servers. A server process provides a **service** and client processes obtain the service by communicating with the server. One type of server is the resource manager. When a user process wishes to obtain a particular resource, for example access to a file, it has to communicate with the appropriate server, in this case the file server. Servers do not have to be associated only with physical resources, for example a mail server which deals with the reception and distribution of user's mail is another common server encapsulates all the resource-dependent information and communication between client and server can be implemented by whatever services are provided by the underlying communication subsystem.

The subject of distributed computing is still in its infancy and there are only relatively few systems in operation. We refer interested readers to the book by Sloman and Kramer in Further Reading for more details. Suffice it to say that distributed systems are much more complex than centralized systems and also less well understood. Therefore, unless there are good reasons, the starting point for design of a computer system should still be centralized rather than distributed.

## 13.6 Summary

In order for a computer to communicate with its environment a protocol has to be defined. The protocol must define how sender and receiver synchronize, how errors are handled, how the flow of information is controlled and how the sender and receiver are identified. The protocol defines the structure of messages passed between sender and receiver and the order in which these messages are passed.

Computers are frequently joined together into networks so that they can share resources, such as printers and files. The networking functions are usually handled by specialized computers called nodes which are connected together in some topology and some of which are connected to the host computers. There are a wide variety of different topologies ranging from total connection to a bus system. Messages sent through the network have to be routed by the nodes to the appropriate destination. The two main routeing schemes are circuit switching and packet switching.

The protocol between computers on a network is usually structured as a hierarchy of protocols. The most common standard is the ISO OSI model which consists of seven levels – physical, data-link, network, transport, session, presentation and application. The lowest three levels are concerned with transferring information across the network and the upper levels with host–host interaction. Software in each node and host deals with the protocols in each layer. Application data passed across the network have to be enveloped in the seven layers of protocol which are stripped off in the receiving host. Each layer is responsible for some of the services and has its own error detection and correction.

Two different types of network are common: wide-area networks and local-area networks. Wide-area networks span a large geographical area and use the PTT data networks, whereas local-area networks are confined to a single building or site and use faster, less-complex communications. Wide-area networks contain host computers which run their own, probably different, operating systems and software. They use facilities on other computers such as files and printers. Local-area networks are usually programmed as a single, distributed system and thus each host computer runs part of a larger task.

## Exercises

13.1   Explain the sequence of actions necessary for a sender to communicate with a remote receiver over a network.

13.2   How does a receiver know that an error has occurred in a communication? What corrective action can the sender take?

13.3   How do the addressing requirements differ between a broadcast and a point-to-point network?

13.4   How would token loss be detected in a token-ring network? Suggest policies by which the token could be regenerated. Would these work in a distributed environment?

13.5   Explain how a user application process could send data to a remote application process using protocols based on the ISO OSI model. What actions are performed by each layer?

13.6   Give examples of client–server models which occur in everyday life. How would you model these on a computer system?

# 14

# New directions in architecture

## 14.1   Introduction

In previous chapters of this book the components of a simple computer system, both hardware and software, have been described with examples from typical microcomputer systems. The hardware and software presented is one possible design of computer but there are many others since the designer has many choices. Also, as technology improves, the tradeoffs to be made by the designer change and new types of architecture become attractive. As discussed in the previous chapter, the emergence of local-area networks has prompted the evolution of distributed computing systems where many processors combine to solve a problem. This is just one of the current trends in computer architecture. In this chapter two other approaches to new architectures are explored.

## 14.2   Architectural considerations and processor design

Some of the designer's choices in so far as processor design is concerned were discussed in Chapter 11. The instruction set may be either three, two, one or zero address or a mixture of several of these. The designer may also choose the number of addressing modes which will be supported. All architectures support direct and indirect addressing, but it is more convenient for the programmer and easier for the compiler writer if more addressing modes are provided. The current trend in conventional architectures appears to be for more and more complex instruction sets with a mixture of addressing types and a large range of different addressing modes. This trend can be seen by comparing the microcomputers produced by a single manufacturer. Comparing, say, the Intel 8085 with the Intel 8086 and with the later Intel 80186, 80286 and 80386, we see that the newer designs are more complex and have more instructions and addressing modes than their predecessors. The reason for this increase in the complexity of the instruction set is that with improvements in technology more complex circuitry can be produced on a chip. Also, to support the compilation of high-level languages designers have traditionally put higher-level, more complex instructions and addressing modes in the processor's repertoire. This both speeds up execution – a hardware implementation is generally faster than an equivalent software one – and makes the compiler writer's job easier. As different high-level languages have been seen traditionally to require different instructions and addressing modes to implement them efficiently, the size and complexity of instructions and addressing modes have continually grown.

## 14.3   RISC architectures

In 1980 some designers began to question this trend towards more and more complex architectures and instruction sets. They set out to investigate alternative types of architecture, called Reduced Instruction Set Computers (RISC), with a reduced number of instructions and addressing modes and the following features

(a) to execute one instruction per cycle,
(b) to make all instructions the same length and fixed format,
(c) to access main memory only with load and store operations,
(d) to efficiently support the execution of high-level languages.

Constraints (a) and (b) mean that the architecture can be simple since all instructions can be treated identically, unlike conventional machines where different instructions often have different lengths and significantly different execution times. Restriction (c) means that execution of most instructions is fast since operations normally take place between registers and these are on the same chip as the arithmetic unit. Restriction (d) is necessary since, for reasons explained previously, most software development is now performed in a high-level language. To implement a high-level language efficiently requires a study of the type of instructions generated by compilers to see which instructions occur most frequently and hence require the most efficient implementation. Patterson and Sequin of the University of California at Berkeley in 1982 studied a range of programs written in both Pascal and C and discovered that the percentages of the different types of instructions in the programs studied, weighted for the number of machine code instructions required to implement each high-level statement, was approximately 45% for procedure call and return, 30% for loops, 15% for assignment and 10% for conditional statements, with the other statements contributing very little. They also discovered that scalar variables were the most frequent data type.

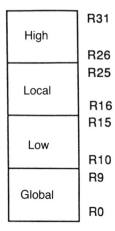

**Fig. 14.1**   Register set for a procedure.

From this they concluded that what is important for a machine to execute high-level languages efficiently is an efficient procedure call/return mechanism and fast access to variables.

To make procedure calls and returns efficient they invented the notion of **register windows**. Invoking a procedure involves copying any parameter from the caller's environment to the called environment, saving the contents of any register which may be used in the called procedure and jumping to the appropriate code. Returning from a procedure involves the reverse operations. Thus to make procedure calls/returns fast requires a mechanism for saving and restoring register contents quickly. Patterson and Sequin's solution was to provide a large number of registers on the processor chip, which can be done since the processor is simple and therefore takes up little chip area. They also arranged for the registers to be divided up into windows and for the windows to be accessible to change on procedure call and return. The windows of the calling procedure and the called procedure overlap to allow for parameter passing. The scheme they suggested divided the register space accessible at any one time into four distinct areas (see Fig. 14.1).

This register set then has to be mapped on to the set of hardware registers provided on the processor chip. The lower area, containing registers $R0$–$R9$, is called the global area and is mapped on to the same registers for all procedures in a program. The area containing registers $R10$–$R15$ is called the low area and contains temporary variables and parameters passed to 'lower' procedures. The local area, registers $R16$–$R25$, contains variables local to the presently executing procedure while the high area, registers $R26$–$R31$, contains parameters from the results to the calling procedure. On each procedure call the register set available for high, local and low slides over the total set of registers

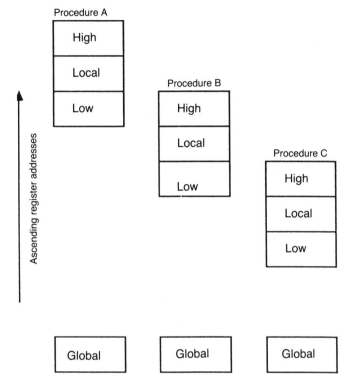

**Fig. 14.2**   Overlapping windows of procedures.

so that the old low area becomes the new high area and new registers are allocated for the new low and local areas, as shown in Fig. 14.2. If the hardware register file is completely allocated then it is extended into main memory, with a consequent loss of performance. However, studies have shown that good performance can be obtained with a register file of about 100 registers.

Because of the need to make all instructions the same size and the same execution time all instructions are simple. In a single instruction cycle operations such as reading a register, storing a register or performing an ALU operation are possible.

In order to make the processor efficient, whilst the current instruction is being executed the next instruction is being decoded. This means that the processor is pipelined. This causes problems for conditional jumps, however, since the next instruction is not known until the present instruction is executed. Conventional high-speed machines use elaborate methods to get around this problem but these techniques are too expensive for RISC machines. The solution used in RISC machines is to delay jumps; they do not take place until

|  |  |  |  |  |  |
|---|---|---|---|---|---|
| CMP | D0,D3 | CMP | D0,D3 | CMP | D0,D3 |
| BNE | L1 | BNE | L1 | BNE | L1 |
| ADD | D1,D0 | NOP | | NOP | |
| JMP | L2 | ADD | D1,D0 | JMP | L2 |
| L1:ADD | D2,D0 | JMP | L2 | ADD | D1,D0 |
| | | NOP | | L1:ADD | D2,D0 |
| | | L1:ADD | D2,D1 | | |

| example code for 'normal' computer | code with **NOP** for pipelined RISC | rearranged code with only one **NOP** |
|---|---|---|

**Fig. 14.3** Delayed jumps.

after the instruction immediately following the jump has been executed. This makes it difficult to program in machine code but these architectures are designed to execute high-level language programs and the compiler takes care of the ordering of the code for delayed jumps. In the worst case a no operation (nop) instruction can be placed after each jump but it is often possible to rearrange the code so that no extra instructions are required and studies have shown that the number of no operations required in typical programs is only a matter of a few per cent. An example of the delayed-jump technique is shown in Fig. 14.3.

Using these techniques it is possible to implement a very simple processor which executes instructions very fast. In fact not all RISC processors use all the techniques described here and some introduce other techniques to produce acceptable performance. Studies have shown that simple RISC architectures can perform as well as the most advanced conventional architectures, excepting supercomputers. This has led to most major manufacturers producing RISC computers. Examples are IBM with the PC RT, Acorn with its RISC chip and Sun Microsystems with its SPARC processor.

## 14.4 CISCs versus RISCs

It is perhaps in the area of processor design that the architect has most choice. Evaluating each architecture is not a simple task and hence choosing the 'best' processor is difficult since so many different factors, for example hardware, software and the applications envisaged, are involved. There is still some debate over whether RISC-based architectures are indeed better than conventional systems with complex instruction sets (CISC). One of the major tasks of the architect is to assign system functionality to implementation levels. RISC designers put the functionality at a higher level in the architecture than CISC designers, assuming that translators will perform an efficient mapping to low-level code. CISC designers build more functionality into the low-level architecture.

The trend for any architecture is to get more complex with time. The reasons for this are many and include:

1. new models of a computer system are required to be upwards compatible, that is they must include as a subset features of previous models so that they can run the same software;
2. reduction in the 'semantic gap' between the user's high-level languages and the low-level machine language is desirable to reduce the complexity of the system software. This requires low-level architectural support of high-level language features;
3. manufacturers strive to make computers faster; one method of achieving this is to migrate functions to hardware from software;
4. tools and technology are continually allowing the designer to increase the size of circuit which can be fabricated on a chip; designers make use of this and produce larger, more complex chips.

This would suggest that any design, even RISCs, will get more complex as time passes and that RISCs and CISCs are just two points in the same design space with architectures having a mixture of both features being possible.

Basically, a RISC machine is a special-purpose design which is optimized to run a particular workload, whereas CISC designs are usually general-purpose and intended to support a wide range of application areas. Because of this it is difficult to directly compare the architectures, especially since raw processing speed is not the only measure of performance. In a transaction processing system, for example, the number of transactions per second which the computer can deal with is a better measure of performance than raw speed and there is no direct relationship between these two quantities.

Perhaps the largest area of debate concerns the influence of the large register file on the performance of the RISC architecture. Would not the use of such a technique speed up the operation of a CISC machine? Undoubtedly it would, but the argument of RISC designers is that such a large register file can only be included on a chip by making the area occupied by the processor small, thus implying a simple architecture, a RISC machine. The CISC designers, on the other hand, argue that the number of components which can be fabricated on a fixed-size chip doubles each year and so efficient use of chip area is becoming less of a constraint thus permitting more complex designs with a large register file.

Although the debate between CISC and RISC designers has been useful in focusing attention on processor design, it would seem that, in the long term, designers will take the best points of RISC and CISC and incorporate them in their designs, bearing in mind the constraints applicable at the time.

## 14.5   The transputer

As has already been mentioned, one of the ways to improve the performance of a computer system is to introduce concurrency in some or all of the architectural levels. For example, by building computing systems with multiple processors it is possible to run several programs at once, concurrently, or to run multiple processes from a single application concurrently. This latter case is normally referred to as distributed computing since the processes are distributed across a set of processors. It is for this latter situation that INMOS designed the transputer, a RISC machine. Strictly the transputer is not a single computer but the name of a range of computers of different sizes and configurations although only two are available at the time of writing: the 32-bit IMS T424 and the 16-bit IMS T414.

The transputer directly implements the process model of computation with message passing between processes along explicitly defined channels. Channels can be set up between processes in adjacent transputers or between processes in the same transputer. Each transputer can timeshare a set of processes so it is possible to map a set of processes in many different ways on to an interconnected set of transputers. Transputers are physically interconnected by hardware links which provide a pair of logical connections, one in each direction. The lowest-level language supported by the transputer is occam, a language derived for this purpose by INMOS. The transputer architecture is a RISC machine specifically optimized to run occam, and hence the need for assembly code programming is eliminated, or so the designers claim.

The IMS T424 transputer, a 32-bit machine with a 10Mip instruction rate, is the first in the compatible range and is implemented in CMOS technology. It consists of a processor, 4K bytes of static memory, specialized interfaces to connect peripherals and external memory and four links to allow connection to up to four adjacent transputers. The links are bit serial transmission pathways with a maximum speed of 20 Mbits s$^{-1}$.

### 14.5.1   Transputer architecture

The intention was that most programmers would program the transputer at the occam level so the programmer's view of the transputer is the occam view. However, for a number of applications, such as implementing compilers and operating systems, occam is not a low enough language and programmers need to know about the underlying architecture. The architecture of the transputer, omitting communication links, is shown in Fig. 14.4. There are six registers in the architecture. A, B and C form an evaluation stack and are the source and destination of most instructions. Loading a value into the A register pushes the current contents of A to B and of B to C. Similarly, storing a value from the A register pops the contents of B to A and C to B. It is the compiler's

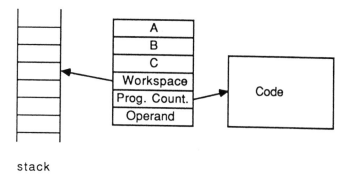

stack

**Fig. 14.4**   Transputer architecture.

responsibility to ensure that no more than three items are required on the stack at any one time. The workspace register contains a pointer to an area of storage used to keep local variables. The next instruction register is a conventional program counter and points to the next instruction to be obeyed. The operand register is used to form the operands of an instruction as described below.

## 14.5.2   Instruction set

The instruction set has been designed to make compilation from occam simple. Each instruction is one byte long, divided into two 4-bit fields. The least significant four bits form a data value and the most significant four bits the function field. This arrangement provides for 16 functions each with a data value between 0 and 15. Thirteen of the function values are used to code up the most frequently used instructions such as the various types of load and store together with jump and call instructions. Two of the remaining function codes are allocated to prefix and negative prefix instructions which allow an operand of any instruction to be extended in length. Fig. 14.5 shows the types of instructions available on the transputer. To explain how these instructions work it is necessary to explain how an instruction is executed. The four data bits of an instruction are loaded into the four least-significant bits of the operand register and are used as the instruction operand. Normally, the operand register is cleared at the end of an instruction but this is not done in the case of prefixing instructions. The prefixing instructions load the data field of the instruction into the operand register and shift the contents up four places. Consequently, by the use of a number of prefixing instructions, operands of any length can be produced subject to the maximum which can be contained in the operand register. This method of generating long operands

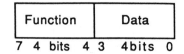

7 4 bits 4 3 4bits 0

Type 1: Direct functions

**These include**

> **load constant**
> **add constant**
>
> **jump**
> **conditional jump**
>
> **call**

Type 2: Prefixing functions

> **prefix**
> **negative prefix**

Type 3: Indirect functions
> **These include**
>
> **add**
> **greater than**

**Fig. 14.5** Transputer instruction types.

from small instructions is dictated by the RISC approach and has the advantage that the operand size is not dictated by the processor wordlength.

The remaining function code, operate, is an indirect function which causes its operand to be interpreted as an operation on values on the evaluation stack. Thus this single function code allows 16 different operations to be encoded in the data field. However, prefixing may also be used with the operate instruction thus allowing the number of operations which may be encoded by the operand instruction to be extended indefinitely, subject to the length of the operand register.

Measurements of programs for the transputer have shown that about 80% are encoded in a single byte and, since a word is the unit of transfer between memory and the processor, the processor does not normally have to wait for an instruction fetch from memory as its two-word internal buffer usually contains at least four instructions.

### 14.5.3   Communications

A novel feature of the transputer is its support of concurrency. A conventional processor has to support an operating system kernel to provide timesharing of concurrent processes. In the transputer this support is provided at the micro-code level so no conventional software kernel is needed. Communication between processes is provided by means of channels which are unidirectional. A channel is implemented between two processes running on the same processor by a single word of memory and by two processes on different processors by direct point-to-point links. The processor supports input-output on channels by the 'input message' and 'output message' instructions. The actual technique of message passing via links is more complicated than message interchange on a single processor since the two communicating processes are executing at the same time in the former case and have to be synchronized. Thus the links utilize a simple protocol to provide the synchronized communication.

The transputer is a RISC but its real claim to fame is its support of concurrency. The RISC approach allows the designers to keep the processor small and fast whilst optimizing the design for the occam language. The transputer was designed for distributing processing applications, that is for use in systems comprising networks of transputers. However, because the T424 is one of the fastest 32-bit processors on the market, at present a number of users have incorporated single transputers in equipment simply because of the transputer's speed. Several vendors, including Meiko, a company which has produced a computer system called the Computing Surface, have produced computer systems based on collections of transputers. These machines are intended to produce performance in the supercomputer league for systems comprising tens of transputers.

## 14.6   Summary

Developments in technology have meant that over the years the amount of circuitry in a processor has gradually increased. Much of this extra functionality has been used to add extra instructions and addressing modes to make the translation and execution of high-level languages easier and faster. This has resulted in so called CISC architecture designs. An alternative approach called RISC has developed over the past decade. The objective of these designs is to make the processor as simple as possible and leave the complexity in an optimizing compiler. There is still a lot of debate as to which is the most effective architecture CISC or RISC since it is very difficult to isolate the instruction set design from the rest of the architecture.

The transputer is a RISC processor but it has been designed for distributed processing applications. It has a very small, simple instruction set, optimized for the language occam. Current versions of the transputer contain four high-speed serial communication links which can be attached to other transputers thus allowing arrays of transputers to be built.

## Exercises

14.1   What are the distinguishing characteristics of a RISC machine? Why does this result in a 'better' architecture?

14.2   In what respects is the transputer a RISC? What is the space liberated by the RISC design used for in the transputer?

# Answers to selected exercises

**2.1** **(a)**

$$\bar{A}.\bar{B} + A.B + \bar{A}.B$$

Combining terms 1 and 3 gives

$$\bar{A}(\bar{B} + B) + A.B = \bar{A} + A.B$$

Using the simplification theorem

$$A + \bar{A}.B = A + B$$

then gives

$$\bar{A} + B$$

i.e.

$$\bar{A}.\bar{B} + A.B + \bar{A}.B = \bar{A} + B$$

The result may be checked by the truth table method.

**(b)**

$$\bar{A}.B.C + A.\bar{B}.C + A.B.\bar{C} + A.B.C$$

The terms A.B.C. can be combined with each of the other terms. If two extra A.B.C. terms are ORed with the original expression, i.e.

$$\bar{A}.B.C. + A.\bar{B}.C + A.B.\bar{C} + A.B.C + A.B.C + A.B.C$$

Then combining terms 1–3, 2–4 and 3–6 gives

$$B.C(\bar{A} + A) + A.C(\bar{B} + B) + A.B(\bar{C} + C) = B.C + A.C + A.B$$

**2.4** Working backwards from the output the expression for Z is

$$Z = \overline{C.(A.(\overline{A} + B))}$$
$$= \overline{C.A.(\overline{A} + B)}$$

Using de Morgan's theorem gives

$$Z = \overline{CA} + A + \overline{B}$$
$$= \overline{C} + \overline{A} + A + \overline{B}$$
$$= \overline{C} + \overline{B} \qquad \qquad (\text{since } \overline{A} + A = 1)$$

i.e. the expression does not depend on A.

**3.1**   The input range of 0 to 7 decimal requires 3 binary inputs, labelled X, Y and Z. The square of the input is obviously a decimal number in the range 0 to 49. The output then requires 6 binary lines, labelled A, B, C, D, E, F. The truth table for the system is:

| *Input* | | *Output* | |
|---|---|---|---|
| *Decimal* | *XYZ* | *Decimal* | *ABCDEF* |
| 0 | 0 0 0 | 0 | 0 0 0 0 0 0 |
| 1 | 0 0 1 | 1 | 0 0 0 0 0 1 |
| 2 | 0 1 0 | 4 | 0 0 0 1 0 0 |
| 3 | 0 1 1 | 9 | 0 0 1 0 0 1 |
| 4 | 1 0 0 | 16 | 0 1 0 0 0 0 |
| 5 | 1 0 1 | 25 | 0 1 1 0 0 1 |
| 6 | 1 1 0 | 36 | 1 0 0 1 0 0 |
| 7 | 1 1 1 | 49 | 1 1 0 0 0 1 |

The outputs required are then

$$A = \Sigma 6,7$$
$$B = \Sigma 4,5,7$$
$$C = \Sigma 3,5$$
$$D = \Sigma 2,6$$
$$E = 0$$
$$F = \Sigma 1,3,5,7 = Z$$

The expressions can be simplified using K-maps, or algebraically as follows:

$$A = XY\overline{Z} + XYZ = XY$$
$$B = X\overline{Y}\overline{Z} + X\overline{Y}Z + XYZ = X\overline{Y} + XYZ$$
$$= X\overline{Y} + XY$$
$$C = \overline{X}YZ + X\overline{Y}Z = Z(\overline{X}Y + X\overline{Y})$$
$$\text{and} \quad D = \overline{X}Y\overline{Z} + XY\overline{Z} = Y\overline{Z}(\overline{X} + X) = Y\overline{Z}$$

The circuit implementation is then

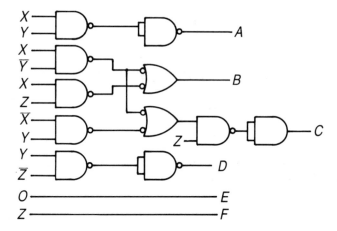

**3.3** The truth table for the 3-input majority function is:

| Inputs | | | Output |
| --- | --- | --- | --- |
| a | b | c | M |
| 0 | 0 | 0 | 0 |
| 0 | 0 | 1 | 0 |
| 0 | 1 | 0 | 0 |
| 0 | 1 | 1 | 1 |
| 1 | 0 | 0 | 0 |
| 1 | 0 | 1 | 1 |
| 1 | 1 | 0 | 1 |
| 1 | 1 | 1 | 1 |

The K-map is:

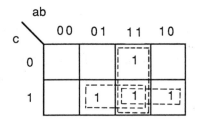

So M = ac + bc + ab. The implementation with NAND gates is:

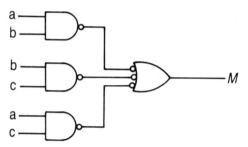

Majority function circuits with 4 or more inputs are best implemented with an iterative circuit.

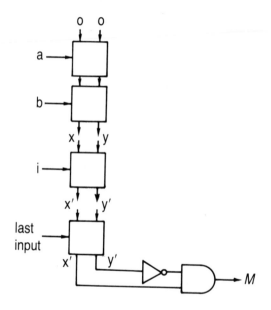

An iterative circuit contains a number of identical cells.

In this example a cell has 3 inputs: input i (for the ith cell), which is an external input (a, b, c ... etc), and two inputs x and y which contain information from the previous cell. The cell has two outputs x' and y' which pass on information to the next cell, according to the following code:

| $x'$ | $y'$ | |
|------|------|---|
| 0 | 0 | No previous inputs are set |
| 0 | 1 | One previous input is set |
| 1 | 1 | Two or more previous inputs are set |

The truth table for the ith cell is then:

| | Inputs | | | Outputs | |
|---|---|---|---|---|---|
| $x$ | $y$ | $i$ | $x'$ | $y'$ | |
| 0 | 0 | 0 | 0 | 0 |
| 0 | 1 | 0 | 0 | 1 |
| 1 | 0 | 0 | 1 | 0 |
| 0 | 0 | 1 | 0 | 1 |
| 0 | 1 | 1 | 1 | 0 |
| 1 | 0 | 1 | 1 | 0 |

Giving the equations:

$$x' = x\bar{y}\bar{i} + \bar{x}yi + x\bar{y}i$$
$$y' = \bar{x}yi + x\bar{y}i$$

For the 1st cell $x = y = 0$.
For the last cell the logic required to generate M is $M = x'y'$

**3.5**  The truth table is

| Input | | | Output | | |
|---|---|---|---|---|---|
| Decimal | BCD | | Decimal | BCD digits | |
| | $x\,y\,w\,z$ | | | $a\,b\,c\,d$ | $e\,f\,g\,h$ |
| 0 | 0 0 0 0 | | 0 | 0 0 0 0 | 0 0 0 0 |
| 1 | 0 0 0 1 | | 5 | 0 0 0 0 | 0 1 0 1 |
| 2 | 0 0 1 0 | | 10 | 0 0 0 1 | 0 0 0 0 |
| 3 | 0 0 1 1 | | 15 | 0 0 0 1 | 0 1 0 1 |
| 4 | 0 1 0 0 | | 20 | 0 0 1 0 | 0 0 0 0 |
| 5 | 0 1 0 1 | | 25 | 0 0 1 0 | 0 1 0 1 |
| 6 | 0 1 1 0 | | 30 | 0 0 1 1 | 0 0 0 0 |
| 7 | 0 1 1 1 | | 35 | 0 0 1 1 | 0 1 0 1 |
| 8 | 1 0 0 0 | | 40 | 0 1 0 0 | 0 0 0 0 |
| 9 | 1 0 0 1 | | 45 | 0 1 0 0 | 0 1 0 1 |

The outputs required are:

$$a = 0$$
$$b = \Sigma(8,9)$$
$$c = \Sigma(4,5,6,7)$$
$$d = \Sigma(2,3,6,7)$$
$$e = 0$$
$$f = \Sigma(1,3,5,7,9) = z$$
$$g = 0$$
$$h = \Sigma(1,3,5,7,9) = z$$

The PLA may be programmed directly from these equations.

If it is necessary to minimize the number of product terms then the expressions for b, c, d and f can be minimized algebraically, or by using the K-map technique.

**4.1**  The first step is to define the state diagram:

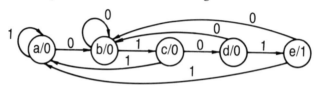

The state diagram is:

| Present state | Input | Next state |
|:---:|:---:|:---:|
| a | 0 | b |
| a | 1 | a |
| b | 0 | b |
| b | 1 | c |
| c | 0 | d |
| c | 1 | a |
| d | 0 | b |
| d | 1 | e |
| e | 0 | b |
| e | 1 | a |

The output z is a 1 if the system is in state e.

Assign the states as follows:    a = 000
b = 001
c = 010
d = 011
e = 100

The state diagram is then re-written:

| Present state ABC | Input x | Next state A'B'C' |
|---|---|---|
| 0 0 0 | 0 | 0 0 1 |
| 0 0 0 | 1 | 0 0 0 |
| 0 0 1 | 0 | 0 0 1 |
| 0 0 1 | 1 | 0 1 0 |
| 0 1 0 | 0 | 0 1 1 |
| 0 1 0 | 1 | 0 0 0 |
| 0 1 1 | 0 | 0 0 1 |
| 0 1 1 | 1 | 1 0 0 |
| 1 0 0 | 0 | 0 0 1 |
| 1 0 0 | 1 | 0 0 0 |

where ABC are the state variables.

Then from the state table:

$$A' = \bar{A}BCx$$
$$B' = \bar{A}\bar{B}Cx + \bar{A}B\bar{C}x$$
$$C' = \bar{x}(\bar{A}\bar{B}\bar{C} + \bar{A}\bar{B}C + \bar{A}B\bar{C} + \bar{A}BC + A\bar{B}\bar{C})$$

The expression for C' can be reduced using a 3-variable K-map to:

$$C' = \bar{x}(\bar{A} + \bar{B}\bar{C})$$
The output is $Z = A\bar{B}\bar{C}$

The implementation is then:

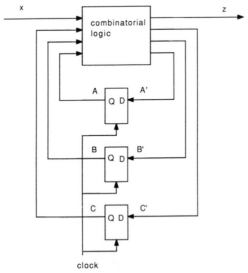

3 D-type flip-flops are required to store the state variables A, B and C. The combinatorial logic can be either random logic or a PLA.

**4.4** The state table for the modulo-3 counter is

| Present state | Next state |
|:---:|:---:|
| 0 | 1 |
| 1 | 2 |
| 2 | 0 |

If the states are represented by
$$0 = 00$$
$$1 = 01$$
$$2 = 10$$

i.e. the normal binary sequence then the state table becomes

| Present state<br>a b | Next state<br>a'b' |
|:---:|:---:|
| 0 0 | 0 1 |
| 0 1 | 1 0 |
| 1 0 | 0 0 |

**(a)**

Two D-type flip-flops are required to store the state variables a and b, which are also the counter outputs. The logic required for the D-inputs is read directly from the state table, and is

$$D_a = \bar{a}b$$
$$D_b = \bar{a}\bar{b}$$

so the implementation is

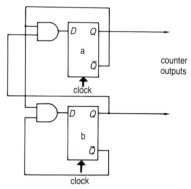

**(b)**

The logic required for the JK flip-flop implementation is determined using the state change table of Table 4.6. The state table becomes:

| Present state | | Next state | | | | | |
|---|---|---|---|---|---|---|---|
| $a$ | $b$ | $a'$ | $b'$ | $J_a$ | $K_a$ | $J_b$ | $K_b$ |
| 0 | 0 | 0 | 1 | 0 | X | 1 | X |
| 0 | 1 | 1 | 0 | 1 | X | X | 1 |
| 1 | 0 | 0 | 0 | X | 1 | 0 | X |
| 1 | 1 | 0 | 0 | X | 1 | X | 1 |

Note that an extra row has been added, namely row 4. If the present state ever becomes ab = 11 then the next state is always 00. In practice state 11 should never be entered, but if it is the counter moves to state 00 on the next clock pulse. The addition of this extra row also simplifies the logic for the J and K flip-flops, namely:

$$J_a = b \quad K_a = 1$$
$$J_b = \bar{a} \quad K_b = 1$$

**6.1** **(a)** 16 address lines are required to access 64K words of memory, since $2^{16} = 65\,536 = 64K$.

**(b)** 20 address lines will address $2^{20} = 1\,048\,576$ words of memory or 1024K.

**6.3** Consider a processor executing 100 instructions. With a hit rate of 0.9, 90 of these will be from the cache memory, and 10 from the main semiconductor memory. The total number of memory read cycles is then

$$(90 \times 3) + (10 \times 5) = 320 \text{ cycles}$$

If there is no cache memory than the total number of read cycles is then $100 \times 5 = 500$.

Thus the speed up factor with cache memory is

$$\left(\frac{500 - 320}{500}\right) \times 100 = 36\%$$

**7.2** The total number of bits transmitted per character is 10, consisting of 8 data bits, 1 start bit and 1 stop bit.

The effective data rate is therefore $9600/10 = 960$ characters/second.

**7.4** When an interrupt occurs the processor has to perform the following tasks:

(a) recognize and acknowledge the interrupt
(b) save the program counter and status register
(c) execute the interrupt handler
(d) restore the status register and program counter.

The total time for all this is $4 + 10 + 70 + 10 = 94$ μs. Interrupts must not occur more frequently than every 94 μs, so the highest interrupt frequency is

$$\frac{1}{94 \times 10^{-6}} = 10\,638 \text{ Hz}, \quad \text{i.e. about 10 kHz.}$$

**8.1** (a) The architecture shown in Fig. 8.1 actually has no direct means of clearing the accumulator. Indirectly it could be done by the instruction AND #0, i.e. ANDing the accumulator with the contents of the next location in memory, zero in this case. In practice the accumulator would probably have an extra control line, which will zero the contents of the accumulator when activated. This line would be controlled by an extra bit in the microinstruction word.

(b) After the processor has fetched and decoded the LDA instruction it has to perform a second fetch to transfer the operand value 10 from memory to the MBR. The microinstruction sequences for the execute cycle are then:
(i) MBR → bus2, bus2 → bus3, bus3 → ACC
(ii) PC → bus1, '1' → bus2, ADD, bus3 → PC

(c) As in (b) above the operand has to be fetched from memory to the MBR. The microinstruction sequences for the execute cycle are then:
(i) ACC → bus1, MBR → bus2, ADD, bus3 → ACC
(ii) PC → bus1, '1' → bus2, ADD, bus3 → PC

Note that it is assumed that data is output from registers such as the ACC or PC on the rising edge of the clock onto bus1 (or bus2 in the case of MAR). Data is latched back into a register on the falling edge of the clock.

**9.1** The original system has a 2K word ROM at addresses 0–2047 and two 256 word RAMs at addresses 2048–2303 and 4096–4357. The memory map is shown on p. 277.

If a 2K ROM is used for the additional ROM memory required, it can be placed at addresses 8192–10239 (2000 to 27FF hex). The extra RAM required can be achieved by using 2 additional 256 word RAMs, at addresses 10240–10495 (2800 to 28FF hex) and 12288–12543 (3000 to 30FF hex).

$A_{15}$ $A_{14}$ $A_{13}$ $A_{12}$ $A_{11}$ $A_{10}$ $A_9$ $A_8$ $A_7$ $A_6$ $A_5$ $A_4$ $A_3$ $A_2$ $A_1$ $A_0$

| | | | | | | | | | | | | | | | | |
|---|---|---|---|---|---|---|---|---|---|---|---|---|---|---|---|---|
| 0 | 0 | 0 | 0 | 0 | x | x | x | x | x | x | x | x | x | x | x | ROM(1) |
| 0 | 0 | 0 | 0 | 1 | 0 | 0 | 0 | x | x | x | x | x | x | x | x | RAM(1) |
| 0 | 0 | 0 | 1 | 0 | 0 | 0 | 0 | x | x | x | x | x | x | x | x | RAM(2) |
| 0 | 0 | 1 | 0 | 0 | x | x | x | x | x | x | x | x | x | x | x | ROM(2) |
| 0 | 0 | 1 | 0 | 1 | 0 | 0 | 0 | x | x | x | x | x | x | x | x | RAM(3) |
| 0 | 0 | 1 | 1 | 0 | 0 | 0 | 0 | x | x | x | x | x | x | x | x | RAM(4) |

**10.1 (a)**   $(27)_{10} = (11011)_2 = (1B)_{16}$

   **(b)**   $(96)_{10} = (1100000)_2 = (60)_{16}$

   **(c)**   $(1032)_{10} = (10000001000)_2 = (408)_{16}$

   **(d)**   $(1111)_{10} = (10001010111)_2 = (457)_{16}$

**10.4 (a)**
```
        0101
        0111 +
  0001  0010
```

   **(b)**
```
  0001  0010
  0000  0011 −
  0000  1001
```

   **(c)**
```
  0010  0000
  0001  0110 +
  0011  0110
  0000  0101 −
  0011  0001
```

   **(d)**  sign
```
  0     0011  0000
  1     0000  0111 −      using −30 + 7 = −(30 − 7)
  1     0010  0011
  0     0001  0010 −
  1     0001  0001
```

(e)   0001   0010
           0101 ×
      0001   0010
      0100   1000
      0110   0000

11.3 (a)   (i) ADD   H
           (ii) MOV   A,C
                ADD   B
                MOV   C,A
           (iii) LDA   2000
           (iv) INX   H              or
                INX   H              MVI   D,0
                INX   H              MVI   E,5
                INX   H              DAD   D
                INX   H              MOV   A,M
                MOV   A,M
           (v) MVI   B,1
                CPI   6
                JZ    L1
                MVI   B,0
           L1:
           (vi) MOV   A,B      SUB:  MVI   B,0
                CPI   2              RET
                CZ    SUB


      (b)   (i) ADD.L    D1,D0
            (ii) ADD.W    2000,D0
            (iii) ADD.B    2000,D1
            (iv) MOVEQ    #1,D1
                 CMPI.I    #3,D0
                 BNE      L1
                 MOVE.Q   #0,D1
            L1
            (v) CMPI.I    #6,D1   SUB   MOVEQ   #0,D1
                BNE      L1            RTS
                JSR      SUB
            L1:

11.5      8085   MOV    A,B
                 ANI    F7
                 HLT

<u>68000</u>   MOVE.L   D0,D1
            ANA       #FFFFFFF7
            STOP

**12.2** In the code the only change would be to put . = 4000 at the start in place of . = 0.

Apart from changing the code or data position the initial values of the assembly location counter (.) would alter the values used for the value of the table in the instruction labelled start and the address of endtable in the cmpa instruction. All the other addresses generated in the code are relative and hence do not depend on the code position.

If the data was located at 2000 and the code at 4000 then the reference to the address of table in the instruction labelled start would be to address 2000 and to endtable in the cmpa instruction to address 2003. The references to the code labels are all coded in relative address mode so they do not depend on the position in memory of the code. Thus the code for the code segment is not sensitive to its position in memory.

**12.4**

| | | | |
|---|---|---|---|
| digittable | dc.w | 2,3,5,7,3 | |
| endoftable | | | |
| start | move.w | #0,D1 | initialize count |
| | movea.w | #digittable,A2 | address of current table element to A2 |
| loop | cmp.w | #endoftable,A2 | at end of table? |
| | stop | | |
| | cmp.w | #3,(A2)+ | is current table value = 3 and increment table pointer |
| | bne | loop | if not 3 go back to consider next element |
| | add.q | #1,D1 | update count |
| | bra | loop | and go back to consider next element in table |
| | end | | |

Improvements to code include

(a) comments added;
(b) identifiers given meaningful names;
(c) **cmp.w** requires round brackets not square ones;
(d) only address registers can be used as index registers – hence change of code to above solution;
(e) an assembled **addq** instruction takes up less space than the equivalent **add** instruction. The same is also true of the **bra** and **jmp** instructions.

**13.2** By checking the parity bits or CRC.

The sender can correct the error by resending the information (backward error correction) or by including enough redundant information with the message for the receiver to reconstitute it (forward error correction).

**13.4** Token loss can be detected in a ring network by the cessation of all activity for a period greater than a specified time, that is, time-out. Token regeneration can be performed simply in a ring network by including a monitor which both detects token loss and then regenerates a token.

Token regeneration in a distributed environment is much difficult since, by definition, no central regeneration can take place. Thus each node must detect token loss and regenerate a token. This can cause the regeneration of multiple tokens which could cause faulty system organization. One algorithm to remove redundant tokens involves each processor being given a unique identity. The task of deciding which processor should issue a new token is then one of election. On detecting token loss a processor sends an elective token to its neighbours specifying its identity. When a processor receives an elective token it sends either its identity or the received identity, depending on which is the highest. A processor receiving back its own identity knows that it has been elected as the token regenerator.

**13.5** User data is encapsulated in 7 levels of protocol, one for each layer, before being physically transmitted from one site to a remote site. Intermediate nodes in the transmission path strip off and replace the outermost three layers, using these for error checking, flow control etc. At the remote site the 7 levels of protocol are stripped off level by level and the original message passed to the receiving process. If any errors are detected in transmission they will be automatically corrected, if possible, with no user process intervention. The actions taken by each level are detailed in section 13.4.6.

**14.2** The transputer is a RISC processor because it has a small instruction set. Some RISC proponents do not consider the transputer to be a RISC processor because it requires a large amount of microcode to implement the instruction set, which is against the RISC philosophy. Instead of using the freed chip area for extra memory, as many RISC processors do, the transputer uses it to implement 4-bit serial links providing fast interconnecting to other processors.

# Further reading

This bibliography contains a list of references to material not dealt with in detail in this book. It is not meant to be exhaustive but contains appropriate references selected by the authors.

## Electronics

Horowitz, P. and Hill, W. (1980) *The Art of Electronics*, Cambridge University Press, Cambridge. This book is an extensive, although easily readable and practical, electronics text aimed at first year undergraduate level. It covers both digital and analogue electronics.

## Very-large-scale integration

Mead, C. and Conway, L. (1980) *Introduction to VLSI systems*, Addison-Wesley. The original book on the design of VLSI circuits. Describes the design and production of a VLSI computer – the OM project. Contains useful material on the internal CPU detailed design.

Mavor, J., Jack, M.A. and Denyer, P.B. (1983) *Introduction to MOS LSI design*, Addison-Wesley. This book is intended to complement the one by Mead and Conway by taking an engineering rather than a systems view of LSI and VLSI. Contains a detailed chapter on the MOS design of combinatorial and sequential circuits.

Pucknell, D.A. and Estraghian, K. (1988) *Basic VLSI Design*, Prentice-Hall. A very good introductory text on VLSI design.

## Digital logic design

Morris Mano, M. (1979) *Digital Logic and Computer Design*, Prentice Hall. This comprehensive textbook covers the whole spectrum of logic design to computer implementation and provides an in depth discussion of most of the topics concerned with designing computers.

Peatman, J.B. (1980) *Digital Hardware Design*, McGraw Hill. This book is aimed at the practical engineer and describes in detail how to implement logic circuits.

Lewin, D. (1985) *Design of Logic Systems*, Van Nostrand Reinhold. This book is a complete text on logic systems, containing all the material required in this area by an electronics undergraduate. It provides a valuable reference for those requiring an in depth analysis of the topics covered in the first three chapters of this book.

## Computer architecture

Lippiat, A.G. (1978) *The Architecture of Small Computer Systems*, Prentice Hall, and Willis, N. and Kerridge, J. (1983) *Introduction to Computer Architecture*, Pitman. Both of these books provide a good introduction to the field of computer architecture. They provide a more detailed study of the information presented here in Chapter 6.

Tanenbaum, A.S. (1984) *Structured Computer Organisation*, Prentice Hall. A book on many topics in computer architecture by concentrating on the software aspects. The chapter on microprogramming is particularly good.

Morris Mano, M. (1982) *Computer Systems Architecture*, Prentice Hall. This book is a very comprehensive account of computer architecture and gives more details than the two books mentioned previously.

Hayes, J.P. (1978) *Computer Architecture and Organisation*, McGraw Hill. This book contains a large section on processor organization and implementation.

Clements, A. (1985) *The Principles of Computer Hardware*, Oxford University Press. Another book by this prolific author. This one deals with many topics in computer architecture and is based around the Motorola 6809 microprocessor.

## Interfacing

Artwick, B.A. (1980) *Microcomputer Interfacing*, Prentice Hall. A good book on interfacing techniques with a wide variety of different types of interface covered.

Stone, H.S. (1983) *Microcomputer Interfacing*, Addison Wesley. An excellent book on interfacing from the detailed electrical level to production circuits.

Peatman, J.B. (1977) *Microcomputer Based Design*, McGraw Hill. Although not specifically on interfacing, much of the book is concerned with how microcomputers are used in instruments; a topic involving much interfacing. The book includes much detail on practical interfacing techniques.

## Digital design including software and hardware

Bywater, R.E.H. (1981) *Hardware/Software Design of Digital Systems*, Prentice Hall. Most digital design involves hardware and software and this book deals specifically with the design of the complete system, hardware and software.

## Motorola 68000

There is the usual manufacturer's literature on this processor, its software and support chips. For beginners a better approach is to consult a textbook such as the ones mentioned below.

Clements, A. (1987) *Microprocessor System Design*, PWS. A predominantly hardware-based text on the 68000 although there is a small amount of material on software. It covers all the hardware characteristics including the bus and support chips.

Bramer, B. (1986) *M68000 Assembly Language Programming*, Arnold. One of the many books on low-level programming of the 68000 processor systems. This is one of the better texts at a moderate price.

## Intel 8085

This Intel processor is rather old now and has been superseded by other processors. However, if the reader needs more information it can be found in the following text as well as the manufacturer's literature.

Leventhal, L.A. (1978) *8080A/8085 Assembly Language Programming*, Osborne and Associates, Berkeley.

## Computer languages

Pratt, T.W. (1984) *Programming Languages: Design and Implementation*, Prentice Hall. This text deals with the main issues of the design of high-level programming languages. The second half of the book discusses many of the common high-level languages, such as Ada, Pascal and Cobol.

MacClennan, B.J. (1983) *Principles of Programming Languages: Design, Evaluation and Implementation*, Holt-Saunders. This text describes and compares most of the common high-level languages available today.

## Macroprocessors

Brown, P.J. (1975) *Macroprocessors and Techniques for Portable software*, Wiley.

## Program proving

Dowsing, R.D., Rayward-Smith, V.J. and Walter, C.D. (1986) *A First Course in Logic and its Applications in Computer Science*, Blackwell Scientific Publications. This book covers both hardware and software applications of logic and one of the chapters provides a good introduction to the subject of program proving.

## Operating systems

Peterson, J.L. and Silberschatz, A. (1985) *Operating System Concepts*, Addison-Wesley. A comprehensive book on all aspects of operating system principles concentrating on the issue of concurrency.

Tanenbaum, A.S. (1987) *Operating Systems: Design and Implementation*, Prentice Hall. A rather different approach to most books in that the whole book is structured around the Minix operating system whose listing comprises almost half the text. The operating system is available in machine readable form for those who wish to experiment with an operating system.

# Networks

Tanenbaum, A. (1981) *Computer Networks*, Prentice Hall. A very comprehensive book on all aspects of computer networking but concentrating on wide area networks.

Black, U. (1987) *Computer Networks: Protocols, Standards and Interfaces*, Prentice Hall. This book considers computer networks mainly from the point of view of protocols. It is notable in that it is one of the few books containing information on recent protocol standards.

Beauchamp, K. (1987) *Computer Communications*, Van Nostrand Reinhold. One of the better recent textbooks, also reasonably priced, on the complete spectrum of computer communications from the signalling level to networks.

# Distributed computing

Sloman, M. and Kramer J. (1987) *Distributed Systems and Computer Networks*, Prentice Hall. As suggested by the title about half this text is devoted to an introduction to loosely coupled distributed systems, mainly architectural and communication aspects, and the remainder to networking with the focus on the ISO model and its use in distributed systems.

Hwang, K. and Briggs, F.A. (1986) *Computer Architecture and Parallel Processing*, McGraw-Hill. Rather than distributed computation this book concentrates on closely coupled multiprocessor systems and describes the architecture and uses of pipeline, array, general purpose multiprocessor and data-flow computers.

# Advanced architecture

Tabak, (1987) *Reduced Instruction Set Computer RISC architecture*, Wiley. This book gives details of the RISC computers developed to the present time.

Brooks, A.B. *et al.* (1988) *The Transputer and its Implementation*, Blackwell Scientific Publications. This book describes the transputer in detail and gives a small amount of coverage of the language occam.

# Data books

Each manufacturer produces a range of literature covering details of all their components. In this text we refer mainly to standard TTL and Intel microprocessor components. The appropriate data books for more information are as follows.

Texas Instruments, (1982) *TTL Data Book*, Fifth Edition.

Intel Corporation, (1983) *Component Data Catalogue*.

# Index